Cyber-Vigilance and Digital Trust

Series Editor
Guy Pujolle

Cyber-Vigilance and Digital Trust

Cyber Security in the Era of Cloud Computing and IoT

Edited by

Wiem Tounsi

WILEY

First published 2019 in Great Britain and the United States by ISTE Ltd and John Wiley & Sons, Inc.

ISTE Ltd
27-37 St George's Road
London SW19 4EU
UK

www.iste.co.uk

John Wiley & Sons, Inc.
111 River Street
Hoboken, NJ 07030
USA

www.wiley.com

Library of Congress Control Number: 2019931457

British Library Cataloguing-in-Publication Data
A CIP record for this book is available from the British Library
ISBN 978-1-78630-448-3

Contents

Chapter 4. Analytical Overview on Secure Information Flow in Android Systems: Protecting Private Data Used by Smartphone Applications 141

Mariem GRAA

Introduction

This book starts by dealing with cyber threat intelligence in Chapter 1. Cyber threat intelligence is an actionable defense and evidence-based knowledge to reduce the gap between advanced attacks and organization defense means in order to aid specific decisions or to illuminate the risk landscape. This chapter classifies and makes distinctions among existing threat intelligence types and focuses particularly on technical threat intelligence issues and the emerging research, trends and frameworks.

Since threat data are sensitive, organizations are often reluctant to share threat information with their peers when they are not in a trusted environment. Trust, combined with new cloud services, is a solution to improve collective response to new threats. To deepen this approach, the second chapter of this book addresses digital trust and identifies mechanisms underlying trust management systems. It introduces basic concepts of trust management and classifies and analyzes several trust management systems. This chapter shows how trust management concepts are used in recent systems to address new challenges introduced by cloud computing.

When threats are not well addressed, any vulnerability could be exploited and could generate costs for the company. These costs can be of human, technical and financial nature. Thus, to get ahead of these threats, a preventive approach aiming to analyze risks is paramount. This is the subject of the third chapter of this book, which presents a complete information system risk analysis method deployed on various networks. This method is

Introduction written by Wiem TOUNSI

applicable to and is based on network security extensions of existing risk management standards and methods.

Finally, a detective approach based on both dynamic and static analysis is defined in the fourth chapter to defend sensitive data of mobile users, against information flow attacks launched by third-party applications. A formal and technical approach based on a data tainting mechanism is proposed to handle control flow in Java and native applications' code and to solve the under-tainting problem, particularly in Android systems.

What is Cyber Threat Intelligence and How is it Evolving?

1.1. Introduction

Today's cyberattacks have changed in form, function and sophistication during the last few years. These cyberattacks no longer originate from digital hacktivists or online thugs. Held by well-funded and well-organized threat actors, cyberattacks have transformed from hacking for kicks to advanced attacks for profit which may range from financial aims to political gains. In that aim, attacks designed for mischief have been replaced with dynamic, stealthy and persistent attacks, known as advanced malware and advanced persistent threats (APTs). The reason is due to the complexity of new technologies. As a system gets more complex, it gets less secure, making it easier for the attacker to find weaknesses in the system and harder for the defender to secure it (Schneier 2000). As a result, attackers have a first-mover advantage, by trying new attacks first, while defenders have the disadvantage of being in a constant position of responding, for example better anti-virus software to combat new malwares and better intrusion detection system to detect malicious activities. Despite spending over 20 billion dollars annually on traditional security defenses (Piper 2013), organizations find themselves faced with this new generation of cyberattacks, which easily bypass traditional defenses such as traditional and next-generation firewalls, intrusion prevention systems, anti-virus and security gateways. Those defenses rely heavily on static malware signatures or lists of pattern-matching technology, leaving them extremely vulnerable

Chapter written by Wiem TOUNSI.

to ever-evolving threats that exploit unknown and zero-day vulnerabilities. This calls for a new category of threat prevention tools adapted to the complex nature of new generation threats and attacks. This leads to what is commonly named cyber threat intelligence (CTI). CTI or threat intelligence means evidence-based knowledge representing threats that can inform decisions. It is an actionable defense to reduce the gap between advanced attacks and means of the organization's defenses. We focus specifically on technical threat intelligence (TTI), which is rapidly becoming an ever-higher business priority (Chismon and Ruks 2015), since it is immediately actionable and is easier to quantify than other TI sub-categories. TTI is also the most-shared intelligence, because of its easy standardization (Yamakawa 2014). With TTI, we can feed firewalls, gateways, security information and event management (SIEM) or other appliances of various types with indicators of compromise (IOC) (Verizon 2015), for example malicious payloads and IP addresses. We can also ingest IOC into a searchable index or just for visualization and dashboards.

Despite its prevalence, many problems exist with TTI. These are mainly related to the quality of IOC (i.e. IP address lifetime, malware signatures) and the massive repositories of threat data given by provider's databases which overwhelms their consumers (e.g. threat analysts) with data that is not always useful, which should be essential for generating intelligence. In many cases, threat feeds can simply amount to faster signatures that still fail to reach the attackers. For example, specific malicious payloads, URLs and IP addresses are so ephemeral that they may only be used once in the case of a true targeted attack.

To date, few analyses have been made on different types of TI and specifically on TTI. Moreover, very little research surveys have been reported on how new techniques and trends try to overcome TTI problems. Most of the existing literature reveals technical reports exposing periodic statistics related to the use of threat intelligence (Ponemon 2015; Shackleford 2015; Shackleford 2016), and also interesting empirical investigations for specific threat analysis techniques (Ahrend et al. 2016; Sillaber et al. 2016).

In order to develop effective defense strategies, organizations can save time and bypass confusions if they start defining what threat intelligence actually is, and how to use it and mitigate its problems given its different sub-categories.

This chapter aims to give a clear idea about threat intelligence and how literature subdivides it given its multiple sources, the gathering methods, the information life-span and who consumes the resulting intelligence. It helps to classify and make distinctions among existing threat intelligence types to better exploit them. For example, given the short lifetime of TTI indicators, it is important to determine for how much time these indicators could be useful.

We focus particularly on the TTI issues and the emerging research studies, trends and standards to mitigate these issues. Finally, we evaluate most popular open source/free threat intelligence tools.

Through our analysis, we find that (1) contrary to what is commonly thought, fast sharing of TTI is not sufficient to avoid targeted attacks; (2) trust is key for effective sharing of threat information between organizations; (3) sharing threat information improves trust and coordination for a collective response to new threats; (4) a common standardized format for sharing TI minimizes the risk of losing the quality of threat data, which provides better automated analytics solutions on large volumes of TTI.

1.2. Background

The new generation threats are no longer viruses, trojans and worms whose signatures are known to traditional defenses. Even social engineering and phishing attacks are now classified as traditional. New generation threats are multi-vectored (i.e. can use multiple means of propagation such as Web, email and applications) and multi-staged (i.e. can infiltrate networks and move laterally inside the network) (FireEye Inc. 2012). These blended, multi-stage attacks easily evade traditional security defenses, which are typically set up to inspect each attack vector as a separate path and each stage as an independent event. Thus, they do not view and analyze the attack as an orchestrated series of cyber incidents.

1.2.1. *New generation threats*

To bring new generation attacks into fruition, attackers are armed with the latest zero-day vulnerabilities and social engineering techniques. They utilize advanced tactics such as polymorphic threats and blended threats (Piper 2013), which are personalized to appear unknown to signature-based tools and yet authentic enough to bypass spam filters. A comprehensive taxonomy of the threat landscape is done by ENISA (The European Network and Information Security Agency) in early 2017 (ENISA 2017). In the following sections, we provide some examples of these new generation threats.

1.2.1.1. *Advanced persistent threats (APTs)*

APTs are examples of multi-vectored and multi-staged threats. They are defined as sophisticated network attacks (Piper 2013; FireEye Inc. 2014) in which an attacker keeps trying until they gain access to a network and stay undetected for a long period of time. The intention of an APT is to steal data rather than to cause damage to the network. APTs target organizations in sectors with high-value information, such as government agencies and financial industries.

1.2.1.2. *Polymorphic threats*

Polymorphic threats are cyberattacks, such as viruses, worms or trojans that constantly change ("morph") (Piper 2013), making it nearly impossible to detect them using signature-based defenses. Evolution of polymorphic threats can occur in different ways (e.g. file name changes and file compression). Despite the changing appearance of the code in a polymorphic threat after each mutation, the essential function usually remains the same. For example, a malware intended to act as a key logger will continue to perform that function even though its signature has changed. The evolution of polymorphic threats has made them nearly impossible to detect using signature-based defenses. Vendors that manufacture signature-based security products are constantly creating and distributing new threat signatures (a very expensive and time-consuming proposition (Piper 2013)), while clients are constantly deploying the signatures provided by their security vendors. It is a vicious cycle which goes to the advantage of the attacker.

1.2.1.3. *Zero-day threats*

Zero-day threats are cyber threats on a publicly unknown vulnerability of an operating system or application. It is so named because the attack was launched on "day zero" or before public awareness of the vulnerability and, in many cases, before even the vendor was aware (Piper 2013). In some cases, the vendor is already aware of the vulnerability, but has not disclosed it publicly because the vulnerability has not yet been patched. Zero-day attacks are extremely effective because they can go undetected for long periods (i.e. for months, if not years), and when they are finally identified, patching the vulnerability still takes days or even weeks.

1.2.1.4. *Composite threats*

Cyberattacks can either be classified as syntactic or semantic attacks. A combination of these two approaches is known as a composite attack or blended attack (Choo *et al.* 2007). Syntactic attacks exploit technical vulnerabilities in software and/or hardware, for example a malware installation to steal data; whereas semantic attacks exploit social vulnerabilities to gain personal information, for example scam solicitations. In recent years, progress has been made using the two approaches to realize composite attacks: using a technical tool to facilitate social engineering in order to gain privileged information, or using a social engineering means to realize a technical attack in order to cause harm to network hosts. Composite attacks include phishing attacks (also called online scams) which frequently use emails to send to carefully selected victims a plausible-looking message including a malicious attachment targeting a zero-day vulnerability. Phishing is positioned in the first three steps of the kill chain (see section 1.2.2.1). Phishing attacks forge messages from legitimate organizations, particularly banking and finance services, to deceive victims into disclosing their financial and/or personal identity information or downloading malicious files, in order to facilitate other attacks (e.g. identity theft, credit card fraud, ransomware (National High Tech Crime Unit of the Netherlands police, Europol's European Cybercrime Centre, Kaspersky Lab, Intel Security 2017)). When the attack focuses on a limited number of recipients to whom a highly personalized message is sent, the technique is named spear phishing. Phishing mostly abuses information found in social media (Fadilpasic 2016). Attackers are always on the lookout for new attack vectors for phishing including smart devices. Such devices are increasingly being used to access and store sensitive accounts and services (Choo 2011).

Obviously, the attack morphology is different depending on the aimed scenario; for example, cybercrime might use stealthy APT to steal intellectual property, while cyber war uses botnets to run distributed denial-of-service (DDoS) attacks (Skopik *et al.* 2016).

1.2.2. *Analytical frameworks*

Some analytical frameworks provide structures for thinking about attacks and adversaries to allow defenders to take decisive actions faster. For example, we name the defensive perspective of a kill chain (Hutchins *et al.* 2011) and the Diamond model used to track attack groups over time. Other standardized frameworks are developed in section 8.4.

1.2.2.1. *Steps of the kill chain defensive perspective*

Kill chain, first developed by Lockheed Martin in 2011 (Hutchins *et al.* 2011), is the best known of the CTI frameworks. It is a sequence of stages required for an attacker to successfully infiltrate a network and exfiltrate data from it (Barraco 2014). By breaking up an attack in this manner, defenders can check which stage it is in and deploy appropriate countermeasures.

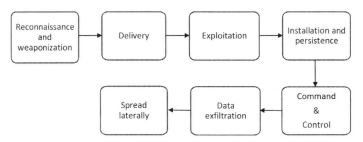

Figure 1.1. *Typical steps of multi-vector and multi-stage attacks by Lookheed Martin's kill chain*

– *Reconnaissance and weaponization*: the reconnaissance consists of research, identification and selection of targets, often by browsing websites (e.g. conference proceedings, mailing lists and social relationships), pulling down PDFs or learning the internal structure of the target organization. The weaponization is realized by developing a plan of attack based on opportunities for exploitation.

– *Delivery*: this consists of the transmission of the weapon to the targeted environment. It is often a blended attack delivered across the Web or email threat vectors, with the email containing malicious URLs (i.e. phishing attack). Whether it is an email with a malicious attachment or a hyperlink to a compromised website or an HTTP request containing SQL injection code, this is the critical phase where the payload is delivered to its target.

– *Exploitation*: most often, exploitation targets an application or operating system vulnerability, but it can exploit the users themselves or leverage an operating system feature that auto-executes a code.

– *Installation and persistence*: a single exploit translates into multiple infections on the same system. More malware executable payloads such as key loggers (i.e. unauthorized malware that records keystrokes), password crackers and Trojan backdoors could then be downloaded and installed. Attackers have built in this stage long-term control mechanisms to maintain persistence into the system.

– *Command and control (C&C)*: as soon as the malware is installed, a control point from organizational defenses is established. Once its permissions are elevated, the malware establishes communication with one of its C&C servers for further instructions. The malware can also replicate and disguise itself to avoid scans (i.e. polymorphic threats), turn off anti-virus scanners, or can lie dormant for days or weeks, using slow-and-low strategy to evade detection. By using callbacks from the trusted network, malware communications are allowed through a firewall and could penetrate all the different layers of the network.

– *Data exfiltration*: data acquired from infected servers are exfiltrated via encrypted files over a commonly allowed protocol, for example FTP or HTTP, to an external compromised server controlled by the attacker. Violations of data integrity or availability are potential objectives as well.

– *Spread laterally*: the attacker works to move beyond the single system and establishes long-term control in the targeted network. The advanced malware looks for mapped drives on infected systems, and can then spread laterally into network file shares.

Typically, if you are able to manage and stop an attack at the exploitation stage using this framework, you can be confident that nothing has been installed on the targeted systems, and triggering a full incident response activity may not be needed.

The kill chain is a good way for defending systems from attacks, but it has some limitations. One of the big criticisms of this model is that it does not take into account the way many modern attacks work. For example, many phishing attacks skip the exploitation phase and instead rely on the victim to open a document with an embedded macro or by double-clicking on an attached script (Pace *et al.* 2018). But even with these limitations, the

Kill Chain is a good baseline to discuss attacks, and find at which stage they can be stopped and analyzed.

1.2.2.2. *The Diamond model of intrusion analysis*

The Diamond model was created in 2013 at the Center for Cyber Intelligence Analysis and Threat Research (CCIATR). It is used to track adversary groups over time rather than the progress of individual attacks. The simplest form of the Diamond model is shown in Figure 1.2.

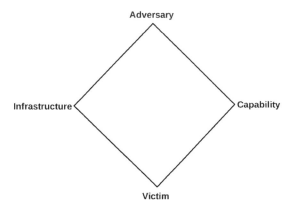

Figure 1.2. *The Diamond model of intrusion analysis*

The Diamond model classifies the different elements of an attack. The diamond for an adversary or a group is not static, but evolves as the adversary changes infrastructure and targets and modifies its TTPs (tactics techniques and procedures). The Diamond model helps defenders to track an adversary, the victims, the adversary's capabilities and the infrastructure the adversary uses. Each point on the diamond is a pivot point that defenders can use during an investigation to connect one aspect of an attack with the others (Pace *et al.* 2018).

One big advantage of the Diamond model is its flexibility and extensibility. It is possible to add different aspects of an attack under the appropriate point on the diamond to create complex profiles of different attack groups. These aspects of an attack include: phase, result, direction, methodology and resources.

This model requires time and resources. Some aspects of the model, especially infrastructure, change rapidly. If the diamond of an adversary is not constantly updated, there is a risk of working with outdated information.

1.3. Cyber threat intelligence

Cyber threat intelligence, also known as threat intelligence, is any evidence-based knowledge about threats that can inform decisions (McMillan 2013), with the aim of preventing an attack or shortening the window between compromise and detection. CTI can also be information that, instead of aiding specific decisions, helps to illuminate the risk landscape (Chismon and Ruks 2015). Other definitions exist, for example, in Steele (2014) and Dalziel (2014). A more rigorous one (Dalziel 2014) states that CTI is an information that should be relevant (i.e. potentially related to the organization and/or objectives), actionable (i.e. specific enough to prompt some response, action or decision) and valuable (i.e. the information has to contribute to any useful business outcome). CTI supports different activities, namely security operations, incident response, vulnerability and risk management, risk analysis and fraud prevention (for more details, see Pace *et al.* (2018)). Depending on the intended activities, the sources of CTI may differ.

1.3.1. *Cyber threat intelligence sources*

Cyber threat intelligence can be generated from information collected from a variety of sources (Holland *et al.* 2013). These commonly include internal sources (i.e. firewall and router logs or other local sensor traffic, such as honeynets, which are groups of interactive computer systems mostly connected to the Internet that are configured to trap attackers), or external sources, such as government-sponsored sources (i.e. law enforcement, national security organizations), industry sources (i.e. business partners), Open Source Intelligence (OSINT i.e. public threat feeds such as Dshield (2017), ZeuS Tracker (2017), social media and dark web forums) and commercial sources (i.e. threat feeds, Software-as-a-Service (SaaS) threat alerting, security intelligence providers).

External sources could provide structured or unstructured information, whereas internal sources are known to provide structured information as it is generated by technical tools. Structured sources are technical, meaning all information from vulnerability databases or threat data feeds, which are machine parsable and digestible and so their processing is simple. Unstructured sources are all that is produced by natural language, such as what we find in social media, discussions in underground forums, communications with a peer, or dark webs. They require natural language processing and machine learning techniques to produce intelligence. Table 1.1 presents these sources with required technologies to process information and transform it into intelligence.

	Internal sources	External sources	
	Structured (mainly)	*Structured*	*Unstructured*
Example	Firewall and router logs, honeynets	Vulnerabilities databases, IP blacklists and whitelists, threat data feeds	Forums, news sites, social media, dark web
Technologies for collecting and processing	Feed parser	Feed/web scraper, parser	Collection: crawlers, feed/web parsers Processing: Natural Language Processing (NLP), machine learning

Table 1.1. *Threat intelligence sources*

After collecting and processing threat information, several initiatives encourage threat information sharing, such as incident response teams and international cooperation (CERTs, FIRST, TF-CSIRT) (Skopik *et al.* 2016), and information sharing and analysis centers (ISACs) (ENISA 2015).

1.3.2. *Cyber threat intelligence sub-domains*

With different sources of threat intelligence and the activities that make use of it, it is useful to have subdivisions to better manage the gathered information and to focus efforts. TI can be categorized into sub-domains. Ahrend *et al.* (2016) divide TI into formal and informal practices to uncover and utilize tacit knowledge between collaborators. It depends on the collaborators' form of interaction. Gundert (2014) and Hugh (2016) categorize TI as strategic and operational depending on the form of analysis used to produce it.

In Chismon and Ruks (2015) and Korstanje (2016), a more refined model divides threat intelligence into four distinct domains: strategic threat intelligence, operational threat intelligence, tactical threat intelligence and technical threat intelligence. This subdivision is also known as the four levels of intelligence analysis (Steele 2007b). It was originally used in a military context as the model of expeditionary factors analysis that distinguishes these four levels (Steele 2007a). In what follows, our study follows the last subdivision. Table 1.2 summarizes the four domains.

– *Strategic threat intelligence* is high-level information consumed by decision-makers. The purpose is to help strategists understand current risks and identify further risks of which they are yet unaware. It could cover financial impact of cyber activity or attack trends, historical data or predictions regarding the threat activity. As a result, a board needs to consider and target possible attacks, in order to weigh risks and allocate effort and budget to mitigate these possible attacks. Strategic TI is generally in the form of reports, briefings or conversations.

– *Operational threat intelligence* is information about specific impending attacks against the organization. It is initially consumed by high-level security staff, for example security managers or heads of incident response team (Chismon and Ruks 2015). It helps them anticipate when and where attacks will take place.

– *Tactical threat intelligence* is often referred to as tactics, techniques and procedures. It is information about how threat actors are conducting attacks (Chismon and Ruks 2015). Tactical TI is consumed by incident responders to ensure that their defenses and investigation are prepared for current tactics. For example, understanding the attacker tooling and methodology is tactical intelligence that could prompt defenders to change policies. Tactical TI is often gained by reading technical press or white papers, communicating with peers in other organizations to know what they are seeing attackers do, or purchasing from a provider of such intelligence.

– *Technical threat intelligence (TTI)* is information that is normally consumed through technical resources (Chismon and Ruks 2015). Technical TI typically feeds the investigative or monitoring functions of an organization, for example firewalls and mail filtering devices, by blocking attempted connections to suspect servers. TTI also serves for analytic tools, or just for visualization and dashboards. For example, after including an IOC in an organization's defensive infrastructure such as firewalls and mail filtering devices, historical attacks can be detected by searching logs of previously observed connections or binaries (Chismon and Ruks 2015).

	Strategic	**Operational**	**Tactical**	**Technical**
Level	High	High	Low	Low
Audience	The board	Defenders	Senior security management; architects	Security Operation Center staff; incident response team
Content	High level information on changing risks	Details of specific incoming attacks	Attackers' tactics, techniques and procedures	Indicators of compromise
Time frame	Long term	Short term	Long term	Immediate

Table 1.2. *Threat intelligence sub-domains*

From their definitions, strategic and tactical threat intelligence are gainful for a long-term use, whereas operational and technical threat intelligence are profitable for a short-time/immediate use. In case technical IOC are for short time use, a key question is: how long we can expect those indicators to remain useful? In the next section, we deal with TTI in more detail.

1.3.3. *Technical threat intelligence (TTI)*

Defenders should not only be aware of threat actors and the nature of attacks they are facing, but also be aware of the data fundamentals associated with these cyberattacks, known as indicators of compromise (IOC). IOC are closely linked to TTI, but are often confused with intelligence. IOC are an aspect that enables the production of intelligence. The feeds by themselves are just data. By conducting the analysis with the internal data intelligence which is relevant to the organization, an actionable decision is able to recover from any incident (Dalziel 2014). IOC are commonly partitioned into three distinct categories (Ray 2015): network, host-based indicators and email indicators.

– *Network indicators* are found in URLs and domain names used for command and control (C&C) and link-based malware delivery. They could be IP addresses used in detecting attacks from known compromised servers, botnets and systems conducting DDoS attacks. However, this type of IOC has a short lifetime as threat actors move from one compromised server to another, and with the development of cloud-based hosting services, it is no longer just compromised servers that are used, but also legitimate IP addresses belonging to large corporations.

– *Host-based indicators* can be found through analysis of an infected computer. They can be malware names and decoy documents or file hashes of the malware being investigated. The most commonly offered malware indicators are MD5 or SHA-1 hashes of binaries (Chismon and Ruks 2015). Dynamic link libraries (DLLs) are also often targeted, as attackers replace Windows system files to ensure that their payload executes each time Windows starts. Registry keys could be added by a malicious code, and specific keys are modified in computer registry settings to allow for persistence. This is a common technique that malware authors use when creating Trojans (Ray 2015).

– *Email indicators* are typically created when attackers use free email services to send socially engineered emails to targeted organizations and individuals. Source email address and email subject are created from addresses that appear to belong to recognizable individuals or highlight current events to create intriguing email subject lines, often with attachments and links. X-originating and X-forwarding IP addresses are email headers identifying the originating IP address of (1) a client connecting to a mail server, and (2) a client connecting to a web server through an HTTP proxy or load balancer, respectively. Monitoring these IP addresses when available provides additional insight into attackers.

Spam is the main means to transport malicious URLs and malware. These are later wrapped in the form of spam and phishing messages (i.e. phishing is positioned in the first three steps of the kill chain.) Phishing attacks forge messages from legitimate organizations to deceive victims into disclosing their financial and/or personal identity information or downloading malicious files, in order to facilitate other attacks). Spam is mainly distributed by large spam botnets (i.e. devices that are taken over and form a large network of zombies adhering to C&C servers (ENISA 2017)). Obfuscation methods (Symantec 2016) were observed in 2015 and continued in 2016 to evade the detection of this type of attack. These methods could be the expedition of massive amounts of spam to a wide IP range to reduce the efficiency of spam filters or the usage of alphanumeric symbols and UTF-8 characters to encode malicious URLs.

1.4. Related work

Cyber threats and attacks are currently one of the most widely discussed phenomena in the IT industry and the general media (e.g. news) (iSightPartners 2014). Figure 1.3(a) shows Google results for cyber "threat intelligence", particularly in terms of research publications, and Figure 1.3(b) shows Google results for "indicators of compromise" in the threat landscape generally and in terms of research publications particularly, in the last five years. These numbers are taken year on year. Even though an exponential interest in threat intelligence and IOC fields is seen, we observe a gap between the evolution of cyber threat intelligence activities and related research work.

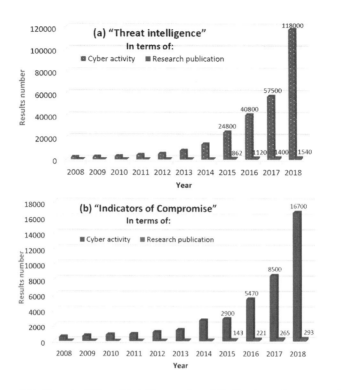

Figure 1.3. *Trend of "threat intelligence" and "indicators of compromise" in cyber activity from the last ten years. For a color version of this figure, see www.iste.co.uk/tounsi/cyber.zip*

Actually, a large number of threat intelligence vendors and advisory papers are found describing very different products and activities under the banner of threat intelligence. The same conclusion is observed with TTI category via the indicators of compromise. However, few research studies have been done to examine and identify characteristics of TI and its related issues. It is also noteworthy that in recent years, significant research progress has been made in this field.

Regarding surveys related to our work, most of them show yearly new trends and statistics which are relevant to strategic intelligence (Ponemon 2015; Shackleford 2015; Shackleford 2016). On the research side, a significant body of work has been dedicated to threat intelligence sharing issues (Moriarty 2011; Barnum 2014; Burger *et al.* 2014; Ring 2014; Skopik *et al.* 2016). Many guidelines, best practices and summaries on existing sharing   standards   and   techniques   have   been   published (e.g. Johnson *et al.* 2016). In contrast, less research has been devoted to areas like TTI problems and how to mitigate them.

This work complements the aforementioned research work by separating TI categories. It specifically analyzes TTI problems per type (i.e. problems of information quantity over quality and specific limitations related to each type of IOC). Then, it shows how to mitigate them. We also survey the reasons behind not sharing threat information with peers and present solutions to share this information by avoiding either attack or business risks for organizations. We show how a common standardized representation of TTI improves the quality of threat information which improves automated analytics solutions on large volumes of TTI suffering from non-uniformity and redundancy. Finally, we evaluate TTI tools which aim to share threat intelligence between organizations.

In the following section, we start by describing the main reasons for not sharing TI.

1.5. Technical threat intelligence sharing problems

The benefits of collective sharing and learning from extended and shared threat information are undeniable. Yet, various barriers limit the possibilities to cooperate. In this section, we detail some of these benefits and expose the reasons for not sharing threat information.

1.5.1. *Benefits of CTI sharing for collective learning*

Many organizations and participants today agree on the importance of threat information sharing for many reasons. First, the exchange of critical threat data has been shown to prevent potential cyberattacks and mitigate ongoing attacks and future hazards. According to Bipartisan Policy Center (2012), leading cybercrime analysts recognize that public-private cyber information sharing can speed identification and detection of threats. Thus, if organizations are able to find an intruder in his/her active phases, they have a greater chance of stopping the attacker before data is stolen (Zurkus 2015).

In addition, threat sharing is a cost-effective tool in combating cybercrime if properly developed (PERETTI 2014; Ponemon 2014). In Gilligan *et al.* (2014), a study on the economics of cyber security identified a number of "investment principles" for organizations to use in developing data security programs with high economic benefit. One of these principles is the participation in multiple cyber security information-sharing exchanges. Advantages of sharing also include a better situational awareness of the threat landscape, a deeper understanding of threat actors and their TTPs, and a greater agility to defend against evolving threats (Zheng and Lewis 2015). This has been proved in a recent survey (Ponemon 2015), where 692 IT and IT security practitioners were surveyed across various industries. Results reveal that there is more recognition that the threat intelligence exchange can improve an organization security posture and situational awareness. More broadly, sharing threats improves coordination for a collective learning and response to new threats and reduces the likelihood of cascading effects across an entire system, industry, sector or sectors (Zheng and Lewis 2015). Many attacks do not target a single organization in isolation, but target a number of organizations, often in the same sector (Chismon and Ruks 2015). For example, a company can be damaged when a competing business's computers are attacked, since the information stolen can often be used against other organizations in the same sector.

1.5.2. *Reasons for not sharing*

Despite the obvious benefits of sharing threat intelligence, a reluctant position in reporting breaches is observed. The issue was seriously highlighted at a pan-European level when ENISA, the EU's main cyber security agency, published a report (ENISA 2013) in 2013, intentionally capitalizing the word "SHARE". The report warned around 200 major CERTs in Europe that "the ever-increasing complexity of cyberattacks requires more effective information sharing" and that organizations were not really involved in doing so. In its last report on threat landscape published in early 2017 (ENISA 2017), ENISA continues to recommend sharing information as a mitigation vector for malwares. Authors recommend the development of methods for the identification and sharing of *modus operandi* without disclosing competitive information.

Many concerns are deterrent to participation in such a sharing initiative. In Table 1.3, we identify by order of importance ten major reasons for not sharing threat information.

Fearing negative publicity is one of the main reasons for not sharing threat information which could result in a competitive disadvantage (Richards 2009; Choo 2011; Peretti 2014; Chismon and Ruks 2015); for example, competitors might use the information against victimized organization. In some sectors, even a rumor of compromise can influence purchasing decisions or market valuations (Bipartisan Policy Center 2012).

Legal rules and privacy issues are also cited among the most important reasons for not sharing (ENISA: European Union Agency for Network and Information Security 2013; PERETTI 2014; Murdoch and Leaver 2015; Skopik *et al.* 2016). Organizations may be reluctant to report an incident because they are often unsure about what sort of information can be exchanged to avoid legal questions regarding data and privacy protection. In the same country legal rules may not be the same for the collaborating parties. Affiliation to a specific sector, for example, might force adherence to specific regulations (ENISA 2006). Regarding international cooperation, confidence between cooperating teams while handling sensitive information is most of the time prevented by international regulations that limit the exchange and usage of such information. Teams working in different countries have to comply with different legal environments. This issue influences the ways the teams provide their services and the way they treat particular kinds of attacks, and therefore limits the possibilities to cooperate, if not making cooperation impossible (Skopik *et al.* 2016).

Quality issues are one of the most common barriers to effective information exchange, according to different surveys realized on CERTs and other similar organizations (ENISA 2013; Ring 2014; Ponemon 2015; Sillaber *et al.* 2016). Data quality includes relevance, timeliness, accuracy, comparability, coherence and clarity. For example, many interviewees report that a great deal of what is shared is usually a bit old and thus not actionable. It is also not specific enough to aid the decision-making process.

Untrusted participants is also cited in recent surveys (ENISA 2013; Murdoch and Leaver 2015; Ponemon 2015) among the crucial obstacles to effective communication between organizations.

1	Fearing negative publicity	Richards (2009), Choo (2011), Peretti (2014), Chismon and Ruks (2015)
2	Legal rules, privacy issues	ENISA (2013), Peretti (2014), Murdoch and Leaver (2015), Skopik *et al.* (2016)
3	Quality issues	ENISA (2013), Ring (2014), Ponemon (2015), Sillaber *et al.* (2016)
4	Untrusted participants	ENISA (2013), Murdoch and Leaver (2015), Ponemon (2015)
5	Believing that the incident is not worth sharing	Choo (2011), Ring (2014), Chismon and Ruks (2015)
6	Budgeting issues	Ring (2014), Skopik *et al.* (2016)
7	Natural instinct to not share	Ring (2014)
8	Changing nature of cyberattacks	Ring (2014)
9	Unawareness of the victimized organization about a cyber incident	Choo (2011)
10	Believing that there is a little chance of successful prosecution	Choo (2011)

Table 1.3. *Reasons for not sharing*

Some interviewees in ENISA (2013) have pointed that trust is undermined when only a few parties are active in a sharing program, without getting much in return from the other parties. Murdoch and Leaver (2015) explain that the conflict involved in the need for sharers to keep anonymity while ensuring that recipients still trust the information (i.e. even when the source is unknown) is a barrier to participation in a threat intelligence sharing platform.

Believing that the incident is not worth sharing is also commonly stated (Choo 2011; Ring 2014; Chismon and Ruks 2015). The victimized organizations simply deal with the incident internally believing that it is not serious enough to warrant reporting it to an external party including law enforcement and other competent agencies.

Budgeting issues are reasons to limit building a valuable level of cooperation (Ring 2014; Skopik *et al.* 2016). Some interviewees have stated that qualified real-time threat intelligence is typically expensive to receive/share. They think that they are mainly dedicated to big organizations. Yet third party providers generally offer a discount to their TI platform subscribers for their willingness to share threat information in addition to its consumption (Piper 2013).

The natural instinct of organizations to not share is another problem of sharing (Ring 2014). In some organizations, there is still the perception of a blame culture (i.e. if something happens, then obviously it is somebody's fault and he/she needs to pay the price). Thus, people are naturally reticent about advertising an incident too widely.

The changing nature of cyberattacks, which are becoming increasingly personalized, is highlighted (Ring 2014). Even though organizations succeed in sharing data on an attack, especially when these organizations fall in the targeting scope of a given adversary (see the Waking Shark II exercise (Keeling 2013)), the issue of personalized attacks do not help them to defend themselves. This sets a different kind of intelligence requirement.

The ignorance of the victimized organization about a cyber incident is another reason for not sharing threat information (Choo 2011). When asked, analysts indicate that they had not experienced any such incidents. Yet the organization has been attacked one or more times.

Believing that there is a little chance of successful prosecution (Choo 2011) discourages organizations from reporting an incident to law enforcement and other competent agencies.

It is worth noting that some of these aforementioned concerns have been alleviated by recent government measures (PERETTI 2014) (e.g. legal rules). However, in all cases, organizations should understand any potential risks associated with exchanging TI and take steps to mitigate such risks. The good news is that organizations are taking strides in sharing threat data. Now the question is: how useful are these shared threats and for how long will they remain worthy of alerting/blocking?

1.6. Technical threat intelligence limitations

While a decade ago no one other than government agencies were talking about threat intelligence, as shown in Figure 1.3, organizations looking to have technical threat intelligence are now overwhelmed with a massive amount of threat data (Chismon and Ruks 2015; Zurkus 2015), leaving them with the huge challenge of identifying what is actually relevant. Thus, a problem of quantity over quality has been developed.

1.6.1. *Quantity over quality*

Most security teams cannot use their threat data in a valuable way because there is just too much. The daily dump of indicators seen as suspicious on the Internet provides information on approximately 250 million indicators per day (Trost 2014), which allows consumers to pivot around and glean their own intelligence. The brain power needed to analyze at the speed at which the threat data is produced is, thus, not humanly possible (Zurkus 2015).

Timeliness of information is also very important when protecting against aggressive attackers and zero-day exploits. According to Ponemon (2013), 57% of surveyed IT professionals state that the intelligence currently available to their enterprises is often out of date, making it difficult for them to understand the motivations, strategies and tactics of attackers and to locate them. In a more recent survey of IT professionals (Ponemon 2014), the authors report that most of the threat information the IT professionals received was not timely or specific enough (i.e. actionable) to meet their perceived need. Finally, according to a recent survey (Ponemon 2015), threat intelligence needs to be timely and easy to prioritize. In this latter survey, 66% of respondents who are only somewhat or not satisfied with current approaches explain that the information is not timely. On the other hand, 46% complain that the threat information is not categorized according to threat types. This has been proved in Ring (2014), where the author explains that qualified real-time threat intelligence is typically expensive; otherwise, most available commercial and open-source threat intelligence products are not effective enough, or provide information that is out of date.

1.6.2. IOC-specific limitations

Let us now deal in more detail with the limitations of each type of indicator of compromise as categorized in section 1.3.3. These TTI types are: network indicators, host-based/malware indicators and email indicators.

1.6.2.1. Network indicators

A number of network indicators can be collected as TTI (as shown in section 1.3.3). In some cases, attackers use different nodes to conduct attacks on a targeted victim. In other cases, they use the same node for multiple victims. Thus, an IP address that has been observed by others, functioning as a C&C (Command and Control) node, can be a useful indicator (see section 1.2.2.1 for more details). However, attackers often use different IP addresses, changing C&C nodes as they are discovered or as victimized computers become unavailable. Regarding domain names, a malware will attempt to connect to a domain name, which can then be pointed to the IP address the attacker is currently using. It is also considered a useful indicator when a malware uses a hard-coded domain. However, it is quite common for malware to use a domain generation algorithm to avoid the need to connect to the same domain twice. In such a case, a domain name has little value as an IOC (Chismon and Ruks 2015). A stark detail in Verizon (2015) illustrates the value of such indicators. The most important experiments conducted in this field are to determine (1) the IP addresses' cumulative uniqueness (i.e. the overlap between the IP address feeds), (2) the time needed for an attack to spread from one victim to another and (3) the time validity of the IP address.

1.6.2.1.1. Cumulative uniqueness observations

For six months, Niddel (Pinto and Sieira 2015) combined daily updates from 54 different sources of IP addresses and domain names tagged as malicious by their feed aggregator TIQ-Test (Niddel Corp. 2014). The company then performed a cumulative aggregation (i.e. if ever two different feeds mentioned the same indicator throughout the six-month experimental period, they would be considered to be in overlap on this specific indicator). To add some context to the indicator feeds being gathered, Niddel separated them into groups of inbound feeds (i.e. information on sources of scanning activity and spam/phishing email) and outbound feeds (i.e. information on destinations that serve either exploit kits or malware binaries, or even locations of C&C servers). The results show significant overlap only in the inbound feeds, which is in some way expected as every feed is probed and scanned all the time. However, despite every feed being generally subjected to the same threats, the overlap in outbound feeds is surprisingly small, even with a long exposure period of six months. This result suggests that either attackers are using huge numbers of IP addresses (i.e. organizations would need access to all threat intelligence indicators in order for the information to be helpful, which is a very hard task) or only a minority of IP addresses contained within the feeds are of intelligence value. It is likely that the truth is a mixture of both explanations (see experience in time validity observations).

1.6.2.1.2. Time spread observations

Experiments on attacks observed by RiskAnalytics (Verizon 2015) display some pretty interesting and challenging results: 75% of attacks spread from Victim 0 to Victim 1 within 24 hours and over 40% hit the second organization in less than an hour. These findings put quite a bit of pressure on the security community to collect, vet and distribute IOC very quickly in order to maximize the collective preparedness. Let us assume that indicators are shared quickly enough to help subsequent potential victims. The next question that needs to be answered is how long we can expect those indicators to remain valid (i.e. malicious, active and worthy of alerting/blocking).

1.6.2.1.3. Time validity observations

RiskAnalytics has already studied the question of IP address validity. Figure 1.4 shows how long most IP addresses were on the block/alert list. The graphic is restricted to seven days of outbound IP address feeds.

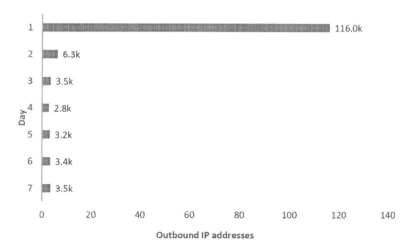

Figure 1.4. *Count of indicators by days as
observed in Verizon (2015) in at least one feed*

While some IP addresses remain valid for some time, most do not last even a day. These findings track well with Niddel's cumulative uniqueness observations where the overlap in outbound feeds is very small. According to Verizon (2015), these results reflect an urgent need to share quickly: "the faster you share, the more you theoretically will stop". Let us recall that these are results from one data source which is geared towards threats of a more opportunistic, high-volume and volatile nature (e.g. brute forcing and web application exploits), rather than more slow targeted attacks. With targeted attacks, sharing IOC faster is not always useful (see section 1.8).

1.6.2.2. *Malware indicators*

A growing sophistication in the evolution of malware has been noted (Choo 2011). Knowing that modified malware does not require great skill or resources, attackers reuse malware to keep ahead of the anti-malware industry and security professionals. They adapt their "products" over time, employing many different obfuscation techniques. The simplest way is to change a single bit in the binary, and then a different hash will be obtained. Attackers can use open-source tools and make more complex modifications to change the hashes. The Zeus bot malware creator kit is an example of an easy-to-use toolkit. It can be bought or found for free on some underground forums (Falliere and Chien 2009) with detailed instructions on how to use such kits. Any individual, including one with limited programming or hacking skills, could use such kits to create sophisticated malware or customize them to his own needs and launch advanced attacks. A study realized by Symantec (Fossi *et al.* 2010) has shown nearly 90,000 unique variants of the basic Zeus toolkit in 2009, which was the second most common new malicious code family observed in the Asia Pacific/Japan region in that year. The widespread availability of such a toolkit facilitates cybercrime. Consequently, there is a marked increase in the number of amateur cyberattackers who make their pocket money from distributing spam or selling stolen credentials and information (Choo 2011). Indicators such as created registry keys or file artifacts can be more useful for threat intelligence as they are less commonly changed by attackers, even though it is still possible to give dropped files a random or pseudorandom component in their names.

1.6.2.3. *Email indicators*

A large number of attacks start with a phishing or spear phishing attack, containing either a document exploit or simply a malware disguised as something benign. Thus, email indicators can provide useful threat intelligence. Attackers often ensure that emails are either targeted or generic (Choo 2011). Sharing generalist feeds of spam email subjects will be less useful than details of phishing emails sent to similar organizations.

1.7. Cyber threat intelligent libraries or platforms

A concept that has emerged recently is the use of threat intelligence libraries, also called threat intelligence platforms (Poputa-Clean and Stingley 2015). Threat intelligence platforms produce data and information, which human analysts can use to produce actionable threat intelligence (RecordedFuture 2017). These libraries solve collection and storing problems of TTI and facilitate sharing with other organizations in the threat intelligence space. They also allow an organization to detect attacks within logs and packet captures. These libraries particularly store indicators and seek links between them (Chismon and Ruks 2015). They are generally large repositories that often use big data technologies (e.g. graph analysis and data warehousing) to draw links between types of TTI, allowing quicker response to detected threats, as well as a historical record of an IOC. The threat library could be seen as the reference system for IOC (Poputa-Clean and Stingley 2015) since it allows the defender to track for a basic observable (e.g. a checksum of a file or a signature), as well as enriching it (e.g. by metadata on the file, notes, campaigns using the file itself and its source). Thus, organization security is no longer dependent on having seen the threat before. It can evaluate any traffic based on the collective knowledge (Williamson 2016) of all the threats that came before it.

1.7.1. *Benefits of CTI libraries based in the cloud*

The cloud is seen as the proper place to host the CTI library, since cloud computing provides computation, storage and distributed capability in support of big data processing used by this library. The TI library is a part of a cloud threat intelligence system (Lightcyber 2016), which is constantly updated with recent IOC. The expected result behind this is, once one entity has detected a new threat in its initial attack state, all other entities connected to the system are protected within minutes. Many call this collective immunity (Piper 2013). But still, organizations should define what cloud model they want to use to be safe and to build trust upon. Whether they are private or public, threat libraries automate in the long term some of the analyst activities (Trost 2014). Their most-known benefits could be seen after a couple of months or a year, when organizations can automatize the inverse engineering by using machine learning techniques. For example, the libraries make it possible to have information associated with one group and to give its evolution, or to know whether attackers are learning from their mistakes, or to know if attackers are changing their TTP and to build an attacker profile. In addition, these libraries allow an operational usage, which helps to define the best metrics by determining what is the best source of intelligence for the organization (i.e. private sources, commercial sources, OSINT) and who is giving the best pool of information to dedicate time and resources. Today, several open-source projects and commercial enterprises are gaining popularity as TTI platforms as they offer a more organized storage of IOC and an improved context around the alerts (Poputa-Clean and Stingley 2015). The most notable open-source intelligence libraries are evaluated in section 1.9.

1.7.2. *Reluctance to use cloud services*

It is hard to deny the benefits of cloud services to host threat intelligence data and networks. However, many businesses are still uncomfortable with the idea of a cloud-based infrastructure. Even though some public cloud providers dedicate infrastructure and services to their customers, offering a virtual private cloud, these businesses want to store their TI-related data in a privately controlled datacenter, where they control at any time where and with whom their data reside.

Some organizations such as healthcare and financial services industries are dealing with data that require more advanced security than what cloud providers can offer. Others have a problem of visibility. In this case, integrating an internal private cloud solution facilitates connection and interaction with other organizations. This could be seen as just an extension of the corporate datacenter which allows internal and external threat data (i.e. OSINT, other partners) to provide context and relevance while the most sensitive data remain safe behind the corporate firewall. Finally, trust issues often remain the most difficult to overcome for IT executives when considering whether or not to move TI into a cloud-based solution maintained by a third-party provider. In fact, trust is difficult to quantify. It depends on the specific needs of the organization, the cloud provider's overall reputation and localization (e.g. European or not, for regulations reasons), and the kinds of service-level agreements to have (OrbIT-Peaple 2016).

1.8. Discussion

1.8.1. *Sharing faster is not sufficient*

As seen before, a variety of security vendors and open-source providers now offer a wide assortment of threat feeds of the latest indicators of compromise (Williamson 2016). The idea behind these threat feeds is generally the same. As attackers are getting faster, security providers find a way to quickly aggregate and share the latest threats that have been noticed. Timeliness of threat information is very important when protecting against aggressive attackers and zero-day exploits, but in many cases, threat feeds of TTI can simply amount to faster signatures that still fail to track the attackers. In fact, a key failing of TTI is that it is relatively simple for an attacker to target a specific organization in a way that ensures no pre-existing indicators are available. For example, specific network indicators may only be used once in the case of a true targeted attack. In addition, a large percentage of malware used in breaches were reported to be unique to the organization that was infected (Shackleford 2015;

Verizon 2015). Clearly, if a threat is only used once, as for targeted attacks, faster sharing of IOC alone is not going to solve the problem. Actually, targeted attacks need a targeted defense as well (Chismon and Ruks 2015).

To defend against this new trend of personalized attacks, organizations need to focus not only on gathering and sharing threat data across their industry sector, but also on their individual threat analysis and incident response (Ring 2014). Obviously, they cannot protect themselves if they do not know what they are protecting against and who their adversaries are (Pepper 2015; Zurkus 2015). To realize such need, internal audit should be done regularly to understand organization's internal and external vulnerabilities. The objective is to make assumptions about what the attacker can do and to get an initial response, a one step forward by focusing on investigating specific devices and attacks.

1.8.2. Reducing the quantity of threat feeds

The other important concern is about the large amounts of data sold as TTI which lack contextual information. Certainly, anything that leads to the discovery of an incident is worthwhile, but in most cases, context is key. Additional context includes indicator role, kill chain stage, originating MD5, malware family and/or adversary group (Trost 2014). Adding, for example, the context in which previously detected attacks have taken place enables a wider audience to make a broader defensive capability. The heart of the issue is that the vast majority of information included in threat feeds is made to answer a question to a particular test. If the question on the test is changed, then the data cease to be useful (Williamson 2016). In such case, an atomic indicator has its own life which has no value in being shared with others.

Facing this challenge, the following solutions could be worth some consideration. Security teams need to contextualize the threat data they collect with the specific internal vulnerabilities and weaknesses (Bellis 2015). For this purpose, they should select the data they collect, or build/purchase large analytics platforms to cope with the quantity of data. There are massive dedicated teams, cleaning the Internet, looking at the targeted attacks, analyzing staff and trying to find associations. This process can also be automated using techniques of artificial intelligence. For example, machine learning approaches are used to build a base knowledge which will be able to infer new relationships (i.e. associations) between entities at hand or predict new events. Following the same idea, it is suggested in Ring (2014) to use managed security services, as an increasing number of organizations start to outsource this area.

Regarding the huge flow of malware variants which is gaining access to networks and computer systems or reaching organizations' honeypots, it is impossible to handle them individually. Identifying the mutations of malware variants is essential in order to recognize those belonging to the same family. Data science and machine-learning models are looking to deliver entirely new ways of searching malware. Instead of taking a 1-for-1 approach where each threat is mapped to a signature and/or IOC, data science models are analyzing a huge number of threats, to learn what they all have in common. Methods of malware analysis, detection, classification and clustering should be either automated or designed in such a way that makes future automation possible (Ghanaei et al. 2016). As for new research work, in Ghanaei et al. (2016), the authors propose a supervised learning method based on statistics to classify new malware variants into their related malware families. In the same vein, VirusBattle (Miles et al. 2014) is a prototype system that employs state-of-the-art malware analyses to automatically discover interrelationships among instances of malware. This solution analyzes malware interrelations over many types of malware artifacts, including binaries, codes, dynamic behaviors and malware metadata. The result is a malware interrelation graph. Cuckoo (Guarnieri et al. 2016) and Malheur (Rieck 2013) are well-known open-source platforms that automate the task of analyzing malicious files in a sandbox environment. Cuckoo uses both a static analysis (i.e. code or binary analysis) and a dynamic analysis (i.e. behavior analysis) (Oktavianto and Muhardianto 2013) whereas Malheur uses a dynamic analysis. To identify a malware family using Cuckoo, one can create some customized signatures that can be run against the analysis results in order to identify a predefined pattern that might represent a particular malicious behavior. This requires a local specialist to investigate the results and classify the analyzed samples. On the other hand, Malheur uses machine learning to collect behavioral analysis data inside sandbox reports and categorizes malware into similar groups called "clusters" (Rieck et al. 2011). Malheur builds on the concept of dynamic analysis, which means that malware binaries are collected in the wild and executed. The execution of each malware binary results in a report of recorded behavior. Malheur analyzes these reports for discovery and discrimination of malware classes using machine learning.

Well-known public sandboxes such as Cuckoo and Malheur have now become highly detectable by malware (Issa 2012; Ferrand 2015). Once such systems are made publicly available, malware authors try to protect themselves and to evade detection by checking whether they are in an emulated environment or in a real one (e.g. by checking the execution time). To face this issue, new research is currently being carried out. For example, in Ferrand (2015), the author shows that with a few modifications and tricks on Cuckoo and the virtual machine, it is possible to prevent malwares from detecting whether they are being analyzed, or at least make this detection harder.

1.8.3. *Trust to share threat data and to save reputation concerns*

Effective sharing requires trust. Since shared threat data might be sensitive (e.g. reveal that an organization has been attacked), organizations will be reluctant to share when they are not in a trusted environment. This is proved in some studies conducted on the economic cost of sharing security data, which have demonstrated that sharing can result in a loss of market due to negative publicity (Campbell *et al.* 2003; Cavusoglu *et al.* 2004). To avoid such consequences, techniques for fine-grained and context-based access control are critical to protect confidentiality and privacy of data (Tounsi *et al.* 2013). Shared threat data could also be contaminated by malicious activity and contain erroneous information. In such a case, establishing trust at least requires authentication of transmissions and encryption of content. To avoid the consequences of identity revelation, anonymous sharing is another solution that provides participants a channel in which they can communicate anonymously. In a recent work (Dunning and Kresman 2013), the authors have developed an algorithm to anonymously share private data between participants.

Trust is also important on another level. It is generally unwise to allow threat actors to learn what you know about them, lest they change their methods. Thus, closed and trusted groups can enable deeper sharing than would otherwise be possible.

Generally, the more a group can trust its members and the security of information within the group, the more effective the sharing tends to be (Chismon and Ruks 2015). However, a certain level of trust in the group should be guaranteed. If a participant believes there is more consumption of the threat information than sharing in the network, the motivation to share information will rapidly decline. To address this issue, some research work has been initiated. In Cascella (2008), the game theory approach using the prisoner's dilemma is employed to model the interactions of rational and selfish nodes in distributed systems. The study shows that by incepting a reputation system, it is possible to distinguish good players (threat sharers) and bad players (threat consumers). In Seredynski *et al.* (2007), a sanction mechanism that makes a decision to discard/forward packets is proposed based on an evolving genetic algorithm. The aim is to enhance trust between several nodes transmitting data packets. However, in voluntary threat sharing mechanisms, the use of sanction and punishment would not be very interesting. Other research has shown that instead of punishing, encouraging good behavior increases the likelihood of participants being more involved in a sharing program in the long run. For example, participants that receive social approval can have a significant positive impact on cooperative behavior (Cook *et al.* 2013). It is also shown that having organizations involved in the quality assurance process improves the cooperation among participants and increases the level of trust (Gerspacher and Lemieux 2010). Finally, Furnell *et al.* (2007) conclude that competitive advantage of threat intelligence can be gained for whichever side employs social factors better, involving human, social and organizational matters that are mostly uncharted on the computer security research agenda. For example, assuming that face-to-face interactions usually occur in a trusted environment (MITRE Corporation 2012), the one-to-one human contacts can be one of the simplest, yet most effective and trusted sources of actionable information (Chismon and Ruks 2015).

1.8.4. *Standards for CTI representation and sharing*

Sharing security knowledge between experts across organizations is an essential countermeasure to recent sophisticated attacks, and organizations can benefit from other organizations' experiences to build a collective knowledge (Williamson 2016).

Organizations have traditionally shared threat information using *ad hoc* solutions such as phone calls, encrypted emails or ticketing systems. More recently, they used portals and blogs, a trend of building interconnected communities with associated platforms to exchange threat information semi-automatically (Sillaber *et al.* 2016). Latent semantic analysis (LSA)

(Landauer *et al.* 1998) was used to find semantically related topics in a web blog corpus. Important keywords of each topic are assigned quantitative measure through probabilistic LSA (PLSA) (Hofmann 1999). The results prove the efficiency of this approach to broadly search security-related news in massive web blogs. However, this approach is limited because of the limitation of web blogs in representing threat scenarios in a real-time and structured manner. Li *et al.* (2007) focus on the problem of true threat identification where network security data are managed at distributed locations. The authors provide several means of finding correlations between alerts arriving from distributed components. The major limitation of this work is once more the lack of standardization as alert data need to be converted to a uniform representation given the multiple TTI sources of information. A concept that has emerged is the use of threat intelligence libraries, also called threat intelligence platforms (Poputa-Clean and Stingley 2015). These libraries were designed to solve the collection and storing problems of TTI and to facilitate sharing threat information with other organizations. However, efficient automation and collection from a diverse set of products and systems require structured and standardized threat information representation (Barnum 2014; Wagner *et al.* 2016), which is expected to be expressive, flexible, extensible, machine-parsable and human-readable (Barnum 2014; Heckman *et al.* 2015).

Several efforts have been made to facilitate threat information sharing in a standardized manner. IODEF (Danyliw *et al.* 2007), RID (Moriarty 2012), STIX (Structured Threat Information eXpression), TAXII (Trusted Automated eXchange of Indicator Information) (Barnum 2014), OpenIOC (Open Incident of Compromise) (Mandiant 2017), CybOX (Cyber Observable Expression) (MITRE 2017e), VERIS (Vocabulary for Event Recording and Incident Sharing) (Verizon 2017), CAPEC (Common Attack Pattern Enumeration and Classification) (MITRE 2017c), MAEC (Malware Attribution and Enumeration Characterization) (MITRE 2017b) and ATT&CK (Adversarial Tactics, Techniques & Common Knowledge) (MITRE 2017a) are popular examples of such standardized efforts. Despite these initiatives of standardization, an interesting survey from SANS (Shackleford 2015) indicates that in 2015, only 38% of organizations were using TI data in standard formats and well-known open-source toolkits. In order to select the right standard for a particular use case, Burger *et al.* (2014) provide an agonistic framework in which standards can be evaluated and assessed. In the following, we briefly examine the aforementioned standards.

STIX and TAXII have appeared as improvement initiatives to IODEF and RID, where RID and TAXII are the transport protocols for IODEF and STIX respectively. Formerly developed by the MITRE corporation, STIX and TAXII are sponsored by the Department of Homeland Security (DHS) office of cyber security and communications. They have been introduced to combine human and machine data for sharing information.

Today, STIX is a commonly used standard even though it is very complex to implement (Kampanakis 2014). STIX is modular and can incorporate other standards efficiently (Burger *et al.* 2014). The STIX architecture is composed of eight core cyber-threat concepts: campaigns, indicators, observables, TTP (tactics, techniques and procedures), incidents, ThreatActors, ExploitTargets and courses of action.

STIX can embed CybOX, IODEF and some OpenIOC extensions, in addition to XML namespaces, extensions for YARA rules (Google Inc. *et al.* 2017), Snort rules (The Snort Team 2017) and non-XML bindings (i.e. using JSON). STIX uses CybOX as a representation of Observables. CybOX is a schema for the specification, capture and characterization of observable operational events. STIX can also include IODEF in place of the IncidentType extension and OpenIOC extensions in place of CybOX, to express non-standard Indicator patterns.

XML namespaces that STIX can embed are the MITRE CAPEC, MAEC and ATT&CK, to cite a few. CAPEC schema attributes characterize how cyber threats are executed and provide ways to defend against these threats. MAEC schema provides a standardized language about malware based on artifacts, behaviors and attack patterns. ATT&CK was released as a framework of adversary post-compromise techniques (Strom 2016). It describes patterns to characterize adversarial behavior on the network and endpoints to achieve its objectives in a standard way. Since CAPEC enumerates a range of attack patterns across the entire cyberattack life cycle (i.e. not just techniques used during post-compromise), the CAPEC ID references are added to the attack pattern descriptions in ATT&CK. For malware researchers using YARA for regular expression matching and analysis or for communities whose interest is intrusion detection using Snort, there are extensions for YARA and Snort rules supported by STIX (Kampanakis 2014). YARA is an engine and language for scanning files and memory blocks. When a rule matches a pattern, YARA presumes to classify the subject according to the rule's behavior. Snort is an open-source packet analyzer with intelligence to match rule sets and trigger actions when there are expression matches (Burger *et al.* 2014). Finally, VERIS system is a characterization of cyber incidents after they have occurred. It is intended for strategic trend analysis, risk management and metrics.

These multiple efforts to obtain different data ontologies for threat information sharing are not without disadvantages. These ontologies often overlap and do not offer a solution to the entire community (Burger *et al.* 2014). There could be duplications and gaps in the threat information ontologies in different communities, which lead to a duplication of effort for effective collaboration. Thus, there is a need for participants to have a common language and toolset to facilitate sharing and threat analytics.

1.8.5. *Cloud-based CTI libraries for collective knowledge and immunity*

1.8.5.1. *Using private/community cloud solutions*

There is no right or wrong answer when choosing to maintain CTI in the cloud via a third-party cloud provider or in a private collaborative solution. Organizations may find that some threat intelligence data have low impact and are relatively easy to transit within the cloud whereas other more critical data may be best kept on site. It all depends on the business, the data that the organization possesses and the comfort level of having a third party managing the risk.

The choice could also be for financial reasons. Private cloud often requires significant capital investment that covers all systems management, patching and future upgrades of hardware and software which are supported by the provider in public cloud solution. Facing such issue, the community cloud-based TI could be the best solution, as each member organization in a community cloud may host some portion, or applications, that all organizations in a community can leverage. However, it is worth noting that the deployment of cloud community requires an extensive and deep long-term relationship between multiple organizations in order to build, govern and operate from a community cloud (Bond 2015). Finally, many technical leaders (Ellison 2014) advocate a hybrid model to threat intelligence-driven security where both coexist (Rouse 2015). In such a case, multiple private/community and/or public cloud providers could interconnect.

1.8.5.2. *Being aware of major security concerns in the cloud*

Some security organizations have released their research findings on major security concerns related to the cloud to assist companies interested in joining cloud computing and security data storage. The aim is to encourage them to make a wise decision while being fully aware of the associated risks. This also encourages new customers to ask the appropriate questions and consider getting a security assessment from a neutral third party before committing to a cloud provider (Khorshed *et al.* 2012).

Since June 2008, the security farm Gartner published a report (Heiser and Nicolett 2008), where it identifies seven specific security issues that customers should raise with providers before selecting the service. The specific issues are privileged user access, regulatory compliance, data location, data segregation, recovery, investigative support and long-term viability.

In November 2009, the European Network and Information Security Agency (ENISA) published another research document for risk and recommendation in cloud computing (Catteddu and Hogben 2009), which is until now referenced by many organizations and certifications (Cloud Security Alliance 2017a). The document lists eight important cloud-specific risks which are: loss of governance, lock-in, isolation failure, compliance risks, management interface compromise, data protection, insecure or incomplete data deletion and malicious insiders. They have also discussed risk management and provided recommendations.

Cloud Security Alliance (CSA) has published via the Top Threats Working Group their most recent research findings on the top threats of cloud computing in February 2016 (Cloud Security Alliance 2016). The purpose is to provide organizations with an up-to-date, expert-informed understanding of cloud security concerns in order to identify major risks and make educated risk-management decisions regarding cloud adoption strategies. In this recent edition of the report, experts identified the following 12 critical issues in cloud security, ranked in order of severity per survey results: data breaches, weak identity, credential and access management, insecure APIs, system and application vulnerabilities, account hijacking, malicious insiders, advanced persistent threats (APTs), data loss, insufficient due diligence, abuse and nefarious use of cloud services, denial of service, and shared technology issues.

Finally, CSA released version 4.0 of its security guidance in cloud computing in December 2017, in which fourteen areas of concerns are identified and categorized into six modules (Cloud Security Alliance 2017b). These are as follows: cloud computing concepts and architectures, governance and enterprise risk management, legal issues, contracts and electronic discovery, compliance and audit management, information governance, management plane and business continuity, infrastructure security, virtualization and containers, incident response, application security, data security and encryption, identity, entitlement, access management, security as a service and related technologies. The documents have quickly become the industry-standard catalogue of best practices for secure cloud computing.

The purpose of all these research works is to assist cloud providers as well as their potential customers in identifying the major risks and to help them decide whether or not to join in cloud infrastructure, and to proactively protect them from these risks.

1.9. Evaluation of technical threat intelligence tools

Now that organizations have found ways to collect huge amounts of information from a wide variety of sources using threat libraries, they are in need of tools to manage the flow of information and convert it into knowledge and actions. Although the existing TI tools need more sophistication (Shackleford 2016), they have been able to achieve a level of maturity that enables organizations to start filtering and sharing information effectively (Brown *et al.* 2015). There are several open-source projects and commercial enterprises offering products to access threat intelligence. These solutions mainly aim at content aggregation and collaborative research such as IBM X-Force Exchange (IBM 2017), Alien-vault OTX Pulse (AlienVault 2007), Recorded Future (Pace *et al.* 2018) and Crowdstrike intelligence exchange (CrowdStrike Inc. 2014). Other solutions are focused on providing TI advanced management options with the possibility of having private instances. These include EclecticIQ (ElecticIQ 2017), Threat-stream (Anomali 2017), ThreatQuotient (ThreatQuotient 2017), ThreatConnect (Threatconnect 2017), MISP (Andre *et al.* 2011), CRITS (MITRE 2017d), Soltra Edge (Soltra 2017), CIF v3 (also called bearded-avenger) (CSIRT Gadgets 2016), IntelMQ (European CERTs/CSIRTs 2014) and Hippocampe (CERT Banque de France 2017). We are focusing on recent open-source tools that offer advanced management options, specifically IntelMQ, Hippocampe and Threatelligence (Phillips 2014). This evaluation complements the previous comparative discussion in Tounsi and Rais (2018), where other free and/or open-source tools can be found.

1.9.1. *Presentation of selected tools*

Some of the aforementioned tools have begun to gain popularity as they promise a more organized storage of IOC and a powerful parsing of the latter. We name IntelMQ, Hippocampe and Threatelligence as examples.

These tools are presented and evaluated according to different functional dimensions (see section 1.9.2). Technical information related to these tools is taken from various sources: official tools sites, white papers, research articles and live interactions with some of the tools' authors.

IntelMQ (European CERTs/CSIRTs 2014) is a community-driven initiative called IHAP (Incident Handling Automation Project) which was conceptually designed by European CERTs units during several InfoSec events in 2014. The solution was designed for CERTs to improve the incident handling processes, using a message queue protocol, to collect and process security feeds, pastebins and tweets.

Hippocampe (CERT Banque de France 2017) is an open-source project released in 2016 by the CERT of the Banque de France. It aggregates feeds from the Internet in an ElasticSearch cluster. It allows organizations to query it easily through a REST API or a Web UI. It is based on a Python script which fetches URLs corresponding to feeds, and parses and indexes them. It is part of the Hive project which is designed to make life easier for SOCs, CSIRTs, CERTs and any information security practitioner dealing with security incidents.

Threatelligence (Phillips 2014) is a cyber-threat intelligence feed collector, using ElasticSearch, Kibana and Python. It was created in 2014 by a professional and very implicated developer in cyber security. It fetches TI data from various custom or public sources into ElasticSearch while enriching them slightly (i.e. looking for geographic locations). It automatically updates feeds and tries to further enhance data for dashboards.

The dashboards that are built using Kibana are used to display data and facilitate searching through them.

1.9.2. *Comparative discussion*

The market maturation is encouraging all the CTI vendors and open-source initiatives to adopt a common set of features. The important features include (Poputa-Clean and Stingley 2015): (1) integration with other security tools (e.g. via an API), (2) data enrichment (i.e. the possibility of integrating other intelligence platforms, for example MISP (Malware Information Sharing Platform) (Andre *et al.* 2011)), (3) integration with other tools created by the same provider and (4) sharing TI features.

Taking into account the aforementioned criteria, we focus our evaluation on the presence of Web API, indexation with MISP (as a standard OSINT feed), interaction with other tools from the same provider, IOC storage and updating, and Web User Interface (UI) capabilities. Table 1.4 summarizes this evaluation.

Criteria/Tool	Hippocampe	IntelMQ	Threatelligence
Project status	Young. Active since 2016	Mature. Active since 2014	Young. Inactive since 2014
Main language	Python	Python	Python
Built in Web API	Yes. Available to retrieve IOCs	No	No
MISP indexing	Not supported, but in the roadmap	A "Collector Robot" for MISP is available	No
Interaction with other products from the same provider	Works seamlessly with Cortex (TI analyzer) and TheHive (incident response tool)	No	No
IOC storage	Uses ElasticSearch: – IOCs are saved in ElasticSearch – IOCs are organized by feed sources	No database required: – Using Redis[1] as data store – IOCs are stored in a JSON file by default. Each IOC from a source corresponds to a JSON record in the file[2]	Uses ElasticSearch: – IOCs are saved in ElasticSearch – IOCs are organized by attack type

IOC updating	For an old IOC record in the database, update only the "last appearance" field. If a new IOC is listed by two feed sources, the IOC will be added to ElasticSearch for each feed	Not clear. The bot "Deduplicator" could filter all duplicated IOC	The same old IOC in the database will be overridden. There is no "First appearance" and "Last appearance" fields
Web UI capabilities	Display the number of IOC by type or by feed Display each feed collector working status (last running time, number of all IOC obtained, number of new IOCs)	Display collector, parser and expert relationship graph. Allow addition or deletion of bots with UI. Allow monitoring and control of bots (start, stop, reload, restart, configure)	N/A

1 https://redis.io/.

2 IntelMQ provides other storage choices, such as ElasticSearch and PostgreSQL.

Table 1.4. *Evaluation of threat intelligence tools*

1.10. Conclusion and future work

As organizations continue to move to the cloud, indicators of compromise (IOC) are also changing. Thus, the impact of cyber security to an organization goes beyond the classic bounds of the technical computer domain. Access to data, their linkage with email accounts, web applications and documents stored in a variety of platforms and mobile devices stretch the need of an organization to protect their data. We have seen that cyber threat intelligence (CTI) has many advantages in supporting several security activities. Discovering covert cyberattacks and new malware, issuing early warnings and selectively distributing TI data, are just some of these advantages. We have given a clear definition of threat intelligence and how literature subdivides it. We have focused on TTI, which is the most-consumed intelligence, and the major problems related to it. We have found that on one hand, timeliness of information is very important when protecting against zero-day exploits. On the other hand, fast sharing of IOC is not sufficient when dealing with targeted attacks, since specific network and host-based indicators may only be used once by the attacker in a true targeted attack. In this case, targeted defenses are also needed where security teams within organizations have to collect and filter threat data with a focus on their internal vulnerabilities and weaknesses. We surveyed new research works, trends and standards to mitigate TTI problems and delivered the most widely used sharing strategies based on trust and anonymity so that participating organizations can do away with the risks of business leak. Clearly, the more a group can trust its organization members, the more effective the sharing tends to be. However, before building community-based organizations, it is worth considering some common factors that are related to business process, stability and cooperation policy. Finally, as security data are shared between participants, aggregated from different sources and linked to other data already present in the datasets, the number of errors will increase. Consequently, a standardized format of threat and a common vocabulary for extra data entry minimizes the risks of data quality issues and provides better automated analytics solutions on large volumes of threat data.

While scalability and accuracy remain an ultimate need for producing actionable IOC, approaches to the collection, processing and analysis of all kinds of intelligence have traditionally relied heavily on the capability of humans to understand references, filter out noise and ultimately make a decision about actions that need to be taken. Today's proliferation of sophisticated cyber attacks and consequently the massive number of indicators of compromise make it paramount to automate at least both information collection and processing, considering the diverse sources of threat data. Artificial intelligence is the best candidate to realize this objective, especially after the advent of cloud computing made access to supercomputer capabilities affordable and opened doors to artificial intelligence being applied to more and more complex problems.

1.11. References

Abuse.ch. (2017). Zeus Tracker [Online]. Available: https://zeustracker.abuse.ch [Accessed January 2017].

Ahrend, J.M., Jirotka, M., and Jones, K. (2016). On the collaborative practices of cyber threat intelligence analysts to develop and utilize tacit Threat and Defence Knowledge. *International Conference on Cyber Situational Awareness, Data Analytics and Assessment (CyberSA)*, IEEE, 1–10.

AlienVault (2007). AlienVault open threat exchange. [Online]. Available: https://www. alienvault.com/open-threat-exchange [Accessed January 2017].

Andre, D., Dereszowski, A., Dulaunoy, A., Iklody, A., Vandeplas, C., and Vinot, R. (2011). MISP: Malware Information Sharing Platform [Online]. Available: http://www. misp-project.org/ [Accessed January 2017].

Anomali (2017). [Online]. Available: https://www.anomali.com/product/ threatstream [Accessed January 2017].

Barnum, S. (2014) Standardizing cyber threat intelligence information with the structured threat information expression (STIX). *MITRE Corporation*, 11, 1–22.

Barraco, L. (2014). Defend like an attacker: Applying the cyber kill chain, [Online]. Available: www.alienvault.com/blogs/security-essentials/defend-like-an-attacker-applying-the-cyber-kill-chain.

Bellis, E. (2015). The problem with your threat intelligence. White paper, Kenna Security, July.

Bipartisan Policy Center (2012). Cyber security task force: Public-private information sharing, National Security Program, July.

Bond, J. (2015). Planning and Architecture. In *The Enterprise Cloud* [Online]. O'Reilly Media, Inc. Available: https://www.safaribooksonline.com/ library/view/the-enterprise-cloud/9781491907832/ch01.html.

Brown, S., Gommers, J., and Serrano, O. (2015). From cyber security information sharing to threat management. *Proceedings of the 2nd ACM Workshop on Information Sharing and Collaborative Security*, ACM, pp. 43–49.

Burger, E.W., Goodman, M.D., Kampanakis, P., and Zhu, K.A. (2014). Taxonomy model for cyber threat intelligence information exchange technologies. *Proceedings of the 2014 ACM Workshop on Information Sharing & Collaborative Security*, ACM, pp. 51–60.

Campbell, K., Gordon, L.A., Loeb, M.P., and Zhou, L. (2003). The economic cost of publicly announced information security breaches: Empirical evidence from the stock market. *Journal of Computer Security*, 11(3), 431–448.

Cascella, R.G. (2008). The "value" of reputation in peer-to-peer networks. *5th IEEE Consumer Communications and Networking Conference, CCNC 2008*, IEEE, 516–520.

Catteddu, D. and Hogben, G. (2009). Benefits, risks and recommendations for information security. *European Network and Information Security*, November.

Cavusoglu, H., Cavusoglu, H., and Raghunathan, S. (2004). How should we disclose software vulnerabilities. *Proceedings of Workshop on Information Technology and Systems*, pp. 243–248.

CERT Banque de France (2017). Hippocampe [Online]. Available: https://github.com/TheHive-Project/Hippocampe [Accessed April 2018].

Chismon, D. and Ruks, M. (2015). Threat intelligence: Collecting, analysing, evaluating. MWR Infosecurity, UK Cert, United Kingdom.

Choo, K.-K.R. (2011). The cyber threat landscape: Challenges and future research directions. *Computers & Security*, 30(8), 719–731.

Choo, K.-K.R., Smith, R.G., and McCusker, R. (2007). *Future Directions in Technology-enabled Crime: 2007–09*. Australian Institute of Criminology, Canberra, Australia.

Cloud Security Alliance (2016). The treacherous 12 – Cloud computing top threats in 2016 [Online]. Available: https://downloads.cloudsecurityalliance.org/assets/research/top-threats/Treacherous-12_Cloud-Computing_Top-Threats.pdf.

Cloud Security Alliance (2017a). Certificate of cloud security knowledge [Online]. Available: https://cloudsecurityalliance.org/education/ccsk.

Cloud Security Alliance (2017b). Security guidance for critical areas of focus in cloud computing v4.0 [Online]. Available: https://downloads. cloudsecurityalliance.org/assets/research/security-guidance/security-guidance-v4-FINAL.pdf.

Cook, K.S., Cheshire, C., Rice, E.R., and Nakagawa, S. (2013). Social exchange Theory. In *Handbook of Social Psychology*, DeLamater, J. and Ward, A. (eds). Springer.

CrowdStrike, Inc. (2014). CSIX: CrowdStrike Intelligence Exchange [Online]. Available: https://www.crowdstrike.com/products/falcon-intelligence/.

CSIRT Gadgets. (2016). Bearded-avenger (CIF v3) [Online]. Available: http://csirtgadgets.org/bearded-avenger [Accessed February 2017].

Dalziel, H. (2014). *How to Define and Build an Effective Cyber Threat Intelligence Capability*. Syngress Publishing.

Danyliw, R., Meijer, J., and Demchenko, Y. (2007). The Incident Object Description Exchange Format (IODEF). *Internet Engineering Task Force (IETF), RFC-5070*.

Dshield (2017). [Online]. Available: https://www.dshield.org [Accessed January 2017].

Dunning, L.A. and Kresman, R. (2013). Privacy preserving data sharing with anonymous ID assignment. *IEEE Transactions on Information Forensics and Security*, 8(2), 402–413.

ElecticIQ (2017). EclecticIQ Platform [Online]. Available: https://www.eclecticiq.com/platform [Accessed January 2017].

Ellison, L. (2014). *Oracle Cloud and Your Datacenter Coexist*. Oracle Media Network.

ENISA: European Union Agency for Network and Information Security (2006). CERT cooperation and its further facilitation by relevant stakeholders.

ENISA: European Union Agency for Network and Information Security (2013). Detect, SHARE, Protect – Solutions for improving threat data exchange among CERTs.

ENISA: European Union Agency for Network and Information (2015). Cyber security information sharing: An overview of regulatory and non-regulatory approaches [Online]. Available: https://www.enisa.europa.eu/publications/cybersecurity-information-sharing/at_download/fullReport.

ENISA: European Union Agency for Network and Information (2017). ENISA threat landscape report 2016–15 top cyber threats and trends.

European CERTs/CSIRTs (2014). IntelMQ [Online]. Available: https://github.com/certtools/intelmq [Accessed April 2018].

Fadilpasic, S. (September 2016). Social media still an important tool for phishing. White paper, ITProPortal.

Falliere, N. and Chien, E. (2009). Zeus: King of the bots. Symantec Security Response. Available: https://www.symantec.com/content/dam/symantec/docs/security-center/white-papers/security-response-zeus-king-of-bots-09-en.pdf.

Ferrand, O. (2015). How to detect the cuckoo sandbox and to strengthen it? *Journal of Computer Virology and Hacking Techniques*, 11(1), 51–58.

FireEye Inc. (2012). Advanced targeted attacks – How to protect against the next generation of cyber attacks. Technical report.

FireEye Inc. (2014). Taking a lean-forward approach to combat today's cyber attacks. Technical report.

Fossi, M., Turner, D., Johnson, E., Mack, T., Adams, T., Blackbird, J., Entwisle, S., Graveland, B., McKinney, D., Mulcahy, J., and Wueest, C. (2010). Symantec global internet security threat report trends for 2009. White paper, symantec enterprise security, 15.

Furnell, S., Clarke, N., Beznosov, K., and Beznosova, O. (2007). On the imbalance of the security problem space and its expected consequences. *Information Management & Computer Security*, 15(5), 420–431.

Gerspacher, N. and Lemieux, F. (2010). A market-oriented explanation of the expansion of the role of Europol: Filling the demand for criminal intelligence through entrepreneurial initiatives. *International Police Cooperation: Emerging Issues, Theory and Practice*. Willan Publishing, Culompton.

Ghanaei, V., Iliopoulos, C.S., and Overill, R.E. (2016). Statistical approach towards malware classification and detection. *SAI Computing Conference*, IEEE, pp. 1093–1099.

Gilligan, J., Heitkamp, K., Dix, R., Palmer, C., Sorenson, J., Conway, T., Varley, W., Gagnon, G., Lentz, R., Venables, P., Paller, A., Lute, J.H., and Reeder, F. (2014). The economics of cybersecurity part II: Extending the cyber-security framework. Technical report, Armed Forces Communications and Electronics Association Cyber Committee.

Google Inc., Bengen, H., Metz, J., Buehlmann, S., and Alvarez Yara V.M. (2017). [Online]. Available: http://virustotal.github.io/yara [Accessed July 2017].

Guarnieri, C., Tanasi, A., Bremer, J., and Schloesser, M. (2016). Cuckoo sandbox [Online]. Available: https://www.cuckoosandbox.org.

Gundert, L. (2014). Producing a world-class threat intelligence capability. White paper, Recorded Future.

Heckman, K.E., Stech, F.J., Thomas, R.K., Schmoker, B., and Tsow, A.W., (2015). *Cyber Denial, Deception and Counter Deception*. Springer.

Heiser, J. and Nicolett, M. (2008). Assessing the security risks of Cloud computing [Online]. Available: https://www.gartner.com/doc/685308/assessing-security-risks-cloud-computing.

Hofmann, T. (1999). Probabilistic latent semantic indexing. *Proceedings of the 22nd Annual International ACM SIGIR Conference on Research and Development in Information Retrieval*, ACM, pp. 50–57.

Holland R., Balaouras S., and Mak K. (2013). Five steps to build an effective threat intelligence capability. Forrester Research, Inc.

Hugh, P. (2016). What is threat intelligence? Definition and examples [Online]. Available: https://www.recordedfuture.com/threat-intelligence-definition.

Hutchins, E.M., Cloppert, M.J., and Amin, R.M. (2011). Intelligence-driven computer network defense informed by analysis of adversary campaigns and intrusion kill chains. *Leading Issues in Information Warfare & Security Research*, 1, 80.

IBM (2017). X-Force exchange [Online]. Available: https://exchange.xforce. ibmcloud.com [Accessed January 2017].

iSightPartners (2014). What is cyber threat intelligence and why do I need it? iSIGHT Partners, Inc.

Issa, A. (2012). Anti-virtual machines and emulations. *Journal in Computer Virology*, 8(4), 141–149.

Johnson, C.S., Badger, M.L., Waltermire, D.A., Snyder, J., and Skorupka, C. (2016). Guide to cyber threat information sharing. Technical report, NIST Special Publication.

Kampanakis, P. (2014). Security automation and threat information-sharing options. *IEEE Security & Privacy*, 12(5), 42–51.

Keeling, C. (2013). Waking Shark II – Desktop cyber exercise – Report to participants. Technical report.

Khorshed, M.T., Ali, A.S., and Wasimi, S.A. (2012). A survey on gaps, threat remediation challenges and some thoughts for proactive attack detection in cloud computing. *Future Generation Computer Systems*, 28(6), 833–851.

Korstanje, M.E. (2016). Threat mitigation and detection of cyber warfare and terrorism activities. *Advances in Information Security, Privacy, and Ethics (AISPE) 2016*.

Landauer, T.K., Foltz, P.W., and Laham, D. (1998). An introduction to latent semantic analysis. *Discourse Processes*, 25(2–3), 259–284.

Li, Z.-T., Lei, J., Wang, L., Li, D., and Ma, Y.-M. (2007). Towards identifying true threat from network security data. *Pacific-Asia Workshop on Intelligence and Security Informatics*, Springer.

Lightcyber (2016) Cloud based threat intelligence [Online]. Available: http://lightcyber. com/glossary/cloud-based-threat-intelligence [Accessed January2017].

Mandiant (2017) OpenIOC [Online]. Available: http://www.openioc.org [Accessed July 2017].

McMillan, R. (2013). *Definition: Threat Intelligence*. Gartner.

Miles, C., Lakhotia, A., LeDoux, C., Newsom, A., and Notani, V. (2014). VirusBattle: State-of-the-art malware analysis for better cyber threat intelligence. *2014 7th International Symposium on Resilient Control Systems (ISRCS)*, IEEE, pp. 1–6.

MITRE (2012). Cyber information-sharing models: An overview. Case no. 11-4486.

MITRE (2017a). ATT&CK: Adversarial Tactics, Techniques & Common Knowledge [Online]. Available: https://attack.mitre.org/wiki/Main_Page [Accessed July 2017].

MITRE (2017b). MAEC: Malware Attribute Enumeration and Characterization [Online]. Available: https://maec.mitre.org [Accessed July 2017].

MITRE (2017c). CAPEC: Common Attack Pattern Enumeration and Classification [Online]. Available: https://capec.mitre.org [Accessed July 2017].

MITRE (2017d). CRITS: Collaborative Research Into Threats [Online]. Available: https://crits.github.io/ [Accessed January 2017].

MITRE (2017e). Cyber Observable eXpression [Online]. Available: http://cyboxproject.github.io [Accessed July 2017].

Moriarty, K.M. (2011). Incident coordination. *IEEE Security & Privacy*, 9(6), 71–75.

Moriarty, K.M. (2012). Real-time inter-network defense (RID). *Internet Engineering Task Force (IETF), RFC-6545*.

Murdoch, S., and Leaver, N. (2015) Anonymity vs. trust in cyber-security collaboration. *Proceedings of the 2nd ACM Workshop on Information Sharing and Collaborative Security*, ACM, pp. 27–29.

National High Tech Crime Unit of the Netherlands police, Europol's European Cybercrime Centre, Kaspersky Lab, Intel Security (2017). No more ransom project [Online]. Available: https://www.nomoreransom.org/index.html [Accessed July 2017].

Niddel Corp (2014). TIQ-Test – Threat Intelligence Quotient Test [Online]. Available: https://github.com/mlsecproject/tiq-test.

Oktavianto, D. and Muhardianto, I. (2013). *Cuckoo Malware Analysis*. Packt Publishing Ltd.

OrbITPeaple (2016). Migrating oracle databases to database cloud service.

Pace, C., Barysevich, A., Gundert, L., Liska, A., McDaniel, M., and Wetzel, J., (2018). *A Practical Guide for Security Teams to Unlocking the Power of Intelligence*. Cyber Edge Press.

Pepper, C. (2015). Applied threat intelligence. Technical report, Securosis.

Peretti, K. (2014). Cyber threat intelligence: To share or not to share – What are the real concerns? Privacy and security report, Bureau of National Affairs.

Phillips, G. (2014). Threatelligence v0.1 [Online]. Available: https://github.com/syphon1c/Threatelligence.

Pinto, A. and Sieira, A. (2015). Data-driven threat intelligence: Useful methods and measurements for handling indicators. *27th Annual FIRST Conference*, June.

Piper, S. (2013). *Definitive Guide to Next Generation Threat Protection*. CyberEdge Group, LLC.

Ponemon (2013). Live threat intelligence impact report 2013. Technical report.

Ponemon (2014). Exchanging cyber threat intelligence: There has to be a better way. Technical report.

Ponemon (2015). Second annual study on exchanging cyber threat intelligence: There has to be a better way. Technical report.

Poputa-Clean, P. and Stingley, M. (2015). Automated defense – Using threat intelligence to augment security [Online]. *SANS Institute InfoSec Reading Room*. Available: https://www.sans.org/reading-room/whitepapers/threats/automated-defense-threat-intelligence-augment-35692.

Ray, J. (2015). *Understanding the Threat Landscape: Indicators of Compromise (IOCs)*. Verisign.

RecordedFuture (2017). Threat intelligence, information, and data: What is the difference? [Online]. Available: https://www.recordedfuture.com/threat-intelligence-data/.

Richards, K. (2009). *The Australian Business Assessment of Computer User Security (ABACUS): A National Survey*. Australian Institute of Criminology.

Rieck, K. (2013). Malheur [Online]. Available: http://www.mlsec.org/malheur.

Rieck, K., Trinius, P., Willems, C., and Holz, T. (2011). Automatic analysis of malware behavior using machine learning. *Journal of Computer Security*, 19(4), 639–668.

Ring, T. (2014). Threat intelligence: Why people don't share. *Computer Fraud & Security*, 2014(3), 5–9.

Rouse, M. (2015). Hybrid Cloud [Online]. TechTarget.

Sauerwein, C., Sillaber, C., Mussmann, A., and Breu, R. (2017). Threat intelligence sharing platforms: An exploratory study of software vendors and research perspectives. *Towards Thought Leadership in Digital Transformation: 13. Internationale Tagung Wirtschaftsinformatik* [Online]. Available: http://aisel.aisnet.org/wi2017/track08/paper/3.

Schneier, B. (2000). Software complexity and security [Online]. Crypto-Gram.

Seredynski, M., Bouvry, P., and Klopotek, M.A. (2007). Modelling the evolution of cooperative behavior in ad hoc networks using a game based model. *IEEE Symposium on Computational Intelligence and Games, 2007*, pp. 96–103.

Shackleford, D. (2015). Who's using cyberthreat intelligence and how? – A SANS Survey. Technical report, SANS Insitute.

Shackleford, D. (2016). The SANS state of cyber threat intelligence survey: CTI important and maturing. Technical report, SANS Institute.

Sillaber, C., Sauerwein, C., Mussmann, A., and Breu, R. (2016). Data quality challenges and future research directions in threat intelligence sharing practice. *Proceedings of the 2016 ACM on Workshop on Information Sharing and Collaborative Security*, ACM, pp. 65–70.

Skopik, F., Settanni, G., and Fiedler, R. (2016). A problem shared is a problem halved: A survey on the dimensions of collective cyber defense through security information sharing. *Computers & Security*, 60, 154–176.

Soltra (2017). Soltra Edge [Online]. Available: http://www.soltra.com/en [Accessed January 2017].

Steele, R.D. (2007a). Open source intelligence. In *Handbook of Intelligence Studies*. Johnson, L.K. (ed.), Routledge.

Steele, R.D. (2007b). Open source intelligence. In *Strategic Intelligence.* Johnson, L.K. (ed.). Praeger.

Steele, R.D. (2014). Applied collective intelligence: Human-centric holistic analytics, true cost economics, and open source everything. *Spanda Journal*, 2, 127–137.

Strom, B. (2016). ATT&CK Gaining Ground [Online]. Available: https://www.mitre.org/capabilities/cybersecurity/overview/cybersecurity-blog/ attck%E2%84%A2-gaining-ground.

Symantec. (2016). Internet security threat report. Technical report.

The Snort team (2017). Snort [Online]. Available: https://www.snort.org [Accessed July 2017].

Threatconnect (2017). Threatconnect platform [Online]. Available: https://www. threatconnect.com/platform [Accessed January 2017].

ThreatQuotient (2017). THREATQ [Online]. Available: https://www.threatq. com/threatq [Accessed January 2017].

Tounsi, W. and Rais, H. (2018). A survey on technical threat intelligence in the age of sophisticated cyber-attacks. *Computers & Security*, 72, 212–233 [Online]. Available: http://www. sciencedirect.com/science/article/pii /S0167404817301839.

Tounsi, W., Cuppens-Boulahia, N., Cuppens, F., and Garcia-Alfaro, J. (2013). Fine-grained privacy control for the RFID middleware of EPCGlobal networks. *Proceedings of the Fifth International Conference on Management of Emergent Digital EcoSystems*, ACM, pp. 60–67.

Trost, R. (2014). Threat intelligence library: A new revolutionary technology to enhance the SOC battle rhythm! Briefing, Blackhat-Webcast.

Verizon (2015). Data breach investigations report. Technical report.

Verizon (2017). Vocabulary for event recording and incident sharing [Online]. Available: http://veriscommunity.net [Accessed July 2017].

Wagner, C., Dulaunoy, A., Wagener, G., and Iklody, A. (2016). MISP: The design and implementation of a collaborative threat intelligence sharing platform. *Proceedings of the 2016 ACM on Workshop on Information Sharing and Collaborative Security*, ACM, pp. 49–56.

Williamson, W. (2016). Distinguishing threat intelligence from threat data [Online]. *Security Week*. Available: http://www.securityweek.com/ distinguishing-threat-intelligence-threat-data.

Yamakawa, N. (2014). Threat intelligence climbs the ladder of enterprise proliferation. Technical report, 451 Research.

Zheng, D.E. and Lewis, J.A. (2015). Cyber threat information sharing – recommendations for congress and the administration. Report Center for Strategic and International Studies (CSIS), Strategic Technologies Program.

Zurkus, K. (2015). Threat intelligence needs to grow up. White paper, CSOfromIDG.

2

Trust Management Systems: a Retrospective Study on Digital Trust

2.1. Introduction

The evolution of communication from standalone systems to open and decentralized ones has driven research to think beyond security. Indeed, the astonishing recent advances in computer systems and networks has boosted the use of the Internet, especially via mobile devices. This new pervasive nature of the Internet has enabled billions[1] of people, distributed worldwide, to intensify their usage by creating, sharing and interacting in many different ways among open and decentralized systems. More than any other form of interaction, collaboration relies on resources, information and knowledge sharing, making security a critical issue (Renzl 2008; Casimir *et al.* 2012).

The concept of trust has been recognized as an interaction enabler in situations of risk and uncertainty (Jøsang *et al.* 2007; Yaich *et al.* 2013). Based on this concept, several trust management systems have been proposed in distributed artificial intelligence and in security. Initially, the concept of *trust management systems* (Blaze *et al.* 1996, 1999b) was introduced by researchers working in access control regarding mechanisms that make use of *credentials* and *policies* to express delegation of rights based on existing *ad hoc* trust relationships. In this approach, it is the resources' owners, and not the security administrators, that are responsible

---

Chapter written by Reda YAICH.
1 List of virtual communities with more than 100 million active users: http://en.wikipedia.org /wiki/List_of_virtual_communities_with_more_than_100_million_active_users.

for specifying who and when access can be granted. Therefore, the role of a trust management system consists of evaluating whether the specified policies and credentials allow us to establish a trust relationship (materialized by the *delegation* chain) between the resources *owner* and the resource *requester*.

This chapter aims to analyze digital trust and identify the mechanisms underlying trust management systems. We also review the different models and systems that have been proposed in the discipline in the last decade. First, in section 2.2, we try to provide a clear definition of trust and clarify how this concept should be understood throughout this chapter. Then, in section 2.3, we propose a historical view on the evolution of such systems from access control to a trust management system. From that first characterization, we provide the reader with the fundamental background concepts supporting this approach. Section 2.5 includes a survey in which the most relevant trust management systems are presented providing an overview of the existing systems. The systems are chronologically presented in order to stress the contribution provided by each system with respect to its predecessors. The systems are also structured by grouping similar systems into three categories: *authorization-based*, *role-based* and *negotiation-based*. This section is followed by section 2.6 with recent applications of trust management systems in cloud infrastructures. Finally, section 2.7 concludes this chapter.

2.2. What is trust?

In the real world as well as in the virtual ones, trust constitutes a fundamental concept for humans, without which they can neither act nor interact. Therefore, unsurprisingly, in the last decades, trust has received much attention from several disciplines. To that aim, a definition section seems essential for the sake of clarification by the disambiguation of its meaning.

According to Gambetta (Gambetta 2000), "trust (or, symmetrically, distrust) is a particular level of the subjective probability with which an agent assesses that another agent or group of agents will perform a given action, both before he can monitor such action (or independently of his capacity ever to be able to monitor it) and in a context in which it affects his own action". First, we note here that Gambetta, who is a sociologist, conceptualized trust as a mathematical concept, making its definition more concrete. Also, the phrase "a particular level" used in the definition means that for Gambetta, trust can be somehow quantifiable. According to Gambetta, 0 means complete distrust and 1 means full trust. Further, this definition makes explicit the idea that trust is subjective and introduces the specificity of trust: trust is made with respect to a specific action to be performed. This definition takes into account uncertainty induced by the behavior of the interacting partner, without which there would be no need for trust. Further, Gambetta states that "if we were blessed with an unlimited computational ability to map out all possible contingencies in enforceable contracts, trust would not be a problem". With this statement, Gambetta highlights the fact that trust involves making decisions in complex situations that are hard to grasp for human minds.

The complex nature of the situations involving trust is further reinforced by the definition provided by *Niklas Luhmann* (Luhmann 1990). According to Luhmann, "the complexity of the future world is reduced by the act of trust". Luhmann approaches trust from a sociological background as he relates the use of trust to interactions among societies, and questions the existence of society without trust (Marsh 1994; Lamsal 2001). He considers trust as one of the most important "internal mechanisms for the reduction of complexity". However, the authors defined complexity in very abstract terms even though generally he used it in reference to *uncertain* situations.

In a computer science context, McKnight (Mcknight and Chervany 1996) defined trust as "the extent to which one party is willing to depend on something or somebody in a given situation with a feeling of relative security, even though negative consequences are possible". According to Grandison and Sloman, trust is "the firm belief in the competence of an entity to act dependably, securely, and reliably within a specified context". Finally, according to Falcone and Castelfranchi, trust is used as "the mental ground and counterpart of delegation" (Falcone and Castelfranchi 2001). Therefore, the authors consider delegation as an action, taking this mental state as an input.

Each of the above definitions advances our understanding of trust and provides important building blocks for the definition of this concept.

However, none of them perfectly matches our conceptualization of trust. In the light of the above definitions, we define trust as:

DEFINITION 2.1. Trust.– *The deliberate decision of an individual/entity A (called a trustor) to be in a situation of vulnerability towards the behavior of an individual/entity B (called a trustee) with respect to an issue X (i.e. trust issue) and within a context C.*

2.3. Genesis of trust management systems

Trust management has its roots in security and more particularly in *access control*. Access control (AC) is the traditional mechanism by which software applications (originally operating systems) answer the question (or request): "can the entity identified as being S manipulate the object O via the action A?" Here, the verb "can" should be understood in terms of rights and not in terms of capabilities. Further, as we may note, this question can be easily contextualized with respect to the trust issue into: "can I trust S enough to allow him performing the action A on the object O?" In this section, we present the different models that have been proposed to answer such questions. Before we proceed, however, we introduce the basic terminology we will rely upon in our descriptions.

2.3.1. *Access control model*

Access control is the mechanism used by applications to determine who will be allowed to manipulate local resources. The abstract model of the access control mechanism is depicted in Figure 2.1.

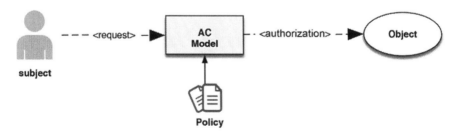

Figure 2.1. *A basic access control model (adapted from Genovese [2012])*

Where:

– the *request* represents the type of interaction for which an authorization is requested (e.g. read, use or login);

– the *subject*, often called the *principal*, is the abstract entity (a human, a program or an artificial agent) requiring authorization;

– the *object*[2] is the abstract artifact representing the resource the requester wants to interact with (e.g. a file or a service);

– the *mechanism* is the scheme that determines whether the requester is authorized to perform the requested interaction.

Thus, the access control mechanism plays the role of guard for the manipulation of sensitive local resources. It determines if a requester should or should not be authorized to manipulate the resource he requested. The specification of the information based on which a requester can be authorized represents permission, and is usually encoded in an *access control policy*. Based on the nature of the policies used to specify permissions, a wide range of mechanisms have been proposed in the past decades to address the access control issue. These mechanisms can, however, be grouped into five categories: *identity-based*, *lattice-based*, *role-based*, *organization-based* and *attribute-based*. The following sections provide an insight into how each mechanism addresses the access control issue.

2.3.2. Identity-based access control

The general access control problem is often split into two main sub-problems: *authentication* and *authorization*. *Authentication* aims to prove that the identity claimed by a principal is authentic, while *authorization* tries to find whether there is a permission that allows this identity to manipulate the requested resource, and how this manipulation can be done. Identity-based access control (IBAC) has made implicit use of a closed world model, in which users and resources are *a priori* known. Under such assumptions, the problem of authorization reduces to one of authentication. Consequently, permissions to access a resource are directly associated with the principal's identifier (e.g. user name, login or public key)

---

2 In the remainder of this chapter, we will interchangeably use the terms subject and principal. We will do so for the concepts of resource and object, too.

as illustrated in Figure 2.2. Access to the resource (an object in Figure 2.1) is only possible when such an association exists.

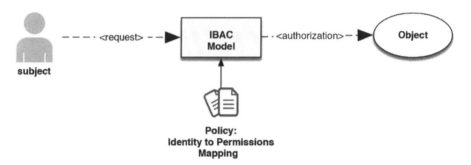

Figure 2.2. *An abstract IBAC model*

Here, the information used in the policy is the *identity* of the principal requesting access to the resource. Therefore, these models are called *identity-based*. A concrete example is the implementation using access control lists (ACL). ACL are the oldest and most basic form of access control commonly found in operating systems such as UNIX. ACL are lists of principals and the actions that each principal is allowed to perform on the resource. Here, the access control policies represent rules that determine whether association between the principal and a permission exists.

In the most general form, a permission is a triple (s, o, a), stating that a user s is allowed to perform an action a on an object o. Let S be the set of all users of the system, O be the set of all objects and A be the set of all possible actions. The access control policies represent a function $f: S \times O \rightarrow A$. Consequently, $f(s, o)$ determines the list of actions that the subject s is allowed to perform over the object o. Table 2.1 illustrates (as a matrix $A = |S| \times |O|$) the access control list of a system, where $S = \{s_1, s_2, s_3\}$, $O = \{o_1, o_2, o_3\}$ and $A = \{a_1, a_2, a_3\}$ (El Houri 2010).

Subject	o_1	o_2	o_3
s_1	$a_1, a_2, -$	a_2	a_2
s_2	a_2, a_2	$-$	$-$
s_3	a_1, a_1, a_2	a_1, a_2	a_1, a_2

Table 2.1. *Example of an access control list*

IBAC models are very easy to implement and use. However, such approaches are unable to scale when the number of users increases (Yuan and Tong 2005). Moreover, the access control decisions are not related to any characteristic of the resource, the subject of the business application, making such approaches very vulnerable to attacks (ACL are easy to corrupt) and identity forgery (identity usurpation) (Chen 2011).

2.3.3. *Lattice-based access control*

Unlike IBAC models, lattice-based access control (LBAC) models (also known as mandatory access control models) are deployed when the access to an object depends on its characteristics and those of the subject, and not on the wills of the object owner (i.e. ACL) (Sandhu 1993). Subjects' and objects' characteristics are represented by security labels (or levels) that are assigned to users and resources of the system. Objects' labels reflect the extent to which a resource is sensitive, while a subject's label reflects the category of objects he is allowed to access. The systems in which LBAC models are implemented are often called *multi-level security systems* as the labels used in these systems represent a partial order (e.g. top secret, secret, confidential and unclassified), which is assumed to form a *lattice*.

In LBAC, the process of access control is reduced to control of data flow. For example, a *read* access to a resource is represented as a flow of data from the object to the subject, while a *write* access represents a flow of data from the subject to the object. In light of this, when used for confidentiality purposes, the LBAC model's objective is to guarantee that data coming from a higher level object never flow to lower-level subjects and that data coming from higher-level subjects never flow down to objects at a lower level. In sum, the label of a subject must be at least as high as the label of the object he wants to read, and to write on an object, the label must be at least as high as the subject's one (Chen 2011). These two security principles are, respectively, called "no-read-up" and "no-write-down" hereafter, as illustrated in Figure 2.3.

The Bell–LaPadula model is the most famous model implementing LBAC. It has been used in both military applications and commercial ones as well as to implement the security mechanisms in the Multics operating systems.

The main limitation of LBAC models is their lack of flexibility and scalability. Indeed, LBAC models are quite efficient and remain relatively manageable in systems with a small number of labels.

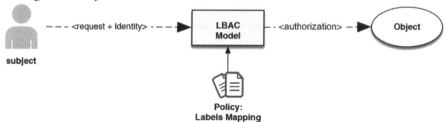

Figure 2.3. *Abstract lattice-based access control model*

2.3.4. *Role-based access control*

Both IBAC and LBAC models have considerable deficiencies: LBAC models are clearly too rigid, while IBAC models are very difficult to maintain and administrate (Becker 2005). This ascertainment has led several researchers in the early 1990s to search for alternative models such as *role-based access control* (RBAC) models (Sandhu *et al.* 1996). The development of RBAC was motivated by the fact that in most of the cases, sensitive resources were generally not owned by users but by the institution wherein users act in the capacity of a role of a job function (Becker 2005; Yao 2004). Therefore, the key components in RBAC models are *subjects*, *roles* and *permissions*, as illustrated in Figure 2.4.

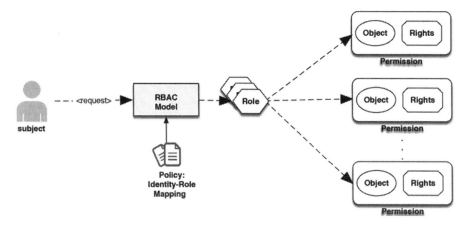

Figure 2.4. *Basic role-based access control model (adapted from Genovese [2012])*

The policy represents here an assignment relation that associates users with the roles they hold, and roles to the permissions they are granted. Thus, roles represent an intermediary layer between subjects and permissions, which makes RBAC a scalable access control mechanism and considerably reduces the complexity of specification and administration of access control policies when the subject's turnover is very high. When a subject joins or leaves the system, only the link between the user identifier and the role has to be updated. Subjects are assigned roles based on their duties, qualifications or competencies in the institution, while permissions are associated with roles based on the institution activities and goals.

RBAC has received in the last twenty years considerable attention that has led to the proposition of a whole family of models (e.g. Sandhu *et al.* 1996; Nyanchama and Osborn 1999; Sandhu *et al.* 2000; Ferraiolo *et al.* 2001; Li *et al.* 2002; Dimmock *et al.* 2004; Boella and van der Torre 2005; Wang and Varadharajan 2007; Finin *et al.* 2008; Ferraiolo and Kuhn 2009). However, most of the researchers would agree on the fact that $RBAC_0$ is the core model (Becker 2005; Chen 2011). $RBAC_0$ is the main and the simplest model. $RBAC_1$ extends $RBAC_0$ with the capability to specify hierarchies of roles, introducing permissions' inheritance between roles. $RBAC_2$ extends $RBAC_1$ with constraints to enforce separation of duties, while $RBAC_3$ is a combination of $RBAC_1$ and $RBAC_2$.

2.3.5. *Organization-based access control*

Organization-based access control (OrBAC) and RBAC have many similar aspects; for example, in both the approaches, the concept of a role is central. Therefore, most of the scholars describe OrBAC as an extension of RBAC (Kalam *et al.* 2003). OrBAC aims to detail the permissions that are used in abstract terms within RBAC. Indeed, RBAC policies define the mapping between identities and roles. Then, based on these policies, the access control mechanism grants permissions to subjects with respect to the role it belongs to. Therefore, the interpretation of permissions remains the responsibility of the administrator and may be very complex to perform; for example, grouping similar rights, preventing inadequate permission and managing conflicting roles are some of the main issues to be addressed (Kalam and Deswarte 2006).

The main concept of OrBAC is entity organization. The policy specification is completely parameterized by the organization. It is characterized by a high level of abstraction. Instead of modeling the policy by using the concrete and implementation-related concepts of subject, action and object, the OrBAC model suggests reasoning with the roles that subjects, actions or objects are assigned in the organization. Thus, a subject is abstracted into role, which is a set of subjects to which the same security rule applies. Similarly, an activity and a view are, respectively, a set of actions and objects to which the same security rule applies.

Figure 2.5 describes the OrBAC model, which introduces two security levels (concrete and abstract). OrBAC defines the context concept. It is a condition that must be satisfied to activate a security rule. A mixed policy can be offered in OrBAC, which defines four types of access: permission, prohibition, obligation and recommendation.

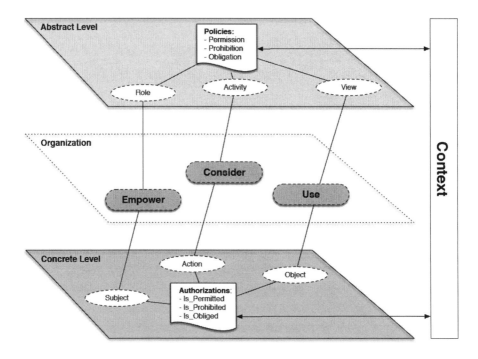

Figure 2.5. *The OrBAC model*

2.3.6. *Attribute-based access control*

The main idea of *attribute-based access control* (ABAC) models is to use policies that rely on the characteristics of authorized individuals instead of their identities, roles or clearances for issuing authorizations (Yuan and Tong 2005; Lee 2008). These policies are then satisfied through the disclosure of credentials issued by third-party attribute certifiers (e.g. organizations, companies and institutions). Consequently, subjects can gain access to resources without being priorly known by the system administrator (or the resource owner), as illustrated in Figure 2.6.

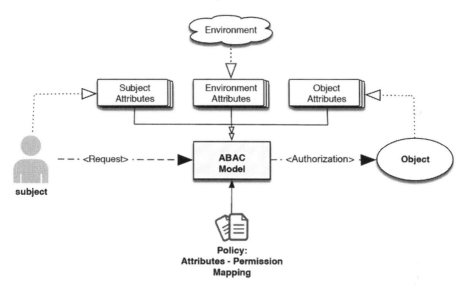

Figure 2.6. *Abstract attribute-based access control model*

Unlike IBAC, LBAC and RBAC, ABAC policies can define permissions based on any relevant characteristic. Characteristics fall into the following three categories (Yuan and Tong 2005):

– *subject attributes.* Subjects are the entities requesting access to objects. Each subject can be characterized via a set of attributes without explicitly referring to its identity. In the ABAC literature, almost all information that can be associated with a subject is considered as an attribute. Such attributes may include subject's name, role, affiliation, address, age and so on. In fact, the subject identity can also be considered as an attribute;

– *object attributes*. Objects are resources that the subject wants to manipulate. Like subjects, resources have properties that are also called attributes in the ABAC model. Resource attributes are also important in access control decision as they can affect the type of the permission accorded (e.g. a read on a text file does not have the same consequence as an execute on a program). Resource attributes may include the name of the resource, its type (text file, image, serve, etc.), the owner and so on. These data are generally made public and can be extracted automatically from metadata;

– *context attributes*. The environment, or more generally the context in which the interaction is undertaken, has been ignored for a long time by the security community. In previous approaches, permissions are attached to individuals (IBAC), roles (RBAC) or labels (LBAC) and derive the same authorization as long as the artifact to which they are attached remains valid (or unless they are revoked by the system administrator). Thus, the context of the interaction never affects the access control decision, whereas environment attributes, such as time, date and threats, are relevant in applying the access control policy.

2.4. Trust management

In this section, we introduce the *trust management* approach that originates from the work of Blaze and colleagues (Blaze *et al*. 1996, 1999a), which tried to address the limits of the above-mentioned traditional access control models with respect to distribution and decentralization limitations. In the remainder of this section, we will first define the concept of *trust management*, and then in section 2.4.3, we will present the primary concepts this approach relies upon.

2.4.1. *Definition*

Trust management has been defined by Blaze and colleagues as "a unified approach to specifying and interpreting security policies, credentials, relationships which allow direct authorisation of security-critical actions" (Blaze *et al*. 1996, 1999a). The main novelty of the approach introduced by Blaze *et al*. is that they unified the concepts of *security policy, credentials* and *authorization* under the concept of *trust management*. However, their definition not very intuitive and too abstract to explain what trust management really is.

According to Jøsang, trust management is "the activity of collecting, codifying, analysing and presenting security relevant evidence with the purpose of making assessments and decisions regarding e-commerce transactions" (Jøsang 2007; Jøsang *et al.* 2007). Despite being broader and more intuitive, this definition was criticized by Grandison in his doctoral thesis to be too domain-specific (i.e. e-commerce) (Grandison 2003). Nonetheless, Grandison reused it to define trust management as "the activity of collecting, encoding, analysing and presenting evidence relating to competence, honesty, security or dependability with the purpose of making assessments and decisions regarding trust relationships for Internet applications" (Grandison 2003; Grandison and Sloman 2003).

The main drawback in Grandison's definition is that the author restricted the nature of the evidences on which the trust relationship can be established. Further, Grandison used the verb "collecting" for evidence, while some evidence cannot be collected but should be requested (e.g. credentials). Therefore, we prefer to adapt the above definitions to provide one that best matches our understanding of trust management.

DEFINITION 2.2. Trust Management.– *The automated activity of collecting, requesting, providing and analyzing information with the purpose of making trust decisions (e.g. access control, delegation and collaboration) based on policies.*

The main aspect we stress in this definition is the automated nature of the trust management process. It is the automation requirement that makes the trust management issue complex and necessitates so much investigation (see section 2.5). Further, we used the term information instead of evidence in order to comply with the analysis we have made previously. Finally, we generalize the purpose of trust management to trust decisions rather than focusing on trust relationships. From our perspective, a relationship implies some kind of continuation in time, while a trust decision better reflects the dynamic nature of trust.

2.4.2. *Trust management system*

Trust management systems (TMSs) were originally designed to solve the problem of deciding whether a request to perform a potentially harmful action on a sensitive resource complies with the access control policy (Blaze *et al.* 1996, 1999a). Nevertheless, these systems are currently used in a broader way to evaluate whether a trust decision complies with the policy or not.

DEFINITION 2.3. Trust Management System.– *An abstract system that processes a symbolic representation of a trust relationship from the perspective of trust decision automation.*

In the above definition, the "symbolic representation of trust" refers to the concepts of credentials and policies by means of which the issuer states that he trusts the entity to which the statement is applicable. In fact, this trust is not generic; thus, in most of the cases, the statement concerns a specific issue (e.g. reading of a document). The symbolic representation of trust relationships can be best illustrated through the everyday ticket experience (Wikipedia 2013). The ticket (let us say a tram ticket) can be considered as a symbol of trust between the tram company and the ticker holder. The ticket acts as a proof that the holder paid for the journey and consequently that he is entitled to get on the tram. Once bought, the ticket can be later given to someone else, thus transferring the trust relationship. On the tram, only the ticket will be verified and not the identity of the holder. Concretely, in the above example, the tram ticket illustrates the importance for credentials while the tram inspector enforces the policy (which is quite simple here).

Thus, a trust management system aims to link the requester and the requested via a trust relationship based on which a trust decision can be made. To that aim, trust management systems provide a language for the specification of *policies* and *credentials* and a *trust management engine* (trust engine for short) that evaluates whether the provided credentials satisfy the specified policy.

2.4.3. *Foundations*

As illustrated in the previous section, trust management systems are made possible thanks to the introduction of *credentials*, *policies* and *trust engines* (Nejdl *et al.* 2004; Lee *et al.* 2009; Ryutov *et al.* 2005; Winsborough and Li 2006; Galinović 2010). These three components are presented in the following sections.

2.4.3.1. *Credentials*

Credentials (or digital credentials) represent the counterpart of the paper credential we use in the real world (e.g. passport, driving license or student card). They represent digital documents or messages that are certified (i.e. signed) by *certification authorities*. They allow user authentication but can also provide additional information such as the user's attributes (see section 2.3.6), memberships or rights. Blaze, in his trust management jargon, defined credential as "a signed message that allows a principal to delegate part of its own authority to perform actions to other principals". It is this definition that we use as a basis in this chapter. For instance, a public key "certificate" is an example of a credential. Public key infrastructures (PKI) have been systemically used by trust management systems to create, distribute, validate, store and revoke credentials. In the following, we review two prominent approaches to PKI, which are *certification authorities (CA)* and *cross-certification (CC)* approaches (Linn 2000). The certification authorities approach relies on the trust that exists between an individual and the organization/institution representing the certification authority, while the cross-certification approach drew trust from the experience of others. We illustrate both approaches with two concrete implementations of these approaches, which are, respectively, *X.509* and *PGP*.

2.4.3.1.1. Certification authorities: X.509

X.509 is a widely used standard for credentials management. Typically, an X.509 certificate contains (but is not limited to) the following information: *issuer name*, *subject name*, *signature algorithm identifier* (e.g. RSA and DSA), *validity period* and optional information, which can be an attribute–value pair (Samarati and Vimercati 2001).

In X.509, the certification management process involves several entities: *certification authorities* (CA), which are the entities that issue and revoke certificates; *registration authorities* (RA), which vouch for the binding of public keys and *repositories*, which store and make available certificates and certificate revocation lists (CRLs); *certificate holders* and *clients*.

The certification process starts when the certificate holder requests a certificate from the registration authority. The RA verifies the future holder identity and/or the attributes for which he wants to be certified (e.g. in the case of driving capabilities, the RA checks whether the entity holds a driving license in the real life). After this step, the RA forwards the request to the CA, who signs the certificate after verifying that the RA really approved the request. Then, the CA sends a copy of the certificate to the repositories so that clients who want to communicate with the requester can get the public key. Analogously, when a certificate needs to be revoked (e.g. a key has been compromised), the CA updates the repositories and adds an entry to the revocation list. Certification authorities are organized in a hierarchical way; the root CA certifies other CAs, which in turn certify other CAs or simple requester. These issues represent the most controversial aspect of X.509 as root CAs are self-certified entities (Yu 2003; Conrad *et al.* 2012).

2.4.3.1.2. Cross-certification: PGP

PGP (Pretty Good Privacy) is a public key infrastructure that has been initially designed to guarantee authenticity, integrity and non-repudiation of exchanged data. Although it can encrypt any data type, PGP has been most commonly used for email exchange. Unlike X.509, in PGP, each user can generate a pair (public key, private key), which is associated with his unique identity. However, the keys are used independently of the identity of the user; thus, PGP guarantees authenticity, integrity and non-repudiation while preserving the confidentiality of the individual identity (i.e. privacy). A PGP certificate includes (but is not limited to) the following information: the *certificate holder*, *holder's information* (e.g. name, ID, email and photo), *digital signature of the holder*, *validity period* and the *encryption algorithm*. Thanks to the holder's information, a unique PGP certificate can contain several pieces of information, which can be certified via the same key (Yu 2003).

In PGP, anyone can freely issue and certify their own certificates; thus, everybody can act as a certification authority. Thus, everyone can certify others' public keys (PGP calls this mechanism introduction), making the trust issues central to PGP. Therefore, PGP relies on a "web of trust", which is the network created by individuals introducing each other's keys. To that aim, PGP uses two distinct metrics: one quantitative (the key validity) and another qualitative (the trust level of a key).

In PGP, a user always trusts his own key, making the level of this key *ultimate*. The other levels used in *PGP* are *complete*, *marginal*, *unknown* and *untrusted* (in decreasing order of trust level). Similarly, the validity of a key can be *valid*, *marginally valid* or *invalid*. The number of individuals signing the public key determines its validity, while the trust level of a key is determined via recommendation. The more a key is trusted, the less validity it requires to be accepted (Gerck 2000; Prohic 2005).

2.4.3.2. Policies

Policies have been extensively used in the computer science literature (e.g. information systems, security and multi-agent systems). Initially, policies have been introduced in computer science to automate tasks and decision-makings (e.g. batch instructions). However, nowadays, the main motivation for using policies is to make systems support dynamic and adaptive behavior. Policies allows a system to change its behavior without being stopped.

Despite their extensive use in the literature, the concept of policies is still hard to define and the provided definitions are either too generic or domain-specific. For instance, Sloman defined policies as "rules governing the choices in behaviour of a system" (Sloman 1994). While this definition captures the meaning of a general policy, it fails in addressing its role, which is to specify the circumstances under which the choices are made (in reaction to which conditions). Further, this definition reduces the form of a policy to a set of rules and thus excludes many of the approaches that do not rely on rules (see section 2.5). Recently, De Coi and Olmedilla have stated that "policies specify who is allowed to perform which action on which object depending on properties of the requester and of the object as well as parameters of the action and environmental factors" (De Coi and Olmedilla 2008). This definition makes explicit the ABAC approach, and thus covers *de facto* IBAC, LBAC, RBAC and OrBAC policies. However, this definition restricts the scope of a policy to situations in which an access request has to be evaluated. Consequently, this definition could not be used to describe situations in which a decision is not merely an access control decision (e.g. delegation). To avoid misunderstandings, we clarify the meaning of trust policy and define it as follows.

DEFINITION 2.4. Policy.– *A policy is a statement that specifies under which conditions an entity (human or artificial) can be trusted for a specific issue (e.g. resource action and task delegation).*

With respect to Definition 2.1, a policy represents the expression of the conditions under which the individual A deliberately makes the decision to trust B. Thus, from our perspective, the role of a policy is twofold: (i) it serves as a means for A to express the policy that its trust management system will rely on and (ii) it is used as a common language that A and B will use to exchange their respective trust conditions. In light of that, the role of the policy specification language is paramount. The language provides the basic syntax to express conditions that represent the building blocks of a policy. Specification languages can be more or less verbal and can have a strong or weak formal basis. Thus, depending on the nature of the policy specification language, policies fall into three categories: *informal*, *semi-formal* and *formal*. In this chapter, we limit our attention to *formal* policies that can be understood by both artificial and human agents. In section 2.5, we present the most important policy languages that have been proposed in the last 15 years.

2.4.3.3. *Trust engine*

The objective of the trust engine is to assess if the credentials provided by the requester are valid and whether they satisfy the specified policy. Importantly, trust management systems are not responsible for making trust decisions. It is always the human or the application using the TMS that decides whether to effectively trust the requester or not[3]. Therefore, the main advantage of using a TMS is to offload applications of the complex and tedious tasks that are *credentials verification* and *policies evaluation*. Figure 2.7 illustrates this principle and shows the basic functioning of a trust management system.

---

3 The study of how trust decisions are made is out of the scope of this chapter.

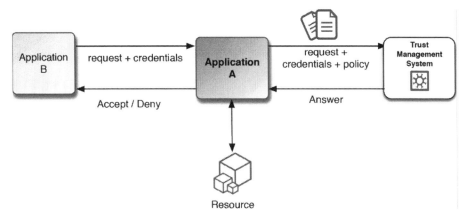

Figure 2.7. *Illustration of the functioning of a trust management system*

In Figure 2.7, the application A invokes the trust management system to determine whether application B can be allowed to perform an operation on a resource. To that aim, the application A provides the TMS with its local policy for the resource concerned by the request and the credentials provided by application B. The TMS produces an answer based on which the application A decides to allow or deny the request of B.

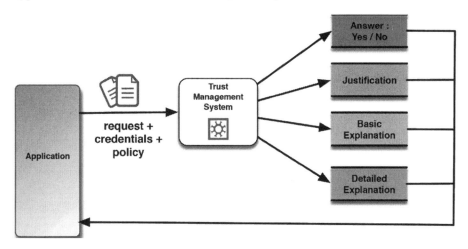

Figure 2.8. *Functioning modes of a trust management system*

Depending on their degree of sophistication, trust management systems can provide more or fewer functionalities. In our work, we are particularly interested in the TMS that outputs detailed answers. Figure 2.8 illustrates the degree of sophistication a TMS can achieve by providing more or fewer elements in its answers.

Based on the type of information provided by the TMS, Seamons and colleagues identified two functioning modes of trust management systems (Seamons *et al.* 2002). In our work, we distinguish four modes, which are summarized as follows:

– *mode 1*: in this mode, the TMS produces a Boolean answer (trust/no trust) that states whether the credentials provided satisfy the policy;

– *mode 2*: in addition to the Boolean answer, in this mode, the TMS provides a *justification*, when the request is denied, that states which conditions in the policy the provided credentials were unable to satisfy;

– *mode 3*: in this mode, the TMS provides an answer, a justification and an *explanation* when the policy is satisfied. The explanation contains all credentials that satisfy the policy;

– *mode 4*: this last mode extends the third mode as it provides a *detailed explanation*. The detailed explanation is obtained by providing all subsets of credentials that satisfy the policy.

Modes 1 and 2 are often used by the resource owner to verify whether the credentials its interlocutor provided satisfy its policy, while modes 3 and 4 are used by the requester to determine whether the credentials it possesses (and which subset of credentials) satisfy the policy stated by the owner of the resource. These latter modes were particularly introduced in the context of trust negotiation that we will address in the following section.

2.4.4. *Automated trust negotiation*

Automated trust negotiation (ATN) is an approach to trust management in which trust is established through the gradual, iterative and mutual disclosure of credentials and access control policies (Yu 2003; Ryutov *et al.* 2005). Unlike the traditional trust management systems that have been presented in the previous section, the automated trust negotiation approach considers credentials as first-class resources that should be protected through *release policies* dedicated to them. Consequently, ATN systems provide users with better fine-grained and flexible control over the disclosure of the potentially sensitive data conveyed by their credentials (Ryutov *et al.* 2005; Yagüe 2006; Lee 2008).

However, negotiation generally refers to the process by which agents can reach an agreement on matters of common interest (Parsons and Wooldridge 2002). We adapt this well-established definition to the *negotiation-based adaptation* of trust policies.

DEFINITION 2.5. Automated Trust Negotiation.– *Automated trust negotiation is an iterative process in which two interacting agents reach an agreement on the credentials they are willing to release to gain each other's trust.*

The introduction of trust negotiation has several benefits. First, it better reflects the asymmetric nature of trust. It allows us also to establish bilateral trust as both participants in an interaction can request credentials from each other. Finally, it allows us to have a more flexible trust management as trust is established gradually and incrementally. Research on trust negotiation has been principally focused on *how to make trust management systems achieve trust negotiation* and *how to make trust negotiation successful*. The first question represents the requirements for trust negotiation, while the second question represents *trust negotiation strategies*. The requirements are further divided into *requirements for trust management systems* and *requirements for policy specification languages*.

Trust negotiation is inherently a strategy-driven process as the choice made by the individual affects the amount of credentials it releases and the time it takes for this task (Lee 2008). Therefore, recent research in the trust negotiation area has been primarily focused on proposing efficient and optimized negotiation strategies and protocols. In general, however, the implemented negotiation strategies fall into three categories: *eager*, *parsimonious* and *prudent* strategies (Grandison 2003):

– *eager strategy:* in the eager strategy, participants in the negotiation adopt a naive position in which they disclose almost all credentials they possess. The negotiation is considered to be successful when each participant has received enough credentials to be assured about the interaction they are engaged in. The major advantage of this strategy is that it does not require the use of *release policies* and it minimizes the time of the negotiation (Ardagna *et al.* 2007). However, this strategy increases the amount of disclosed credentials and thus the sensitive date they convey;

– *parsimonious strategy:* with this strategy, participants exchange only credentials requests (no credential is released) and try to find a possible sequence of credentials disclosure that can lead to a successful negotiation (Grandison 2003). Also, in the parsimonious strategy, only credentials that are explicitly requested are released. Unlike the eager strategy, the parsimonious strategy minimizes the credentials exposure but considerably increases the time of the negotiation without any guarantee of success;

– *prudent strategy:* it is a mix of the above two strategies. An eager strategy is applied to credentials that are not sensitive, and a parsimonious strategy is used for the sensitive ones. This strategy has been proved to outperform the other strategies in situations where the negotiation involves the disclosure of sensitive and non-sensitive credentials (Yu *et al.* 2000).

2.5. Classification of trust management systems

Given the multiplicity of trust management systems[4], we may argue that a comparison among them is neither possible nor desirable. However, we think that from a higher perspective and with a good abstraction level, a comparison of all these systems is not only possible but also worth carrying out.

In this section, we review a selection of trust management systems. These systems are split into *decentralized trust management (DTM) systems* and *automated trust negotiation systems*. DTM systems are further divided into *authorization-based TMS (ABTMS)* and *role-based TMS*. These systems are presented in the chronological order in which they were published. We think that respecting this chronological causality helps the reader to understand key elements that motivated the contribution of each system.

Each system is described with respect to the trust management key concepts that we presented above, namely *credentials*, *policies* and *trust engines*. For *credentials*, we are interested in the nature of information used

---

4 Judging from the list of surveys devoted to this subject; e.g. (Grandison 2003; Yu 2003; Yao 2004; Ruohomaa and Kutvonen 2005; Gray 2006; Yagüe 2006; Bandara *et al.* 2007; Fernandez-Gago *et al.* 2007; Jøsang 2007; Jøsang *et al.* 2007; Krukow *et al.* 2008; Artz and Gil 2010; Braghin 2011; Saadi *et al.* 2011; Liu 2011; Firdhous *et al.* 2012).

by each system to derive trust and the formalism used to express it. For *policies*, we will focus on the type, semantics, expressiveness and flexibility of the formalism used to represent policies. Finally, for *trust engines*, we will stress the negotiation ability and response mode.

2.5.1. *Authorization-based TMSs*

The *authorization-based TMSs* category relates to systems that pioneered the trust management approach. While most of these systems are considered nowadays as obsolete, the mechanisms they proposed remain valid and can be found at the basis of most of modern trust management systems. They inherit from IBAC and ABAC models. They build a trust chain in order to map a credential holder to the authorization it can be trusted for.

PolicyMaker (Blaze et al. 1996)

PolicyMaker is the first application stamped as a trust management system. This system introduces the concept of programmable credentials and policies by means of an assertion language. The syntax of an assertion is:

```
Source ASSERTS Subject WHERE Filter              [2.1]
```

The above syntax can be used to specify both credentials and policies. Here, the statement represents a credential by means of which a *source* authorizes a *subject* to perform actions that are accepted by the *filter* (i.e. interpreted program). The main difference between a credential and a policy is that in policies the keyword *policy* is always used as the source of the assertion. For instance, we can use the assertion given below to authorize the entity holding the public key ''rsa:123'' to access all resources shared among the community.

```
policy ASSERTS ''rsa:123'' WHERE filter to access
all shared resources                             [2.2]
```

In PolicyMaker, an assertion (whether credential or policy) is used to state that the source (or the local application in the case of a *policy*) trusts the key holder to perform the actions accepted by the filter. However, the formalism used to encrypt keys is left to the application using PolicyMaker, thus PolicyMaker is generic with respect to the keys encryption scheme. The semantics of the operations and the enforcement of the trust evaluation decisions are also left to the application.

Typically, the application provides to the PolicyMaker trust engine a set of requested actions, a set of credentials and a policy. The objective of PolicyMaker is to check whether the credentials form a delegation chain by means of which the action can be linked to the key of the keys. PolicyMaker then replies with an answer (``Trust'' or ``False'') and it is up to the application to interpret the answer and make the appropriate decision. The functioning of the PolicyMaker engine is similar to the architecture we described in Figure 2.7 (see section 2.4.2). PolicyMaker does not support *negotiation*. Policies are evaluated in a static and context-independent way. Finally, PolicyMaker cannot be used to manage resources that are owned by more than one individual.

In PolicyMaker, the choice of the policy specification language is left open, which makes policy evaluation undecidable in most of the cases (Grandison 2003). KeyNote (Blaze *et al.* 1999b), its successor, overcomes this drawback and imposes that the policies must be written in a specific language. KeyNote also makes the cryptographic verification, which was left to the application in PolicyMaker.

REFEREE (Chu et al. 1997)

REFEREE (Rule-controlled Environment For Evaluation of Rules and Everything Else) is a W3C and AT&T joint trust management system used for web document access control. The system was developed based on the PolicyMaker architecture, but the functioning of the system is somehow different. Here, the resource providers (i.e. authors of web content) are trying to gain the trust of the resource consumer (i.e. the site visitor). The system was essentially used to prevent minors from accessing illegal content. The system uses PICS (Platform for Internet Content Selection) labels as credentials that the REFEREE trust engine (a browser plug-in) evaluates with respect to a local policy.

Profiles-0.92 is a rule-based policy language that was designed for REFEREE. As illustrated in Listing 2.1, each policy is an "s-expression" that is evaluated in a top-down manner.

```
(((invoke "load-label" STATEMENT-LIST URL
"http://www.emse.fr/")
(false-if-unknown
(match
(("load-label" *)
(service "http://www.emse.fr/CA.html") *
(ratings (RESTRICT > trust 2)))))
STATEMENT-LIST))
```

Listing 2.1. *Example of a policy specified in Profiles-0.92 (adapted from Chu et al. [1997])*

The above policy states that any document that has a label (certified by *emse*) with a trust rating greater than 2 can be viewed by the user. The matching between labels and the conditions specified in the policy is purely syntactic. Thus, it remains up to the application and the labeling institution to define its semantic.

The REFEREE trust engine evaluates the above policy in two steps. First, it tries to find and download labels provided by the server, the URL of which has been specified in the policy. Then, a pattern-matcher is run to find a label with a trust rating. If the rating is greater than 2, then the result of the evaluation would be `true`, if not, then the result would be `false` and if no label was found, the result would be `unknown`. Thus, the REFEREE trust engine implements a three-valued logic, especially for the management of the meaning of `unknown` (Chu *et al.* 1997; Grandison 2003).

Binder (DeTreville 2002)

Binder is the first trust management system that uses a logic-based policy language (DeTreville 2002). The particularity of Binder lies in its explicit specification of right delegation through the extension of Datalog with the `says` construct (Ceri *et al.* 1989). In Binder, credentials represent keys that holders use to sign delegation assertions. Then, policies are used to filter these assertions and map them to their authors. The specification language proposed in Binder allows us to express two types of declarations: *beliefs* and *policies*. For instance, the following declaration is used by an individual A to state that another individual B can be trusted for joining his community and for reading his personal files.

```
can(B, read, MyFile).

can(B, join, MyCommunity).

can(X, join, MyCommunity) :-Y says trust(Y,X),
can(Y,join,MyCommunity)
```

Listing 2.2. *Examples of Binder declarations (beliefs and policies)*

The above example also illustrates the declaration of policies in Binder. In this example, the policy states that if A trusts an individual Y to join his community and that Y trusts another individual X, the latter can also be trusted to join the community. Worth noting in this policy is the use of the says construct.

The role of the Binder trust engine is to evaluate policies with respect to local assertions (i.e. beliefs) and assertions made by others (i.e. others' beliefs). The main novelty of the system lies in the addition of the says construct each time an assertion is received from others. Indeed, each time an individual sends an assertion, the Binder trust engine transforms this assertion into a certificate, which is signed with the private key of the issuer. Then, these assertions are sent to other Binder engines in order to make trust decisions. When an assertion is received, Binder verifies the validity of the certificate and automatically quotes the assertion with the says construct to distinguish them from local assertions.

SULTAN (Grandison 2003)

SULTAN (Simple Universal Logic-based Trust Analysis) is a TMS that has been proposed for the specification and analysis of trust and recommendation relationships (Grandison 2003). In SULTAN, credentials represent certified statements about identity, qualification, risk assessment, experience or recommendations. The system is provided with a policy specification language in which policies are used to specify two types of policies: *trust/distrust* policies and *positive/negative* recommendation policies. In fact, trust policies correspond to the classical meaning of policies used here, while recommendation policies are statements by means of which individuals make recommendations to others. In the following, we provide the syntax used to specify both types of policies:

$$P olicyN ame: \textbf{trust}(Tr, Te, As, L) \leftarrow C s. \tag{2.3}$$

The above policy represents a trust policy by means of which a trustor (Tr) trusts (or does not trust) to some extent (L – the level of trust) a trustee (Te) with respect to an action set (As) and if the conditions hold (Cs). Similarly, the recommendation policy defined hereafter specifies that the recommender (Rr) recommends at a recommendation level (L) the recommended agent (Re) to perform the action (As) if the conditions (Cs) hold.

$$P\ olicyN\ ame\text{: } \mathbf{recommend}(Rr, Re, As, L) \leftarrow C\ s. \qquad [2.4]$$

The SULTAN trust engine is responsible for collecting the information required for the policy evaluation, making trust relationship decisions and monitoring the environment from the perspective of re-evaluating existing trust relationships.

Ponder (Damianou et al. 2001)

Ponder is merely a policy language for which there was no associated trust management system (Damianou *et al.* 2001). Ponder is the first object-oriented policy language that adopts a role-based approach. Nevertheless, many of the features proposed by this language inspired other systems, which explains our motivation to review it. Ponder is a declarative language, which can be used for the specification of four types of policies, namely *authorization*, *obligation*, *refrain* and *delegation*. Ponder pioneered the use of a deontic approach, which was reused later by other languages such as Rei (Kagal *et al.* 2003) and KAos (Uszok *et al.* 2003, 2004). Furthermore, the main novel aspect of Ponder lies in the constructs it provides for updating, organizing and handling policies on runtime according to the environment context.

For instance, the following example is an instantiation of a positive authorization policy type called `rights`. The policy specifies that `members` (the subjects of the policy) can *modify* the target objects of type file that are stored in the common space of the community `com`.

```
type auth+ rights(member, target <file> com)
{action modify(); }                                      [2.5]
```

Another interesting aspect of Ponder policies lies in the fact that subjects and objects to which a policy applies can be grouped. For instance, in the above example, the policy concerns all members of the community and all files, making factorization of rights implicit and more efficient than what can be expressed in RBAC models or any other role-based trust management systems. Further, the authors assume that their language is flexible, scalable and extensible; flexible as it allows us to reuse policies since many instances of the same policy can be created for many different conditions, scalable as it allows the definition of composite policies; and extensible as it accepts the definition of new types of policies that can be considered as sub-classes of existing policies, thanks to the object-oriented approach. However, due to the absence of implementation, none of these properties have been proved to be valid.

Recently, Ponder has been redesigned, as *Ponder2*, to increase the functionality of authorization policies (e.g. operators for all managed objects have been added). In contrast to the previous version, which was designed for general network and systems management, Ponder2 has been designed as an entirely extensible framework that can be used at different scales: from small embedded devices to complex services and virtual organizations.

2.5.1.1. *Role-based TMSs*

In *authorization-based TMSs*, the delegation of authority is used in a very restrictive way. For instance, in PolicyMaker, a community member cannot simply specify that "all members of my community can access my resources". In these systems, the solution would be for the community member to delegate the right to the members they know and authorize these members to further delegate the right to each member they know. This approach makes trust decision complex and difficult to manage and control (e.g. a member can delegate the right to non-members).

In response, a new generation of *role-based* trust management systems that take advantage of the strength of RBAC and trust management approaches have been used. From RBAC, role-based TMSs borrow the concept of role, and from trust management, they borrow delegation and distributed credentials certification. The combined use of roles and distributed credentials management makes these systems convenient for large-scale systems such as virtual communities.

IBM Trust Establishment (Herzberg et al. 2000)

IBM Trust Establishment (IBM-TE) is a role-based trust management system developed by IBM for e-commerce applications. The main objective of IBM-TE is to map credential holders to groups. Credentials are specified in a generic language, but the system provides transcoding mechanisms to handle X.509. Credentials are used to authenticate users, while policies are used to express restrictions on how a credential holder could belong to a group. Groups are used in the sense of roles, which are mapped to authorizations (see section 2.3.4). IBM-TE comes with a dedicated XML-based policy specification language called *Trust Policy Language* (TPL). An example that illustrates the TPL syntax is given in Listing 2.3.

```
<GROUP NAME="Community">
<RULE>
<INCLUSION ID="reco"
TYPE="Recommendation"
FROM="members"
REPEAT="2">
</INCLUSION>
<FUNCTION>
<GT>
<FIELD ID="reco" NAME="Level"></FIELD>
<CONST>1</CONST>
</GT>
</FUNCTION>
</RULE>
</GROUP>
```

Listing 2.3. *A fragment of a TPL policy specifying a membership rule*

The above policy is used to add a new member to the group Community (role). The policy states that a new member can be admitted if he can provide two recommendations of existing members. For that, two XML tags are used: *inclusion* and *function*. Inclusion tag defines the credentials that the requester must provide (e.g. two recommendation credentials), while the function tag allows us to define additional conditions over requested credentials (e.g. recommendations must be greater than, GT, 1). The trust engine processes credentials in a traditional way. Along with his request, the requester provides the set of credentials he possesses. These credentials are then evaluated by the engine to determine to which group the requester can be mapped (Herzberg *et al.* 2000).

Role-based trust management framework (Li et al. 2002)

The *role-based trust management framework* (*RT*) was initially designed to support trust decision-making in collaborative environments (Li *et al.* 2002).

In *RT*, roles are represented as attributes, so an individual is said to belong to a role if it possesses a credential in which the role identifier is specified. Unlike IBMTE, *RT* uses an extension of Datalog (Ceri *et al.* 1989) to represent both credentials and policies. In *RT*, the terms credential and policy are used interchangeably. However, *RT* uses the term *certificate* in reference to the meaning of credential we use. The formalism used to specify certificates has not been defined, but some approaches proved the compatibility of *RT* with both X.509 and PGP and any certification mechanisms using PKI. The syntax used to specify policies is defined as follows:

$$C \text{ om.evaluator}(?X) \leftarrow C \text{ om.recommender}(?X) \land C \text{ om.M ember} \quad [2.6]$$

The above policy states that any member of the community that recommended another member is allowed to evaluate it. The *RT* policy specification language comes in five flavors RT_0, RT_1, RT_2, RT^T and RT^D (Li *et al.* 2002). RT_0 is the basic language that supports roles hierarchies, delegation of authorities over roles, roles intersection and attribute-based delegation of authority. RT_1 adds to RT_0 the possibility adding parameters to roles (e.g. in the previous policy, the evaluator and the recommender roles are endowed with parameters), and RT_2 adds to RT_1 logical objects. They represent a way to (logically) group resources of access modes in order to ease the specification of policies. RT^T adds thresholds to roles, while RT^D supports delegation of roles activation (i.e. roles that are active only within a specific context).

Cassandra (Becker and Sewell 2004)

Cassandra is a TMS that aims to enable individuals involved in potentially large-scale systems (e.g. P2P systems) to share their respective resources under the restriction of local policies (Becker and Sewell 2004). The system has been principally deployed in the context of electronic health records access control. Cassandra is role-based and supports X.509 credentials. Policies in Cassandra are expressed in a language based on Datalog with constraints (Ceri *et al.* 1989). For instance, a policy can state that an individual A can delegate the role of *moderator* as long as he commits to the role *admin*. This policy is specified using the constructor canActivate() as follows:

$$\text{canActivate}(B, moderator) \leftarrow \text{hasActivated}(A, admin) \quad [2.7]$$

Cassandra provides flexible delegation mechanisms, which facilitate the explicit specification of delegation lengths (Becker and Sewell 2004; De Coi and Olmedilla 2008). In addition, Cassandra proposes a mechanism for role revocation, including cascade role revocation (e.g. if an individual is revoked from its role, all individuals to which he delegated the role are revoked too). Finally, the Cassandra policy language facilitates the specification of roles hierarchies. The Cassandra trust engine is only available as a proof-of-concept implementation in OCaml. The main feature of the engine is the implementation of the semantics of Cassandra policies for their evaluation.

2.5.2. *Automated trust negotiation systems*

In trust management, a trust decision comes after a complex interaction process, where parties exchange policies and credentials. Traditionally, in early TMS, trust is established in a unidirectional way: the resource owner is assumed to be trusted by the requester. Consequently, before manipulating the resource, the requester must provide its credentials to know whether its request is accepted or not. Therefore, if the request was not accepted, the requester would have uselessly released its credentials (which contains sensitive data such as its id, age or address). Therefore, due to privacy considerations, such an approach is not acceptable. To that aim, several *negotiation-based TMSs* have been proposed.

TrustBuilder (Yu et al. *2003)*

TrustBuilder was the first TMS to introduce the concept of trust negotiation. TrustBuilder uses X.509 certificates and TPL policies (see section 2.5.1.1). The authors reused also the IBM-TE engine for the evaluation of policies. Therefore, TrustBuilder can be considered as an extension of IBM-TE to include negotiation features. The main novelty of this system lies in its rational management of credentials disclosure. To that aim, the trust engine is endowed with a negotiation module in which strategies are used to determine safe credentials disclosure for both parties involved in the interaction.

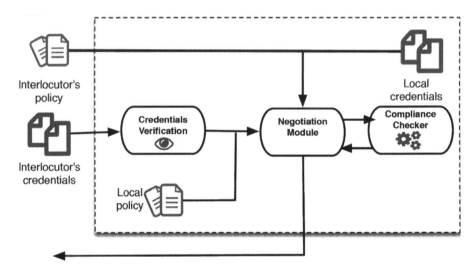

Figure 2.9. *Architecture of the TrustBuilder TMS*

As illustrated in Figure 2.9, TrustBuilder engine is split into three sub-modules: *credentials verification module, negotiation module* and *compliance checker module*. The core element of this architecture is the negotiation module that is responsible for enforcing negotiation strategies. The objective of a negotiation strategy is to minimize credentials disclosure. To that aim, TrustBuilder iteratively evaluates the policy of the interlocutor and the set of local credentials to compute the minimal set of credentials that satisfy the policy (as depicted in Figure 2.9).

Recently, Lee and colleagues have proposed an extension of TrustBuilder that they called TrustBuilder2 (Lee *et al.* 2009). This extension aims to endow the TMS with four main functionalities: support of arbitrary policy languages, support of arbitrary credentials format, integration of interchangeable negotiation strategies and flexible policies and credentials management.

Fidelis (Yao 2004)

Fidelis is a TMS that originates from the OASIS (Open Architecture for Secure, Interworking Services) distributed authorization architecture project. Fidelis makes use of keys X.509 and PGP as credential, and policies and credentials are systematically specified by distinct entities. Fidelis distinguishes two types of entities: *simple* and *composite* principals. Simple principals are in fact public keys, while composite principals are groups of public keys (e.g. groups or communities).

The Fidelis policy language (FPL) is the core element of the system. The language is able to express recommendations and trust statements. The syntax of the language is presented in the following example.

```
any-statement: ind -> statement
asserts any-statement: self -> statement
where ind == 0x14ba9b925 || ind == 0x5918b01a ||...
```

Listing 2.4. *A blind delegation policy in Fidelis*

This policy represents a special type of delegation policy, called *blind delegation*. It is used to make an individual "blindly" trust and assert all assertions made by other individuals. In this example, the group of trusted individuals is constrained by the variable ind.

In addition to the FPL, the authors developed a trust negotiation framework in which meta-policies are used to specify negotiation strategies. Meta-policies are designed to express four types of conditions about when a credential could be disclosed: designated principal disclosure, context-specific disclosure, trust-directed disclosure and mutual exclusion (Yao 2004). For instance, the following meta-policy is used to disclose the trust statement T2(a, b): self -> p (which is used as a credential here) when negotiating with the 0xb258d29f key holder.

```
negotiator(): self -> 0xb258d29f
grants disclose(T2(a, b): self->p)
```

Listing 2.5. *A credential disclosure meta-policy in Fidelis*

Fidelis does not support standard negotiation strategies. Thus, termination property is not guaranteed, making the evaluation of a policy not decidable in many situations. Finally, Fidelis distinguishes between *static* policies and *live* policies. Static policies do not depend on environment variables (e.g. date and time) to be evaluated, while live polices must be queried dynamically and tailored to each request. Nevertheless, live policies were only used in the context of negotiation as presented above and no adaptation mechanisms have been proposed as the description may suggest.

Trust-X (Bertino et al. 2003)

Trust-X is a TMS that was designed for trust negotiation in peer-to-peer systems (Bertino *et al.* 2003, 2004). It is built upon two blocks: *X*-profiles and *X*-TNL. *X*-profiles are data structures used to store user's credentials along with uncertified declarations containing information about them (e.g. age, mail and address). *X*-TNL stands for *XML-based trust negotiation language*. *X*-TNL has been developed for the specification of Trust-X certificates and disclosure policies.

```
<policySpec>
<properties>
<certificate targetCertType= Corrier_employee>
<certCond>
//employee number[@code=Rental Car.requestCode]
</certCond>
<certCond> /.../[position=driver]
</certCond>
</certificate>
</properties>
<resource target="Rental_Car"/>
<type value="SERVICE"/>
</policySpec>
```

Listing 2.6. *Example of X-TNL policy specification*

The code in Listing 2.6 shows an example of an *X*-TNL policy defined by a rental car agency. The agency is aimed at drivers of the Corrier society, which is part of the agency to rent cars without paying. This policy can be satisfied by providing a credential, which is specified using the *X*-TNL too. The syntax of a credential is described in the example provided in Listing 2.7.

```
<Corrier Employee credID='12ab', SENS= 'NORMAL' >
<Issuer HREF='http://www.Corrier.com' Title=Corrier
Employees Repository/>
<name>
<Fname> Olivia </Fname>
<lname > White </lname>
</name>
<address> Grange  Wood 69 Dublin </address>
<employee number code=34ABN/>
<position> Driver </position>
</Corrier Employee>
```

Listing 2.7. *Example of X-TNL profile*

The Trust-X engine provides a mechanism for negotiation management. The main strategy used in Trust-X consists of releasing policies to minimize the disclosure of credentials. Therefore, only credentials that are necessary for the success of a negotiation are effectively disclosed (Squicciarini *et al.* 2007). Thus, Trust-X makes use of a prudent strategy (see section 2.4.4).

The primary novel aspect proposed in Trust-X consists of the use of *trust tickets*. Trust tickets are issued upon the successful completion of a negotiation. These tickets can later be used in subsequent negotiations to speed up the process in case the negotiation concerns the same resource. Additionally, Trust-X provides a mechanism to protect sensitive policies. This is achieved using *policy-precondition*; policies are logically sorted so that the satisfaction of a policy is the precondition of the disclosure of the subsequent policies.

Recently, Braghin (2011) has proposed an interesting extension in which the framework is used to handle negotiations between groups of individuals instead of only between two individuals.

XACML

The *XML Access Control Markup Language* (XACML) (Humenn 2003; Cover 2007) is a generic trust management architecture. Even though in most of the works X.509 certificates are used with XACML. This framework accepts any credential format and thus is also generic with respect to credentials. XACML is also a standardized and interoperable policy specification language for expressing and exchanging policies using XML. The syntax of an XACML rule is defined as follows:

```
<Policy PolicyId="owner">
<Rule RuleId="owner-r" Effect="Permit">
<Condition>
<Apply FunctionId=
    "urn:oasis:names:tc:xacml:1.0:function:string- equal">
<SubjectAttributeDesignator DataType=
    "http://www.w3.org/2001/XMLSchema#string">
        urn:oasis:names:tc:xacml:1.0:subject:subject-id
</SubjectAttributeDesignator>
<ResourceAttributeDesignator DataType=
    "http://www.w3.org/2001/XMLSchema#string">
        urn:emc:edn:samples:xacml:resource:resource-owner
</SubjectAttributeDesignator>
</Apply>
</Condition>
</Rule>
</Policy>
```

Listing 2.8. *A simple "owner" policy in XACML*

The above policy states that anybody can do anything with their own records. Therefore, in XACML, the policy's building blocks are rules. Each rule is composed of three main components: a *target*, a *condition* and an *effect* (see Listing 2.8). The target defines the rule scope (i.e. subject, actions and resources that the rule applies to); the condition specifies restrictions on the attributes of the subject and defines the applicability of the rule and the effect is either `permit` (the rule is then called a permit rule) or `deny` (the rule is then called a deny rule). When a request meets the rule target and satisfies the rule condition, the rule is applied and the decision specified in the effect is built, otherwise, the rule is not applicable and the request yields the decision `NotApplicable` (Li *et al.* 2009). Policies group rules that relate to the same target and policy sets group policies that relate to the same target.

The trust engine architecture is composed of several points, each representing a separate module: the policy decision point (PDP) is the core of the architecture where policies are evaluated and decisions are made; the policy enforcement point (PEP) is the point in which decisions are applied (e.g. issuing an authorization); the policy retrieval point (PRP) is the point in which policies are selected and retrieved from repositories; the policy information point (PIP) is the point in which information is collected from the perspective of policies evaluation; and the policy administration point (PAP) is the point in which policies are administrated (e.g. specified, updated, activated and deactivated).

Typically, the functioning of the XACML engine can be summarized as follows. The requester sends a request to the PEP (typically the application using the TMS), which is then sent to the PDP, which extracts the applicable policies using the PRP. The PIP is then requested to collect and retrieve the credentials required for the evaluation of the policy. For that, the PIP interacts with the requester, the resources and the environment to extract each entity's attributes. Based on these data, the PDP evaluates the policy and provides an answer along with an optional obligation. This result is transmitted to the PEP which applies the obligation and grants access to the requester if the evaluation was positive.

Recently, Abi Haidar and colleagues (Abi Haidar *et al.* 2008) have used an extended RBAC profile of XACML in the context of XeNA (the XACML negotiation of access), an access negotiation framework. XeNA brings together negotiation for trust establishment and access control management within the same architecture. The XeNA trust engine is based on TrustBuilder2 extended to support XACML access control and negotiation policies.

ATNAC (Ryutov et al. 2005)

Adaptive Trust Negotiation and Access Control (ATNAC) is an integrated TMS that combines two existing systems: GAA-API and TrustBuilder (already presented earlier in section 2.5.2). GAA-API is a generic authorization and access control system that captures dynamically changing system security requirements. The system uses X.509 credentials to convey information between negotiating partners. ATNAC uses TPL to express trust policies that, in addition to the partner's properties, explicitly refer to the context suspicion level (SL). In ATNAC, several policies are specified and used to protect the same resource. Therefore, the main novelty of the system lies in the trust engine that monitors the environment suspicion level (thanks to GAAI-API) and adapts the selected policy based on that suspicion level. This mechanism is used in ATNAC to provide adaptive trust negotiation in order to counter malicious attacks.

	Suspicion level		
	Low	*Medium*	*High*
R_1	freely	freely	freely
R_2	freely	freely	C_1
R_3	freely	C_1	C_1 and C_2

Table 2.2. *Example of policies used in ATNAC (adapted from Ryutov et al. (2005))*

Table 2.2 illustrates the adaptive approach advocated by ATNAC. In this example, the resource R_1 is non-sensitive and thus it is disclosed independently of the suspicion level. In contrast, R_3 can be freely disclosed in the context of a *low* SL, which requires a credential C_1 when the SL is *medium* but requires both C_1 and C_2 when the SL is *high*.

PROTUNE (Bonatti et al. 2008)

The *PROvisional TrUst NEgotiation* (PROTUNE) *framework* is a system that provides distributed trust management and negotiation (Bonatti and Olmedilla 2005; Bonatti *et al.* 2008) features to web services. The PROTUNE framework provides (a) a trust management language,

(b) a declarative meta-language for driving decisions about information disclosure, (c) a negotiation mechanism that enforces the semantics of the meta-language, (d) a general ontology-based approach to support the policy language extension and (e) an advanced policy explanation mechanism that is able to output *why*, *why not* and *how to* answers that are important during a negotiation process. One of the main advances made by PROTUNE lies in the use of *declarations* along with credentials during the policy evaluation process. Declarations are the unsigned equivalent of credentials. They can also be considered as statements that are not signed by a certification authority. However, the most novel part of the project remains the policy specification language, which combines access control and provisional-style business rules.

In PROTUNE, policies are specified using the rule language defined in Bonatti and Olmedilla (2005). The language is based on logic program rules extended with an object-oriented syntax[5].

```
allow(X,access(Resource))  :-
goodReputation(X), validID(C).
validID(C)  :-
credential(identity, C[subject:X]). goodReputation(X)  :-
declaration(Y,X,reputation(R)), Y!= X, R > 50.
```

Listing 2.9. *Example of a PROTUNE access policy*

The above PROTUNE policy states that an individual must provide a valid credential proving their identity and that they must have a good reputation to be granted access to a resource. This kind of policy is called access policy. Similarly, PROTUNE implements negotiation strategies through *release* policies, which states under which conditions a credential can be released. An example of such resource is provided hereafter.

```
allow(release(credential(C[type:identity])))
:credential(ta, Cred[issuer:'Trusted Authories']).
```

Listing 2.10. *Example of a PROTUNE release policy*

---

5 *A.at*: *v* means that the individual A has the attribute *at* and that this attribute has the value *v*. This expression is in fact an abbreviation of the logic predicate *at*(*A*, *v*).

This policy states that identity credentials can only be released to individuals providing a credential that proves that they belong to the "*Trusted Authorities*" group.

2.6. Trust management in cloud infrastructures

In this section, we review an example of recent applications of trust management mechanisms. We are particularly interested in reviewing trust models in cloud infrastructures. Trust in cloud computing has been addressed in the literature from two different perspectives: the cloud service consumer (CSC) and the cloud service provider (CSP). In this section, we classify existing approaches from both perspectives.

2.6.1. *Credentials-based trust models*

These models draw their inspiration from the approach advocated in DTM systems presented previously (see section 2.5.1). In these models, trust is established between CSP and CSC using credentials (i.e. certificates and/or keys) issued by trusted third parties or certification authorities. An entity A trusts another entity B if and only if it receives the adequate credentials to build a chain of trust that links B to A. This model reproduces the Web of Trust (WoT) approach, in which each member vouches for each other (Abdul-Rahman 1997; Abdul-Rahman and Hailes 2000).

2.6.2. *SLA-based trust models*

In Noor and Sheng (2011), the authors proposed the "Trust as a Service" (TaaS) framework, in which they introduced an *adaptive credibility model* that distinguishes between credible trust feedbacks and malicious feedbacks by considering cloud service consumers' capability and majority consensus of their feedbacks. In this work, trust has been addressed from the perspective of users.

In Habib *et al.* (2011), the authors proposed a multi-face model to manage trust in cloud computing marketplaces. The model collects several attributes to assess the trustworthiness of a cloud service provider. These attributes correspond to service level objectives defined within active SLAs. Feedback information is also collected from different sources and used alongside SLA metrics to derive a trust score for each CSO.

The authors refer to the CAIQ (Consensus Assessments Initiative Questionnaire; https://cloudsecurityalliance.org/articles/ccm-caiq-v3-0-1-soft-launch/) as a way to extract SLA compliance information.

In the joint risk and trust model (JRTM) developed in the context of the A4Cloud (accountability for cloud) (Cayirci 2013), statistical data (i.e. proofs and indicators) collected from third-party services (i.e. a TaaS Provider) are accumulated and computed to estimate the trust that a cloud customer puts on a specific cloud service provider. The model relies on the assessment of the cloud service security and privacy risk to derive a trust metric. The information used includes, for instance, statistics on the number of security and privacy incidents that the CSP was subject to.

2.6.3. *Feedback-based trust models*

In these models, trust is built upon feedbacks, ratings and opinions that CSP and CSC express based on their past experience with each other. In these models, each entity (CSP and CSC) is responsible for collecting, processing and sharing a reputation measure. In general, feedbacks are expressed with respect to business (e.g. QoS) and security parameters. Thus, the object of a feedback can be any property that CSP and CSC can rate each other on. Feedbacks are more generally compared to reputation. However, the models used in reputation-based trust models are comparable to the model used for feedback management. Reputation is the social evaluation of a group, a community or a society of agents towards the trustworthiness of an individual (Sabater and Sierra 2001).

In DAI, and more particularly in multi-agent systems, reputation has been considered as a substantial dimension of trust (Jøsang and Ismail 2002). In the following, we review some predominant reputation models.

ReGreT (Sabater and Sierra 2001) is a well-known decentralized trust and reputation model for e-commerce. Proposed by Sabater and Sierra in 2001, the main objective of ReGreT was to make more accurate trust evaluations. To that aim, the authors used three factors based on which trust was computed: *the direct experience*, *the global reputation* and an ontological *fine-grained reputation*, which defines reputation values for each trait of the individual using the ontology. In ReGreT, the network to which the agent belongs is used to assess the credibility of the information provided by each agent. Social relationships are presented in the form of fuzzy rules, which are later used to determine whether the witness information provided by an agent should be considered or not.

Jøsang (Jøsang and Ismail 2002) proposed a reputation model (called the beta reputation system) for decision-making in the context of e-commerce transactions. The authors used the concept of reliability along with the probability of success to determine the trustworthiness of a partner. The reliability of an individual is assessed in direct and indirect ways. The direct reliability is computed based on previous knowledge about the partner, while the indirect reliability is given by recommendation from other trusted third parties. The indirect reliability is then computed by averaging all the recommendations weighted by the recommender trust degree. Then, this value is combined with the direct reliability in order to derive a trust degree. Once this trust degree is obtained, it forms a belief that is described as a set of fuzzy propositions such as "A believes that B is very trustworthy".

FIRE (Huynh *et al.* 2006) is another important model designed by Huynh and colleagues for multi-agent systems. They compute trust based on past experiences, the role of the agent, its reputation and a kind of certified reputation. Roles are used to determine to what degree an agent that has a certain position in the society could be trusted. The main idea is that trust depends on the fulfillment of the role ascribed to the agent. Also, the authors make a distinction between witness reputation and certified reputation. Certified reputation is a reputation that comes from a certified, presumably trusted witness, while normal reputation comes from every agent of the society.

2.6.4. *Prediction-based trust models*

In Xie *et al.* (2013), the authors defined a similarity-based prediction model. Entities (i.e. cloud users and cloud providers) are represented using a vector of capabilities and interests. The more these vectors are similar, the more likely trust can be established between them.

In Habib *et al.* (2011), the authors presented a behavior-based trust model, in which the trust value depends on the expected behavior of the cloud provider. The behavior of the provider is assessed with respect to specific attributes such as security measures, compliance and customer support. Here again, the authors focus on the perspective of the user that tries to select the best provider.

2.7. Conclusion

In this chapter, we introduced basic concepts of trust management. We also reviewed and analyzed several trust management systems that we classified along basic components of trust management systems, namely *credentials*, *policies* and *trust engines*. In the last section, we presented how these concepts have been used in recent systems to address new challenges introduced by cloud computing.

All reviewed systems rely on credentials in their trust management process. Credentials are used between the *trustors* and *trustees* to exchange *information* based on which trust can be established. With respect to that, credentials are essentially used as a means for bootstrapping trust between individuals that know little about each other.

In terms of information, systems are split into three categories. In the first category, systems use credentials to support authentication. These systems inherit from IBAC models and use credentials to convey the identity of the holder (generally a key). Other systems such as PolicyMaker use credentials to represent a *delegation of rights*. Finally, the last generation of TMS (e.g. TrustBuilder) makes use of fine-grained credentials, in which all attributes of the holder can be represented (e.g. age, address, rights and roles). These systems inherit from ABAC and raise the *credentials privacy* issue, which motivated *negotiation trust management systems*.

In terms of condition expressiveness, all reviewed policy languages proceed in the same way. Conditions are stated to set minimal values that are accepted for each information. Then, policies are expressed by a conjunction or a disjunction of these conditions. This approach has a limited expressiveness as all conditions stated by a policy are considered to be equally important.

Moreover, many policy languages we reviewed adopted a binary evaluation, in which either all conditions are satisfied or no condition is considered to be satisfied (e.g. early TMS). With respect to this, trust negotiation systems (e.g. TrustBuilder, Trust-X and PROTUNE) are more flexible as the evaluation of a policy is progressively achieved. Nevertheless, no system considered partial policy evaluation in which the policy satisfaction level is computed even though all conditions are not met.

2.8. References

Abdul-Rahman, A. (1997). The PGP Trust Model EDI-Forum. *The Journal of Electronic Commerce*, 10(3), 27–31.

Abdul-Rahman, A. and Hailes, S. (2000). Supporting trust in virtual communities. In *Proceedings of the 33rd Hawaii International Conference on System Sciences Volume 6*, HICSS '00, Washington, DC. IEEE Computer Society. p. 6007. ISBN 0-7695-0493-0. Available: http://dl.acm.org/citation.cfm?id= 820262.820322.

Abi Haidar, D., Cuppens-Boulahia, N., Cuppens, F., and Debar H. (2008). XeNA: An access negotiation framework using XACML. *Annals of Telecommunications*, 64(1–2), 155–169. ISSN 0003-4347. doi: 10.1007/s12243-008-0050-5. Available: http://link.springer.com/10.1007/s12243-008-0050-5.

Ardagna, C.A., Damiani, E., Capitani di Vimercati, S., Foresti, S., and Samarati, P. (2007). Trust management. In *Security, Privacy, and Trust in Modern Data Management*, Data-Centric Systems and Applications, Petković, M. and Jonker, W. (eds). Springer, Berlin, Heidelberg, pp. 103–117. ISBN 978-3-540-69860-9. doi: 10.1007/978-3-540-69861-6_8. Available: http://dx.doi.org/10.1007/978-3-540-69861-6_8.

Artz, D. and Gil, Y. (2010). A survey of trust in computer science and the Semantic Web. *Web Semantics: Science, Services and Agents on the World Wide Web*, 5(2), 58–71. ISSN 15708268. doi: 10.1016/j.websem.2007.03.002. Available: http://linkinghub.elsevier.com/retrieve/pii/S1570826807000133.

Bandara, A., Damianou, N., Lupu, E., Sloman, M., and Dulay, N. (2007). Policy-based management. In *Handbook of Network and System Administration*, Bergstra, J., and Burgess, M. (eds). Elsevier Science.

Becker, M.Y. (2005). Cassandra: Flexible trust management and its application to electronic health records. Technical Report UCAM-CL-TR-648, University of Cambridge.

Becker, M.Y. and Sewell, P. (2004). Cassandra: Distributed access control policies with tunable expressiveness. In *Proceedings of the Fifth IEEE International Workshop on Policies for Distributed Systems and Networks*, POLICY '04, Washington, DC. IEEE Computer Society. ISBN 0-7695-2141-X. Available: http://dl.acm.org/citation.cfm?id=998684.1006922.

Bertino, E., Ferrari, E., and Squicciarini, A. (2003). X -tnl: An xml-based language for trust negotiations. In *Proceedings of the 4th IEEE International Workshop on Policies for Distributed Systems and Networks*, POLICY '03, Washington, DC. IEEE Computer Society. ISBN 0-7695-1933-4. Available: http://dl.acm.org /citation.cfm?id=826036.826848.

Bertino, E., Ferrari, E., and Squicciarini, A.C. (2004). Trust-x: A peer-to-peer framework for trust establishment. *IEEE Trans. on Knowl. and Data Eng.*, 16(7), 827–842. ISSN 1041-4347. doi: 10.1109/TKDE.2004.1318565. Available: http://dx.doi.org/10.1109/TKDE.2004.1318565.

Blaze, M., Feigenbaum, J., and Lacy, J. (1996). Decentralized trust management. In *Proceedings of the 1996 IEEE Symposium on Security and Privacy*, SP '96, Washington, DC. IEEE Computer Society. ISBN 0-8186-7417-2. Available: http://dl.acm.org/citation.cfm?id=525080.884248.

Blaze, M., Feigenbaum, J., Ioannidis, J., and Keromytis, A.D. (1999a). The role of trust management in distributed systems security. In *Secure Internet Programming*, Vitek, J. and Jensen C.D. (eds). Springer-Verlag, London, pp. 185–210. ISBN 3-540-66130-1. Available: http://dl.acm.org/citation.cfm?id=380171.380186.

Blaze, M., Feigenbaum, J., and Keromytis, A. (1999b). Keynote: Trust management for public-key infrastructures. In *Security Protocols*, vol. 1550 of Lecture Notes in Computer Science, Christianson, B., Crispo, B., Harbison, W., and Roe, M. (eds). Springer Berlin Heidelberg. pp. 59–63. ISBN 978-3-540-65663-0. doi: 10.1007/3-540-49135-X_9. Available: http://dx.doi.org/10.1007/3-540-49135-X_9.

Boella, G. and van der Torre, L. (2005). Role-based rights in artificial social systems. In *Proceedings of the IEEE/WIC/ACM International Conference on Intelligent Agent Technology*, IAT '05, Washington, DC. IEEE Computer Society. pp. 516–519. ISBN 0-7695-2416-8. doi: 10.1109/IAT.2005.123. Available: http://dx.doi.org/10.1109/IAT.2005.123.

Bonatti, P. and Olmedilla, D. (2005). Driving and monitoring provisional trust negotiation with metapolicies. In *Proceedings of the Sixth IEEE International Workshop on Policies for Distributed Systems and Networks*, POLICY '05, Washington, DC. IEEE Computer Society. pp. 14–23. ISBN 0-7695-2265-3. doi: 10.1109/POLICY.2005.13. Available: http://dx.doi.org/10.1109/POLICY.2005.13.

Bonatti, P., Juri, L., Olmedilla, D., and Sauro, L. (2008). Policy-driven negotiations and explanations: Exploiting logic-programming for trust management, privacy & security. *Logic Programming*, pp. 779–784. Available: http://link.springer.com/chapter/10.1007/978-3-540-89982-2_76.

Braghin, S. (2011). Advanced languages and techniques for trust negotiation. PhD Thesis, University of Insubria.

Casimir, G., Lee, K., and Loon, M. (2012). Knowledge sharing: Influences of trust, commitment and cost. *Journal of Knowledge Management*, 16, 740–753. doi:10.1108/13673271211262781.

Cayirci, E. (2013). A joint trust and risk model for msaas mashups. In *Simulation Conference (WSC), 2013 Winter*, December, pp. 1347–1358. doi:10.1109 /WSC.2013.6721521.

Ceri, S., Gottlob, G., and Tanca, L. (1989). What you always wanted to know about datalog (and never dared to ask). *IEEE Trans. on Knowl. and Data Eng.*, 1(1), 146–166. ISSN 1041-4347. doi: 10.1109/69.43410. Available: http://dx.doi.org/ 10.1109/69.43410.

Chen, L. (2011). Analyzing and developing role-based access control models. PhD Thesis, Royal Holloway, University of London. Available: http://digirep.rhul. ac.uk/file/817519d1-0731-c09f-1522-e36433db3d2c/1/liangcheng.pdf.

Chu, Y.-H., Feigenbaum, J., LaMacchia, B., Resnick, P., and Strauss, M. (1997). Referee: Trust management for web applications. *World Wide Web J.*, 2(3), 127–139. ISSN 1085-2301. Available: http://dl.acm.org/citation.cfm?id =275079.275092.

Conrad, E., Misenar, S., and Feldman, J. (2012). *CISSP Study Guide*. Syngress.

Cover, R. (2007). Extensible Access Control Markup Language (XACML). Available: http://xml.coverpages.org/xacml.html.

Damianou, N., Dulay, N., Lupu, E., and Sloman, M. (2001). The ponder policy specification language. In *Proceedings of the International Workshop on Policies for Distributed Systems and Networks*, POLICY '01, London. Springer-Verlag. pp. 18–38. ISBN 3-540-41610-2. Available: http://dl.acm.org/citation.cfm? id=646962.712108.

De Coi, J.L. and Olmedilla, D. (2008). A review of trust management, security and privacy policy languages. In *SECRYPT 2008, Proceedings of the International Conference on Security and Cryptography, Porto, Portugal, July 26–29, 2008*, INSTICC Press, pp. 483–490.

DeTreville, J. (2002). Binder, a logic-based security language. In *Proceedings of the 2002 IEEE Symposium on Security and Privacy*, SP '02, Washington, DC. IEEE Computer Society. ISBN 0-7695-1543-6. Available: http://dl.acm.org/ citation.cfm?id=829514.830540.

Dimmock, N., Belokosztolszki, A., Eyers, D., Bacon, J., and Moody, K. (2004). Using trust and risk in role-based access control policies. In *Proceedings of the Ninth ACM Symposium on Access Control Models and Technologies*, SACMAT '04, New York, NY. pp. 156–162. ISBN 1-58113-872-5. doi: 10.1145/ 990036.990062. Available: http://doi.acm.org/10.1145/990036.990062.

El Houri, M. (2010). A formal model to express dynamic policies access control and trust negotiation a distributed environment. PhD Thesis, Paul Sabatier University.

Falcone, R. and Castelfranchi, C. (2001). Social trust: A cognitive approach. In *Trust and Deception in Virtual Societies*, Castelfranchi, C. and Tan, Y.-H. (eds). Kluwer Academic Publishers, Norwell, MA. pp. 55–90. ISBN 0-7923-6919-X. Available: http://dl.acm.org/citation.cfm?id=379153.379157.

Fernandez-Gago, M.C., Roman, R., and Lopez, J. (2007). A survey on the applicability of trust management systems for wireless sensor networks. In *Third International Workshop on Security, Privacy and Trust in Pervasive and Ubiquitous Computing (SecPerU 2007)*. IEEE, July. pp. 25–30. ISBN 0-7695-2863-5. doi: 10.1109/SECPERU.2007.3. Available: http://ieeexplore.ieee.org/lpdocs/epic03/wrapper.htm?arnumber=4279766.

Ferraiolo, D.F. and Kuhn, D.R. (2009). Role-based access controls. *arXiv preprint arXiv:0903.2171*, pp. 554–563. Available: http://arxiv.org/abs/0903.2171.

Ferraiolo, D.F., Sandhu, R., Gavrila, S., Kuhn, D.R., and Chandramouli, R. (2001). Proposed NIST standard for role-based access control. *ACM Transactions on Information and System Security*, 4(3), 224–274. ISSN 10949224. doi: 10.1145/501978.501980. Available: http://portal.acm.org/citation.cfm?doid=501978.501980.

Finin, T., Joshi, A., Kagal, L., Niu, J., Sandhu, R., Winsborough, W., and Thuraisingham, B. (2008). Rowlbac: Representing role based access control in owl. In *Proceedings of the 13th ACM symposium on Access control models and technologies*, SACMAT '08, New York, NY. ACM. pp. 73–82. ISBN 978-1-60558-129-3. doi: 10.1145/1377836.1377849. Available: http://doi.acm.org/10.1145/1377836.1377849.

Firdhous, M., Ghazali, O., and Hassan, S. (2012). Trust management in cloud computing: A critical review. *International Journal on Advances in ICT for Emerging Regions (ICTer)*, 4(2).

Galinović, A. (2010). Automated trust negotiation models. In *Proceedings of the 33rd International Convention*, MIPRO, pp. 1197–1202.

Gambetta, D. (2000). Can we trust trust? In *Trust: Making and Breaking Cooperative Relations*, Chapter 13, Gambetta, D. (ed.). Department of Sociology, University of Oxford. pp. 213–237. Available: http://citeseerx.ist.psu.edu/viewdoc/download?doi=10.1.1.24.5695&rep=rep1&type=pdf.

Genovese, V. (2012). Modalities in access control: Logics, proof-theory and applications. PhD Thesis, University of Luxembourg and University of Torino.

Gerck, E. (2000). Overview of certification systems: X.509, ca, pgp and skip. Technical Report, Meta-Certificate Group. Available: http://rustie.thebell.net/papers/ certover.pdf.

Grandison T.W.A. (2003). Trust management for internet applications. PhD Thesis, Imperial College of Science, Technology and Medicine, University of London. Available: http://www.doc.ic.ac.uk/~mss/Papers/Grandison-phd.pdf.

Grandison, T.W.A. and Sloman, M. (2003). Trust management tools for internet applications. In *Proceedings of the 1st International Conference on Trust Management*, iTrust'03, Berlin, Heidelberg. Springer-Verlag. pp. 91–107. ISBN 3-540-40224-1. Available: http://dl.acm.org/citation.cfm?id=1759008.1759015.

Gray, E. (2006). A trust-based reputation management system. PhD Thesis, Department of Computer Science, Trinity College Dublin. Available: https://www.tara.tcd.ie/handle/2262/24260.

Habib, S., Ries, S., and Muhlhauser, M. (2011). Towards a trust management system for cloud computing. In *Trust, Security and Privacy in Computing and Communications (TrustCom), 2011 IEEE 10th International Conference*, November, pp. 933–939. doi: 10.1109/TrustCom.2011.129.

Herzberg, A., Mass, Y., Michaeli, J., Ravid, Y., and Naor, D. (2000). Access control meets public key infrastructure, or: Assigning roles to strangers. In *Proceedings of the 2000 IEEE Symposium on Security and Privacy*, SP '00, Washington, DC. IEEE Computer Society. ISBN 0-7695-0665-8. Available: http://dl.acm.org/citation.cfm?id=882494.884417.

Humenn, P. (2003). The formal semantics of XACML. Technical Report, Syracuse University. Available: http://citeseerx.ist.psu.edu/viewdoc/download?doi=10.1.1.152.8864&rep=rep1&type=pdf.

Huynh, T.D., Jennings, N.R., and Shadbolt, N.R. (2006). An integrated trust and reputation model for open multi-agent systems. *Autonomous Agents and MultiAgent Systems*, 13(2), 119–154. ISSN 1387-2532. doi: 10.1007/s10458-005-6825-4. Available: http://dx.doi.org/10.1007/s10458-005-6825-4.

Jøsang, A. (2007). Trust and reputation systems. In *Foundations of Security Analysis and Design IV*, Aldini, A. and Gorrieri, R. (eds). Springer-Verlag, Berlin, Heidelberg. pp. 209–245. ISBN 3-540-74809-1, 978-3-540-74809-0. Available: http://dl.acm.org/citation.cfm?id=1793914.1793923.

Jøsang, A. and Ismail, R. (2002). The beta reputation system. In *Proceedings of the 15th Bled Electronic Commerce Conference*, vol. 160, pp. 324–337. doi: 10.1.1.60.5461.

Jøsang, A., Ismail, R., and Boyd, C. (2007). A survey of trust and reputation systems for online service provision. *Decision Support Systems*, 43(2), 618–644. ISSN 01679236. doi: 10.1016/j.dss.2005.05.019. Available: http://linkinghub.elsevier.com/retrieve/pii/S0167923605000849.

Kagal, L., Finin, T., and Joshi, A. (2003). A policy based approach to security for the semantic web. In *The Semantic Web ISWC 2003*, vol. 2870 of Lecture Notes in Computer Science, Fensel, D., Sycara, K., and Mylopoulos, J. (eds). Springer, Berlin, Heidelberg. pp. 402–418. ISBN 978-3-540-20362-9. doi: 10.1007/978-3-540-39718-2_26. Available: http://dx.doi.org/10.1007/978-3-540-39718-2_26.

Kalam, A.A.E. and Deswarte, Y. (2006). Multi-OrBAC: A new access control model for distributed, heterogeneous and collaborative systems. In *8th International Symposium on System and Information Security (SSI'2006)*, Sao Paulo, Brazil, 8–10 November. Available: http://homepages.laas.fr/deswarte/Publications/06427.pdf.

Kalam, A.A.E., Benferhat, S., Miège, A., Baida, R.E., Cuppens, F., Saurel, C., Balbiani, P., Deswarte, Y., and Trouessin, G. (2003). Organization based access control. In *Proceedings of the 4th IEEE International Workshop on Policies for Distributed Systems and Networks*, POLICY '03, Washington, DC. IEEE Computer Society. ISBN 0-7695-1933-4. Available: http://dl.acm.org/citation.cfm?id=826036.826869.

Krukow, K., Nielsen, M., and Sassone, V. (2008). Trust models in ubiquitous computing. *Philosophical Transactions of the Royal Society*, 366(1881), 3781–3793. doi: 10.1098/rsta.2008.0134. Available: http://rsta.royalsociety publishing.org/content/366/1881/3781.short.

Lamsal, P. (2001). Understanding trust and security. Technical Report, Department of Computer Science, University of Helsinki, Finland.

Lee, A.J. (2008). Towards practical and secure decentralize attribute-based authorisation systems. PhD Thesis, University of Illinois.

Lee, A.J., Winslett, M., and Perano, K.J. (2009). Trustbuilder2: A reconfigurable framework for trust negotiation. In *Trust Management III*, vol. 300 of IFIP Advances in Information and Communication Technology, Ferrari, E., Li, N., Bertino, E., and Karabulut, Y. (eds). Springer, Berlin, Heidelberg. pp. 176–195. ISBN 978-3-642-02055-1. doi: 10.1007/978-3-642-02056-8_12. Available: http://dx.doi.org/10.1007/978-3-642-02056-8_12.

Li, N., Mitchell, J.C., and Winsborough, W.H. (2002). Design of a role-based trust management framework. In *Proceedings of the 2002 IEEE Symposium on Security and Privacy*, SP '02, Washington, DC. IEEE Computer Society. ISBN 0-7695-1543-6. Available: http://dl.acm.org/citation.cfm? id=829514.830539.

Li, N., Wang, Q., Qardaji, W., Bertino, E., Rao, P., Lobo, J., and Lin, D. (2009). Access control policy combining: Theory meets practice. In *Proceedings of the 14th ACM Symposium on Access Control Models and Technologies*, SACMAT '09, New York, NY. ACM. pp. 135–144. ISBN 978-1-60558-537-6. doi: 10.1145/1542207.1542229. Available: http://doi.acm.org/10.1145/1542207.1542229.

Linn, J. (2000). Trust models and management in public-key infrastructures. Technical Report, RSA Laboratories. Available: http://storage.jak-stik.ac.id/rsasecurity/PKIPaper.pdf.

Liu, W.W. (2011). Trust management and accountability for internet security. PhD Thesis, Department of Computer Science, Florida State University. Available: http://etd.lib.fsu.edu/theses/available/etd-07222011-212723/.

Luhmann, N. (1990). Familiarity, confidence, trust: Problems and alternatives. In *Trust: Making and Breaking Cooperative Relations*. Basil Blackwell. pp. 15–35.

Marsh, S. (1994). Formalising trust as a computational concept. PhD Thesis, Department of Computing Science and Mathematics, University of Stirling. Available: http://scholar.google.com/scholar?hl=en&btnG=Search&q=intitle:Formalising+Trust+as+a+Computational+Concept#0.

Mcknight, D.H. and Chervany, N.L. (1996). The Meanings of trust. Technical Report 612, University of Minnesota.

Nejdl, W., Olmedilla, D., and Winslett, M. (2004). Peertrust: Automated trust negotiation for peers on the semantic web. In *Secure Data Management*, vol. 3178 of Lecture Notes in Computer Science, Jonker, W. and Petković, M. (eds). Springer, Berlin, Heidelberg. pp. 118–132. ISBN 978-3-540-22983-4. doi: 10.1007/978-3-540-30073-1_9. Available: http://dx.doi.org/10.1007/978-3-540-30073-1_9.

Noor, T.H. and Sheng, Q.Z. (2011). Trust as a service: A framework for trust management in cloud environments. In *Proceedings of the 12th International Conference on Web Information System Engineering*, WISE'11, Berlin, Heidelberg. Springer-Verlag. pp. 314–321. ISBN 978-3-642-24433-9. Available: http://dl.acm.org/citation.cfm?id=2050963.2050992.

Nyanchama, M. and Osborn, S. (1999). The role graph model and conflict of interest. *ACM Transactions on Information and System Security*, 2(1), 3–33. ISSN 10949224. doi: 10.1145/300830.300832. Available: http://portal.acm.org/citation.cfm?doid=300830.300832.

Parsons, S. and Wooldridge, M. (2002). Game theory and decision theory in multiagent systems. *Autonomous Agents and Multi-Agent Systems*, 5(3), 243–254. Available: http://link.springer.com/article/10.1023/A%3A1015575522401.

Prohic, N. (2005). Public Key Infrastructures – PGP vs. X. 509. In *INFOTECH Seminar Advanced Communication Services (ACS)*. Available: http://www.linecity.de/INFOTECH_ACS_SS05/acs5_top6_paper.pdf.

Renzl, B. (2008). Trust in management and knowledge sharing: The mediating effects of fear and knowledge documentation. *Omega*, 36(2), 206–220. ISSN 0305-0483. doi: http://dx.doi.org/10.1016/j.omega.2006.06.005. Special Issue on Knowledge Management and Organizational Learning.

Ruohomaa, S. and Kutvonen, L. (2005). Trust management survey. In *Trust Management*, vol. 3477 of Lecture Notes in Computer Science, Herrmann, P., Issarny, V., and Shiu, S. (eds). Springer, Berlin, Heidelberg. pp. 77–92. ISBN 978-3-540-26042-4. doi: 10.1007/11429760_6. Available: http://dx.doi.org/10.1007/11429760_6.

Ryutov, T., Zhou, L., Neuman, C., Leithead, T., and Seamons, K.E. (2005). Adaptive trust negotiation and access control. In *Proceedings of the Tenth ACM Symposium on Access Control Models and Technologies*, SACMAT '05, New York, NY. ACM. pp. 139–146. ISBN 1-59593-045-0. doi: 10.1145/ 1063979.1064004. Available: http://doi.acm.org/10.1145/1063979.1064004.

Saadi, R., Rahaman, M., Issarny, V., and Toninelli, A. (2011). Composing trust models towards interoperable trust management. *Trust Management V*, 358, 51–66. Available: http://link.springer.com/chapter/10.1007/978-3-642-22200-9_7.

Sabater, J. and Sierra, C. (2001). Regret: Reputation in gregarious societies. In *Proceedings of the Fifth International Conference on Autonomous Agents*, AGENTS '01, New York, NY. ACM. pp. 194–195. ISBN 1-58113-326-X. doi: 10.1145/375735.376110. Available: http://doi.acm.org/10.1145/375735.376110.

Samarati, P. and Vimercati, S.D.C.d. (2001). Access control: Policies, models, and mechanisms. In *Revised versions of lectures given during the IFIP WG 1.7 International School on Foundations of Security Analysis and Design on Foundations of Security Analysis and Design: Tutorial Lectures*, FOSAD '00, London. Springer-Verlag. pp. 137–196. ISBN 3-540-42896-8. Available: http://dl.acm.org/citation.cfm?id=646206.683112.

Sandhu, R. (1993). Lattice-based access control models. *Computer*, 26(11), 9–19. ISSN 0018-9162. doi: 10.1109/2.241422. Available: http://dx.doi.org/10.1109 /2.241422.

Sandhu, R., Coyne, E., Feinstein, H., and Youman, C. (1996). Role-based access control models. *Computer*, 29(2), 38–47. doi: 10.1109/2.485845. Available: http://ieeexplore.ieee.org/xpls/abs_all.jsp?arnumber=485845.

Sandhu, R., Ferraiolo, D., and Kuhn, R. (2000). The NIST model for role-based access control: Towards a unified standard. In *Proceedings of the Fifth ACM Workshop on Role-based Access Control*, RBAC '00, New York, NY. ACM. pp. 47–63. ISBN 1-58113-259-X. doi: 10.1145/344287.344301. Available: http://doi.acm.org/10.1145/344287.344301.

Seamons, K., Winslett, M., Yu, T., Smith, B., Child, E., Jacobson, J., Mills, H., and Yu, L. (2002). Requirements for policy languages for trust negotiation. In *Proceedings of the 3rd International Workshop on Policies for Distributed Systems and Networks (POLICY'02)*, POLICY '02, Washington, DC. IEEE Computer Society. ISBN 0-7695-1611-4. Available: http://dl.acm.org/citation.cfm?id=863632.883487.

Sloman, M. (1994). Policy driven management for distributed systems. *Journal of Network and System Management*, 2(4).

Squicciarini, A., Bertino, E., Ferrari, E., Paci, F., and Thuraisingham, B. (2007). Pp-trustx: A system for privacy preserving trust negotiations. *ACM Trans. Inf. Syst. Secur.*, 10(3). ISSN 1094-9224. doi: 10.1145/1266977.1266981. Available: http://doi.acm.org/10.1145/1266977.1266981.

Uszok, A., Bradshaw, J., Jeffers, R., Suri, N., Hayes, P., Breedy, M., Bunch, L., Johnson, M., Kulkarni, S., and Lott, J. (2003). Kaos policy and domain services: Toward a description-logic approach to policy representation, deconfliction, and enforcement. In *Proceedings of the 4th IEEE International Workshop on Policies for Distributed Systems and Networks*, POLICY '03, Washington, DC. IEEE Computer Society. ISBN 0-7695-1933-4. Available: http://dl.acm.org/citation.cfm?id=826036.826850.

Uszok, A., Bradshaw, J.M., Johnson, M., Jeffers, R., Tate, A., Dalton, J., and Aitken, S. (2004). Kaos policy management for semantic web services. *IEEE Intel Ligent Systems*, 19(4), 32–41. ISSN 1541-1672. doi: 10.1109/MIS.2004.31. Available: http://dx.doi.org/10.1109/MIS.2004.31.

Wang, Y. and Varadharajan, V. (2007). Role-based recommendation and trust evaluation. In *The 9th IEEE International Conference on E-Commerce Technology and the 4th IEEE International Conference on Enterprise Computing, E-commerce and E-services (CEC-EEE 2007)*. IEEE, July. pp. 278–288. ISBN 0-7695-2913-5. doi: 10.1109/CEC-EEE.2007.83. Available: http://ieeexplore.ieee.org/lpdocs/epic03/wrapper.htm?arnumber=4285225.

Wikipedia (2013). Trust management (information system). Available: http://en.wikipedia.org/wiki/Trust_management.

Winsborough, W.H. and Li, N. (2006). Safety in automated trust negotiation. *ACM Trans. Inf. Syst. Secur.*, 9(3), 352–390. ISSN 1094-9224. doi: 10.1145/1178618.1178623. Available: http://doi.acm.org/10.1145/1178618. 1178623.

Xie, F., Chen, Z., Xu, H., Feng, X., and Hou, Q. (2013). Tst: Threshold based similarity transitivity method in collaborative filtering with cloud computing. *Tsinghua Science and Technology*, 18(3), 318–327. doi: 10.1109/TST.2013.6522590.

Yagüe, M. (2006). Survey on xml-based policy languages for open environments. *Journal of Information Assurance and Security*, 1, 11–20. Available: http://www.softcomputing.net/jias/a2.pdf.

Yaich, R., Boissier, O., Picard, G., and Jaillon, P. (2013). Adaptiveness and social compliance in trust management within virtual communities. *Web Intelligence and Agent Systems*, 11(4), 315–338.

Yao, W. (2004). Trust management for widely distributed systems. Technical Report UCAM-CL-TR-608, University of Cambridge Computer Laboratory.

Yu, T. (2003). Automated trust establishment in open systems. PhD Thesis, University of Illinois at Urbana-Champaign, Champaign, IL. AAI3102006.

Yu, T., Ma, X., and Winslett, M. (2000). Prunes: An efficient and complete strategy for automated trust negotiation over the internet. In *Proceedings of the 7th ACM Conference on Computer and Communications Security*, CCS '00, New York, NY. ACM. pp. 210–219. ISBN 1-58113-203-4. doi: 10.1145/352600.352633. Available: http://doi.acm.org/10.1145/352600.352633.

Yu, T., Winslett, M., and Seamons, K.E. (2003). Supporting structured credentials and sensitive policies through interoperable strategies for automated trust negotiation. *ACM Transactions on Information and System Security*, 6(1), 1–42. ISSN 10949224. doi: 10.1145/605434.605435. Available: http://portal.acm.org/citation.cfm?doid=605434.605435.

Yuan, E. and Tong, J. (2005). Attributed based access control (ABAC) for Web services. In *IEEE International Conference on Web Services (ICWS'05)*. IEEE. ISBN 0-7695-2409-5. doi: 10.1109/ICWS.2005.25.

Risk Analysis Linked to Network Attacks

3.1. Introduction

Securing enterprise information systems (IS) is a vital, complex and difficult task to undertake. Some IS threats, if they materialize, can be fatal for a company. These threats are intended to alter one of the key security attributes: integrity, authenticity, availability and confidentiality. In a simpler way, they can undermine the availability of systems and data, destroy data, corrupt or falsify data, steal or spy on confidential data, try to misuse the system or network, or use the compromised system to attack other targets.

Threats can have impacts that generate different costs for the company: human, technical and financial. Examples of impacts include: loss of confidentiality of sensitive data, unavailability of infrastructure and data, damage to intellectual property, loss of notoriety, etc. The risks of such threats can occur if the IS and the networks that support them are vulnerable. Generally, the risk can be described by a function with two parameters: probability of occurrence (likelihood) and threat impact. A widely used function is the product function of Impact and Occurrence Probability: *Risk = Impact × Occurrence Probability.*

Enterprise IS security is increasingly being addressed using risk-based approaches. These approaches can significantly reduce the impact of threats due to IS vulnerabilities. IS security and risk analysis have been the subject of several standards summarized below (Bloch *et al.* 2007):

Chapter written by Kamel KAROUI.

– ISO 27000: security vocabulary for ISS information systems;

– ISO 27001: security management system for ISMS information systems;

– ISO 27002 (previously 17799): security measures;

– ISO 27003: ISMS implementation;

– ISO 27004: ISMS follow-up indicators;

– ISO 27005: risk management and processing;

– ISO 27006: ISMS certification;

– ISO 27007: ISMS audit.

There are few IS risk assessment methods that take into account network security, network architectures and components. Among these methods, we can mention (Pons 2014): attack graphs, the CHASSIS method, the BDMP method, etc. These methods, although they can be very useful as risk indicators, are more or less simple and cannot be considered as complete risk analysis methods.

The objective of this chapter is therefore to summarize IS security from a risk perspective by integrating the network dimension and its various threats, that is, to propose a complete method for risk analysis of IS deployed on networks. This method is applicable and is based on existing risk management standards.

After the introduction, section 2 provides the reader with an introduction to risk definitions and terminology. It will also cover the main existing methodologies such as EBIOS, MEHARI and OCTAVE. This section ends with a comparison of these methods.

In section 3, we study risk analysis in the context of computer networks. In this section, we will try to propose a detailed and practical methodology to illustrate the different phases proposed by the ISO 27005 standard (Bahtit and Regragui 2012). We will apply our methodology to the case of the network architecture of an e-commerce company.

Finally, we will conclude this chapter with a brief conclusion summarizing the standards, methodology and processes presented in this chapter.

3.2. Risk theory

In this section, we will define the key terms associated with risk analysis (SGDN 2017). Next, we will present the main methodologies of risk analysis.

3.2.1. *Risk analysis terminology*

In the following, we will define the frequently used vocabulary in risk management. Figure 3.1 shows the relationship between the different terms used in risk management.

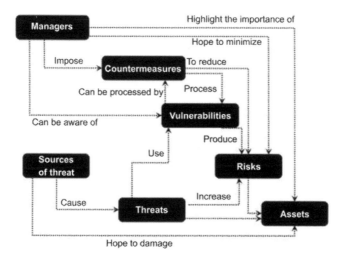

Figure 3.1. *Risk terminology*

The vocabulary of risk management includes:

– *asset*: a physical, software, or simply information resource that can be of particular importance in an information system;

– *importance of assets*: each asset has a certain material, and/or moral, and/or sentimental value, etc. This value is associated with assets and is called the importance of the resource or asset. Some assets are vital while others are optional for the proper functioning of a company's information system. The importance is pre-defined by the information systems managers;

– *IS Security managers*: by managers we mean all the IS actors of a company who can, on the one hand, evaluate the importance of assets, and, on the other hand, take decisions concerning the security of the IS and its most important assets against possible threats;

– *threats*: represent the possibility that a source or agent of threats may physically, logically or morally damage an IS's resources. A threat that is actually implemented is called an attack. A successful attack is called an intrusion. Threats can be classified in different ways: accidental/deliberate, passive/active, etc.;

– *sources of threats or threat agent or risk factor*: any entity that may pose a threat to IS assets. Sources can be classified in different ways: internal/external, malevolent/non-malevolent, automatic/manual, etc. The source can also be qualified as deliberate, if it is deliberately caused by an attacker, or unintentional if it appears spontaneously following normal use of the IS (e.g. software failure);

– *vulnerabilities*: weakness or flaw in security procedures, administrative controls, or internal controls of a system that could be exploited by a threat source to corrupt the IS, that is, compromise the confidentiality, and/or integrity and/or availability of the IS;

– *impact*: an estimate of all the material, logical or moral consequences that the information system may suffer following the realization of a threat (advent of a successful attack);

– *countermeasures*: a set of security measures that are adopted by the company to prevent a threat from materializing;

– *security policy*: a global system whose implementation ensures that the information system is secure against threats and the misuse of company assets;

– *risk*: the possibility that a particular source of threats exploits the vulnerabilities of one or more assets to damage a company's IS. Risk can therefore be considered as a multi-variable function that depends on the probability of occurrence (or likelihood), the impact and the countermeasures adopted by a company to deal with a given threat. This function is therefore proportional to the probability of occurrence and the impact of a threat, that is, the higher the probability of occurrence and the impact increases, the higher this function increases. On the other hand, it is inversely proportional to countermeasures, that is, the more effective the countermeasures are, the more this function decreases;

– *likelihood or probability of occurrence of a threat*: an estimate of the possibility or probability that a threat will be exploited in practice to become an attack against a company's IS;

– *risk management*: also called risk analysis. Risk management is defined by ISO (Bahtit and Regragui 2012) as the set of coordinated activities aimed at directing and leading an organization towards risk. In general, three purposes of risk management are identified:

– to improve the security of an IS,

– to justify the budget allocated to securing an IS,

– to prove the credibility of an IS.

3.2.2. *Presentation of the main risk methods*

Risk management is mainly described in ISO 27005 (Bahtit and Regragui 2012), which supports the general concepts specified in ISO 27001 (Brenner 2007). A standard is a reference document established to formally describe an industrial or economic issue. The ISO 27005 standard sets out all the steps of the risk management process used to secure information systems. It explains how to conduct, assess and deal with the risks incurred by IS. It also provides generic instructions to address information security risks. This standard distinguishes between the concepts of risk assessment, analysis, identification, estimation and evaluation. ISO 27005 can be used as a guide by an IS Security Officer. It describes the risk management process from setting the context to risk monitoring, risk assessment and risk treatment. According to this standard, the information security risk management process consists of the following stages:

– *context setting*: allows the criteria for the evaluation, impact and level of risk acceptance of IS to be defined;

– *risk assessment*: this phase allows the risks of an IS to be analyzed and evaluated in order to organize them in relation to the evaluation criteria set out in Stage 1;

– *risk treatment:* a process of implementing the security measures to be undertaken in response to IS security risks. This phase takes into account the priorities and risk ranking adopted in Stage 2;

– *risk acceptance*: involves approval by the responsible parties or by a designated approval authority of the choices made when processing the risk;

– *risk communication*: a regular process that allows the information on risks defined in the previous phases to be shared with the relevant stakeholders;

– *risk monitoring*: this phase makes it possible to control and ensure the adaptation and relevance of the security measures adopted in response to risks. It takes into account the safety objectives set by the company.

The main phases of standard 27005 are not based on specific methods or a detailed process that shows how to apply these stages. On the other hand, a method is a set of ordered activities that effectively achieve a specific and desired result without necessarily relying on a consensual reference document such as a standard, for example. Standards and methods are therefore complementary and it is preferable to combine them together, so that the method is used to implement the standard. Thus, to effectively implement ISO 27005, it is necessary to rely on a risk management method such as MEHARI, OCTAVE, EBIOS, etc. It is up to companies to choose to adopt standard 27005 rather than another one. In the following sections, we will present some risk management or analysis methods.

3.2.2.1. EBIOS

Expression des Besoin et Identification des Objectifs de Sécurité or EBIOS (Défense Nationale 2010) is a French risk analysis method. It was created in 1995 by the DCSSI (Direction Centrale de la Sécurité des Systèmes d'Information) of the French Ministry of Defence (Vasquez *et al.* 2012). EBIOS was updated in 2010 by the Agence Nationale de la Sécurité des Systèmes d'Information (Vasquez *et al.* 2012) and the EBIOS Club. This update makes it possible to take into account feedback and changes in standards. EBIOS can be used by the organization in two complementary ways: identifying the risks of an IS and proposing a security policy adapted to needs.

The EBIOS method consists of the following five steps (see Figure 3.2):

– *context study*: allows the study's target information system to be identified. It defines the limits of the risk study: presentation of the company, architecture of the information system, technical and regulatory constraints and commercial issues. It also studies details concerning the company's equipment, software and the company's human organization;

– *expression of security needs*: during this step, IS users (identified in step I) express their security needs according to the impacts they consider unacceptable;

– *threat study*: as its name suggests, this step makes it possible to identify IS threats according to the information system's technical architecture. This step requires the involvement of specialists to identify IS vulnerabilities and the threats they can generate based on them, the hardware used, the network architecture and the software used. The identification of vulnerabilities should be as comprehensive as possible. It must be independent of the origin (human, material, environmental, etc.), cause (intentional, accidental), etc., of vulnerabilities;

– *identification of security objectives*: this step makes it possible to compare the security needs identified at the needs expression stage with the vulnerabilities and threats identified at the threat study stage. The result of such a confrontation produces a list of IS risks against which one must protect oneself and which will be used to write security specifications. The specifications will express the choices that must be made to counter threats based on security requirements;

– *determination of security requirements*: this last step defines the risk management strategy that the company will adopt. It will set out in a risk plan the strategy to be adopted for each risk (accept, reduce or reject). This is because a company generally cannot have enough resources to deal with all the types of risks identified. To do this, it prioritizes the risks identified in the previous step. Indeed, for economic and strategic reasons, some risks must be ignored because, on the one hand, the cost of protection is exorbitant and, on the other hand, the probability of occurrence and the impacts are ultimately considered insignificant.

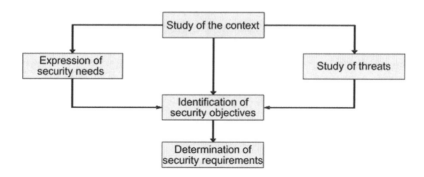

Figure 3.2. *Overall EBIOS approach (Culioli et al. 2009)*

It can therefore be said that EBIOS makes it possible to create a security policy based on a risk analysis based, in turn, on the company's context and the vulnerabilities related to its information system. In addition, to facilitate its application, the EBIOS method proposes the use of free software that allows the application of the methodology explained above. The software makes it possible to automate the creation of summary documents. In addition, the software connects to a knowledge base to take advantage of the predefined description of a set of specific vulnerabilities, security constraints and attack methods. This knowledge base can be easily enriched (feedback) via the software.

3.2.2.2. *MEHARI*

MEthode Harmonisée d'Analyse de Risques or MEHARI (Syalim *et al.* 2009) is a risk management method used by many public and private companies. It fully complies with the guidelines of ISO 31000 (Purdy 2010). Mehari provides an approach focused on the company's business continuity needs and uses a methodological guide to provide standard deliverables. The approach used by this method is based on that of two other methods that are no longer used, Melisa and Marion (Eloff *et al.* 1993). MEHARI is maintained by CLUSIF (Club de la Sécurité des Systèmes d'Information Français) via its Working Group dedicated to the maintenance of this method.

Regardless of the safety approach chosen by a company, the application of the MEHARI method involves the following generic activities (see Figure 3.3):

– *analysis of security issues*: this activity consists of gathering, for each major IS resource (hardware, software and information), the types of dysfunctions or vulnerabilities feared. Then the effects or impacts of these vulnerabilities on the resource are classified in relation to:

- the three basic attributes of security which are confidentiality, integrity and availability,

- the cause, which may be accidental, malicious, or due to an IS vulnerability,

- the consequences or impacts of these dysfunctions, which may be financial, technical or other, on the company;

– *security services audit*: this is the verification and control of the proper functioning and effectiveness of IS security services in order to possibly deduce vulnerabilities not mentioned in the previous activity;

– *detection of risk situations*: for each security threat, this activity consists of taking into consideration the probability of occurrence and potential impacts, as well as the security services to counter this threat, to deduce the severity of the associated risk.

In Mehari, the application of the previous activities aims to produce the following three deliverables also called the following plans (see Figure 3.3):

– *SSP (a strategic security plan)*: it is in this deliverable that the security objectives are set as well as the methods and metrics to evaluate the degree of achievement of these objectives. Thus, it is in this plan that the risks facing the company are assessed and the security policy that the company will have to adopt to secure its information system will be defined;

– *OPS (an operational security plan)*: a plan is defined for each major IS resource related to a given security risk. Its objective is to assess the security measures that exist or must be put in place to counter a threat. To define these measures, scenarios are developed to implement these threats, and the response of IS services is analyzed. Scenarios will be linked to vulnerabilities if the response of the security services is inadequate or insufficient to counteract these situations. These plans therefore make it possible to identify IS vulnerabilities. This allows the company to audit these security capabilities and properly assess the risks and identify the security needs to be undertaken;

– *COP (a company's operational plan)*: this plan can be considered as a dashboard. It allows us to control and monitor the company's overall IS security. This is done by using identified risk indicators and monitoring the worst-case scenarios of dangerous threats (probability, impact) from which to protect oneself.

In summary, MEHARI is based on a set of IS activities and audits that allow the development of a security policy. This policy is intended to counteract threats and vulnerabilities extracted in the Operational Security Plans and to ensure an acceptable level of security that corresponds to that presented in the Strategic Security Plan (see Figure 3.3). To achieve these objectives, the MEHARI methodology is based on guides, knowledge bases and quantitative evaluation processes:

– *guides*:

- sensitive resource classification guide,

- security services audit guide,

- risk analysis guide,

- guide to the development of safety objectives;

– *knowledge bases*:

- security services base,

- security services audit base,

- risk scenario base,

- base for analyzing risk scenarios based on actual security services,

- base for the analysis of risk scenarios by direct assessment of risk factors;

– *quantitative evaluation processes*:

- assessment of the quality of security services,

- assessment of risk factors,

- assessment of the potentiality and impact of a risk scenario,

- assessment of the severity of a risk.

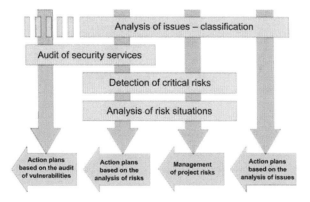

Figure 3.3. *General outline of the Mehari method (Ghazouani et al. 2014)*

3.2.2.3. OCTAVE

Operationally Critical Threat, Asset and Vulnerability Evaluation or OCTAVE (Alberts and Dorofee 2002) is a method that was initially proposed for large companies. It was developed in 1999 by the Software Engineering Institute (SEI) of Carnegie Mellon University through its CERT program. Currently, OCTAVE has three versions: OCTAVE (more than 300 employees), OCTAVE-S (less than 100 employees) and OCTAVE-Allegro (cut-down version of OCTAVE) (Caralli *et al.* 2007). OCTAVE-Allegro aims to enable a small structure to carry out its IS risk analysis based on a multidisciplinary team comprising members from all the company's departments. The OCTAVE application allows managers to improve their knowledge of the company and share knowledge on good security practices. OCTAVE describes the steps in detail and provides practical risk analysis tools such as risk spreadsheets and questionnaires.

The effectiveness of the OCTAVE method has allowed it to be quite widespread in North America. OCTAVE's objectives are to secure resources and manage staff from a technical and organizational point of view. The OCTAVE method consists mainly of the following three phases or views preceded by a preparation step (see Figure 3.4):

– *organizational view*: this is the study of the security needs linked to the company's resources. This phase aims to identify the assets and security threats that threaten the proper functioning of each entity in the company. It combines resources and threats with the company's vulnerabilities, which are enhanced by risk scenarios that threaten these resources. This leads to deducting the security needs related to each resource from the security objectives imposed by management and the current measures adopted by the company;

– *technical view*: this is the study of vulnerabilities and the identification of the technical components corresponding to each resource (identified in the organizational view). It is in this phase that priority resources are identified and audited to determine their vulnerabilities;

– *development of the security and strategy plan,* also called *the security strategy*: in this phase, the risks identified in the previous views are assessed and countermeasures are proposed to mitigate them. It is in this phase that a risk reduction plan is developed and organized.

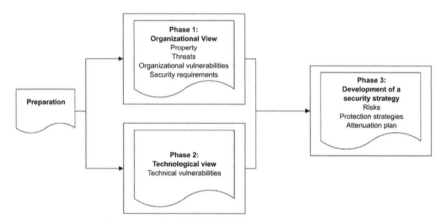

Figure 3.4. *Phases of the OCTAVE method (Bou Nassar 2012)*

3.2.3. *Comparison of the main methods*

Each of the risk analysis methods has its own specificities and differences (ANSI 2014). These methods also share the following common points:

– *a methodological approach*: these methods are based on processes consisting of phases and ordered activities. The objectives of these phases are to identify the company's significant risks and resources and to decide on appropriate countermeasures;

– *reference documents*: these methods help the various stakeholders in risk analysis by providing them with a reference document that lists and classifies the company's resources. Each resource is associated with its own threats and vulnerabilities.

These risk analysis methods also present differences that can lead to the choice of one or the other. These differences can be classified according to the following criteria (ANSI 2014):

– *language*: the language and vocabulary used by a risk analysis method is very important to understand and better use a method;

– *tools and knowledge base*: each risk analysis method has tools and knowledge base to facilitate the use of the method;

– *documentation*: the complexity of a risk analysis method can be mitigated by the quality of the documentation accompanying the method;

– *sustainability*: this attribute combines the criteria of permanence, stability and continuity of the risk analysis method. These criteria are important in choosing one method over another. This is the assurance that the publishers regularly updates and improves their method;

– *compatibility*: the risk analysis method must be consistent and not contradict international standards;

– *feedback*: the experience following the use of a method should be used to enrich the method. This can be a strength and leads to choosing one method over another;

– *complexity of implementation:* the ease of use of a method is a criterion that can be the strength of a method. This criterion depends not only on the methodology adopted by the method, but also on other attributes such as language, tools, documentation and feedback.

Below is a comparative table of the methods presented previously (ANSI 2014). This table is based on the criteria mentioned above. We can note, for example, that only EBIOS and MEHARI are compatible with the ISO 27005 standard.

Criteria Methods of operation	Documentation	Tools	Features	Complexity of implementation
EBIOS Language: French Country: France Conformity: ISO 31000, 27001, 27005	Rich in free downloads at http://www.ssi. gouv.fr/fr/guide s-et-bonnes- pratiques/outils-methodologiques/	EBIOS 2010 software, free and available at: https://adull act.net/projects/ebios2010/	– Risk analysis – ISS Maturity: DCSSI provides a document describing a methodological approach for determining the appropriate level of maturity for information system security (http://www.ssi. gouv.fr/IMG/pdf/maturitessi-methode-2007-11-02.pdf).	The implementation of this method is facilitated by the availability to users of rich and expandable knowledge bases, free and open source software to simplify the application and automate the creation of synthesis documents. In addition, an EBIOS user club was created in 2003 and constitutes a community of experts for sharing experiences.
MEHARI Language: French, English, German Country: France Conformity: ISO 27001, 27002,	Rich and available for free at https://www.clusif.asso.fr /fr/production/mehari/pre sentation.asp	A first level of tool is directly included in the method's knowledge base, using Excel and Open Office formulas. A reference manual, which is free of charge, explains its use. It is possible to adapt the knowledge database to the specific areas of activity, maturity level, scope and size	– Risk Analysis – Dashboard – ISS Maturity Indicators: the method gives indications of the maturity of the organization's ability to manage information security in all its forms. It makes it possible to measure the maturity level of information system security through several indicators	The implementation of MEHARI can only be carried out in conjunction with dedicated software or spreadsheets. The start of the analysis requires a somewhat complicated adaptation of the "knowledge base". In addition, a "MEHARI-Pro" version, which mainly targets small-and medium-sized

Criteria Methods of operation	Documentation	Tools	Features	Complexity of implementation
27005		of the company. In addition, several independent efforts are being made to develop additional tools such as RISICARE, developed by BUCSA, which is the most compliant and comprehensive.	(e.g. efficiency, resilience, continuity aspects).	organizations, private or public, is available at http://www.clusif. asso.fr/en/production/mehari/pr esentation.asp
OCTAVE **Language: English** **Country: USA** **Compliance: ISO 31010**	Catalogue of security practices and other documents are available for free download at http://www.cert.org/resili ence/products- services/octave/index.cf m	Paid software	– Risk Analysis – Dashboard – ISS Maturity Indicators: the method gives indications of the maturity of the organization's ability to manage information security in all its forms. It makes it possible to measure the maturity level of information system security through several indicators (e.g. efficiency, resilience, continuity aspects).	The OCTAVE methods are designed to be used by small, interdisciplinary teams of the organization's staff; the use of external experts for specific activities is sometimes necessary.

Table 3.1. *Comparative table of risk analysis methods (ANSI 2014)*

3.3. Analysis of IS risk in the context of IT networks

Information systems are generally based on distributed architectures that allow the IS of the company to be used by the network's various users: customers, internal users, suppliers, decision-makers, partners and/or administrative agents. Networking and exchanges between the various stakeholders can lead to new vulnerabilities in the company's information system. Network security is therefore a key component of information system security. In this chapter, we will adopt the risk management approach proposed by ISO 27005 and apply it to Information Systems (IS) deployed on computer networks. We remind you that this standard is a generic approach that does not provide any specific methodology for managing risks related to IS and network security. We also recall that ISO 27005 proposes a generic risk management approach based on six steps (see section 3.2.2): Setting the Context, Risk Assessment, Risk Treatment, Risk Acceptance, Risk Communication and Risk Monitoring.

In the following sections, we will detail the different steps of our methodology (Karoui 2016) for IS risk analysis deployed in computer networks. We will adopt the six-step approach of the 27005 standard. We will explain each of these steps and apply it to the case of an e-commerce company that can face a DDoS attack on its computer network and particularly on its web server. The choice of this example is used to demonstrate the usefulness of the IS risk management process in a network context.

3.3.1. *Setting the context*

An IS deployed in a network is associated with several important hardware and software resources that must be protected against possible cyberattacks. The protection of these resources can be initiated by an analysis of the risks to which these resources are exposed. Most of the work on risk (WEF 2012, ENISA 2013, OWASP 2018a, etc.) has demonstrated that the risk is based on two main parameters: the *Impact* and the *Probability of occurrence* of threats or attacks. In this section, we will present the resources to be protected, the risk parameters and the classification that will be adopted in the risk analysis.

3.3.1.1. *Resources to be protected*

An IS deployed in a network consists of a multitude of resources and components, each of which is of particular importance to the company. The complexity and number of these components make it fanciful to fully protect the IS. To this end, priority will be given to protecting the most important resources. First, resources and components will be identified and ranked in terms of their importance to the business. Subsequently, for each of these resources, an attempt will be made to identify the threats they may face.

3.3.1.1.1. Resource identification

The information system is an organized set of resources for collecting, storing, processing and distributing information. The most important components of an IS are applications, servers and databases. To secure these components, it is not enough to protect them directly, but also to protect the underlying technologies that support them and support the exchanges necessary for the normal operation of the IS. Figure 3.5 summarizes this for web applications.

3.3.1.1.2. Threats to resources

For each important resource of the company, we try to identify the threats that can affect its operation. For example, in the case of an e-commerce company, the website is of paramount importance to it. Indeed, the financial aspect of the company depends largely on the sales and financial operations carried out through the website. According to Figure 3.5, attacks are of different types. In the following, we will present the threats by dividing them into three categories: application, network and host. For each of these three categories, we will give some examples of threats that can affect the proper functioning of an e-commerce company's online sales website:

– *application threats*: these are all threats that can affect a company's applications or websites (Charpentier and Torstenson 2013). These threats include those on databases, application servers and database servers. The document (OWASP 2018b) provides a list of the 10 most common attacks on web applications and possible countermeasures. These attacks include: *Injection, Broken Authentication, Sensitive Data Exposure, XML External Entities (XXE), Broken Access Control, Security Misconfiguration, Cross Site Scripting (XSS), Insecure Deserialization, Using Components with Known Vulnerabilities, Insufficient Logging, HHTP flood, DDoS*, etc. (Charpentier and Torstenson 2013);

– *network threats*: there are two types of network equipment. The first type, consisting of equipment such as routers or switches, is used to route data from one point on the network to another. The second type, consisting of security equipment such as firewalls, IDSs and IPSs, is used to secure exchanges. Missing, misconfigured or misplaced network equipment can lead to vulnerabilities that can be exploited by an attacker. Common vulnerabilities include: low installation settings, inadequate access control and equipment that is not updated with the latest security patches. Microsoft's report (Microsoft 2018) discusses the following main types of threats: Information gathering, Sniffing, Spoofing, Session hijacking, Denial of service, etc.;

– *host threats*: the host is the end point of a network. From the host you can request, receive or update a network service. If a host is compromised, it can not only cause poor access to the IS, but it can also compromise the entire IS. According to Burke and Mouton (2018), there can be several types of threats such as: Malware, Password attacks, Arbitrary code execution, Unauthorized access, Privilege escalation, Backdoor attacks and Physical security threat.

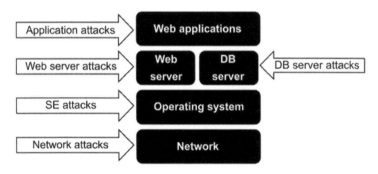

Figure 3.5. *Different classes of attacks on a web application of an IS*

3.3.1.2. *Risk model*

For the representation of risk parameters, we will use the approach presented by OWASP (OWASP 2018a). In this work, *Risk* is modeled in relation to these two main parameters: the *Impact* and the *Probability of occurrence* of threats. Each of these two parameters is modeled as a hierarchy of factors. We will call any particular ordering of this hierarchy of factors a model. In the following, we will present the two models associated with the *Impact* and *Probability of occurrence* of threat parameters.

3.3.1.2.1. Impact model

The impacts of an attack on an IS can be classified into two categories (OWASP 2018a): impacts on the company's *business* and *technical* impacts. The impacts on *Business* are, in turn, broken down into several sub-attributes or factors: *Secrets*, *Finance* and *Reputations*. On the other hand, the *Technical Impacts* are composed of the following factors: *Confidentiality*, *Integrity*, *Availability* and *Accounting*. This hierarchy of attributes and factors of the *Impact* can be represented by the tree shown in Figure 3.6. The list of these attributes and factors may vary from one institution to another and from one context to another.

For a given level of the *Impact* tree, more importance can be assigned to one factor or attribute than to another. A risk specialist may give more importance to the *Business Impact* attribute than to the *Technical Impact*. Similarly, *Business Impact* factors can be classified by importance as follows: *Financial*, *Reputation* and *Secrets*. We assume that importance follows a strict order (i.e. attributes or factors cannot have the same importance). Significance is independent of threats. In the *Impact* tree, importance is associated with all the direct descendants of a node, independently of the other nodes. Our notion of significance is the equivalent of the *weighted average* function coefficients used in several *Impact* estimation studies such as OWASP (2018a).

We will call the *Impact Model* the *Impact* tree sorted according to the selected importance of the nodes. Figure 3.6 illustrates an *Impact Model* where, at the first level, the *Business Impact* is considered to be of higher priority than the *Technical Impact*. When evaluating the *Impact*, using the same model avoids obtaining several different results for the same context. Several other benefits can result from the use of the models.

3.3.1.2.2. Probability of an occurrence model

The attributes or factors characterizing the *Probability of occurrence* of an attack can be classified into two categories (OWASP 2018a): *Threat* and *Vulnerability Agents*. The *Threat Agent's* attribute is composed of several factors: *Knowledge*, *Motivation*, *Size* and *Opportunity*. The *Vulnerability* attribute is composed of the following factors: *Ease of Operation*, *Ease of*

Discovery, *Awareness* and *Detection Systems*. This hierarchy of attributes and factors of the *Probability of occurrence* can be represented by the tree in Figure 3.6. The list of these attributes and factors may vary from one institution to another.

Similarly, the attributes and factors of the *Probability of occurrence* parameter will be ordered according to their importance. We will call the *Probability of Occurrence Model* the *occurrence probability* tree sorted according to the selected importance of the nodes. Figure 3.6 illustrates a *Probability of Occurrence Model*. When assessing *Probability of occurrence*, using the same model avoids obtaining several different results for the same context.

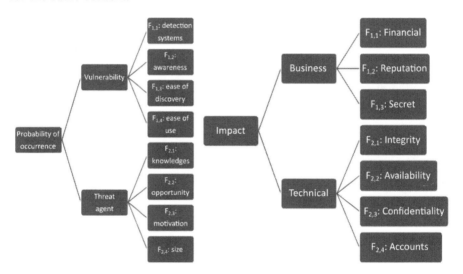

Figure 3.6. *Models of the Impact and Probability of occurrence parameters*

3.3.1.3. *Risk classification*

We propose to use the following risk classification scale composed of four ordered classes (best to worst) as follows (see Figure 3.7): *Low, Medium, High* and *Critical*.

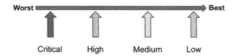

Figure 3.7. *Proposed risk classification*

3.3.1.3.1. Classification of risk parameters

The classification adopted will be as shown in Figure 3.7. If we note I the *impact* and O the *Probability of occurrence*, we can decompose the values of each of these two parameters into classes by dividing their respective value intervals into sub-intervals. The decomposition into sub-intervals is performed using limit values for each parameter. These limit values or thresholds are chosen from the outset. For example, for parameter I, whose values belong to an interval $[0, I_{max}]$, we choose three threshold values: SI_B, SI_M, and SI_E associated with the *Low, Medium, High* and *Critical* classes. We thus obtain four classes denoted by I_{++}, I_{+-}, I_{-+} and I_{--}. These classes are derived from the following decomposition (see Figure 3.8):

I_{++} if $0 \leq I < SI_B$

$I{+}{-}$ if $SI_B \leq I < SI_M$

$I{-}{+}$ if $SI_M \leq I < SI_E$

$I{-}{-}$ if $SI_E \leq I \leq I \leq I_{max}$

The same approach will be adopted for parameter O and three threshold values of O are chosen: SO_B, SO_M, and SO_E, thus obtaining the classification presented in Figure 3.8.

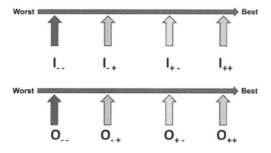

Figure 3.8. *Classification of Impact and Probability of occurrence*

3.3.1.3.2. Risk classification

Once the *Impact* and *Probability of occurrence* have been classified, this can be used to categorize the *Risk*. For this purpose, two global threshold classes *CGSI* and *CGSO* associated with the two parameters I and O will be defined. *CGSI* or *CGSO* represents the threshold class of I or O that the risk analyst considers acceptable (e.g. $CGSI = I_{+-}$). These two global threshold classes will divide the values of I (or O) into two categories that will be noted I^+ (or O^+) and I^- (or O^-) defined as follows:

– I^+ (or O^+) if class I is equal to or better than *CGSI* (or *CGSO*);

– I^- (or O^-) if class I is worse than *CGSI* (or *CGSO*).

The classes of I and O thus obtained will be used to classify the risk. There will be four possibilities representing the following four risk classes:

– class 1 rated I^+O^+: this is the class where the impact belongs to I^+ and the occurrence to O^+;

– class 2 noted I^+O^-: this is the class where the impact belongs to I^+ and the occurrence to O-;

– class 3 noted I^-O^+: this is the class where the impact belongs to I^- and the occurrence to O^+;

– class 4 noted I^-O^-: this is the class where the impact belongs to I^- and the occurrence to O^-.

To give a better meaning to this *Risk* classification, we can order these classes from the best to the worst. The best and worst class will be I^+O^+ and I^-O^-, respectively. On the other hand, to discriminate between classes I^+O^- and I^-O^+, a manager must decide which *risk* parameter has the highest priority. For example, if I is considered to be a higher priority than O, the following ranking will be given (see Figure 3.9):

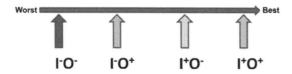

Figure 3.9. *Risk classification*

3.3.2. *Risk assessment*

In the context setting step, we proposed to represent each of these risk parameters as a tree of attributes and factors (see Figures 3.6). To estimate the value of one of the risk parameters, we will first assign a criticality value to these factors represented by the leaves of the tree. The criticality value that will be assigned will be either 0 (in binary 00) if the criticality of this factor is low, or 1 (in binary 01) if the criticality is medium, or 2 (in binary 10) if the criticality is high, or 3 (in binary 11) if the criticality is very high or critical. The criticality values of the factors will be aggregated at the parent node and so on until they reach the root of the tree. The value obtained at the root level is representative of the criticality of the *Risk* parameter. The method used to aggregate factor criticality values is called the bit alternation method (Karoui 2016). In what follows, we will first introduce the bit alternation method, then we will show how to use it to assess the *Impact*, the *Probability of occurrence*, and finally the risk.

3.3.2.1. *Bit alternation method for aggregating criticality values*

This method is based on a binary algorithm that aggregates several factor values to construct a single metric. The particularity of such a metric is that it is reversible. If necessary, it allows the criticality values of the components or factors used to build the metric to be restored.

The bit alternation method consists of aggregating binary words, representing the criticality of factors, into a single sequence representing a single metric. Aggregation takes into account the importance of factors. It is accomplished by alternating the bit sequences of the factors from the most important to the least important. Figure 3.10 shows the case of the aggregation of four factors F_1 ='10' (high criticality), F_2 ='11' (extreme criticality), F_3 ='01' (medium criticality) and F_4 ='00' (low criticality); the order of importance will be F_1, F_2, F_3 and F_4. By applying the bit alternation to F_1, F_2, F_3 and F_4, we obtain the sequence M='11000110', whose equivalent decimal value is 198 (see Figure 3.10).

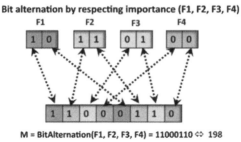

M = BitAlternation(F1, F2, F3, F4) = 11000110 ⇔ 198

Figure 3.10. *Bit alternation. For a color version of this figure, see www.iste.co.uk/tounsi/cyber.zip*

The bit alternation method is reversible. From a binary sequence (associated with a decimal value), if we know the model, that is, the number of factors, their order of importance and their respective sizes, we can reproduce them. Inversion is an iterative process that reads the unique sequence bit by bit and assigns the bit read, in turn (depending on importance), to one of the factors. This is repeated until the end of the sequence. If we take the previous sequence, $M =$ '11000110'. During the first iteration, the first bit 1 is assigned to $F_1=$'1', the second bit 1 to $F_2=$'1', the third bit 0 to $F_3=$'0', and the fourth bit 0 to $F_4=$'0'. In the second and last iteration, the fifth bit 0 is assigned to $F_1=$'10', the sixth bit 1 to $F_2=$'11', the seventh bit 1 to $F_3=$'01', and finally the eighth bit 0 to $F_4=$'00'.

3.3.2.2. *Impact assessment*

After explaining the bit alternation method, we will now show how to extend it to use it in the estimation of the *Impact* parameter. The *Impact* assessment will be carried out for each major resource (asset) of the company and for each of the related threats.

The Impact Model is a tree consisting of the root (level 0) plus two levels (level 1 and level 2). First, the bit alternation method will be applied at level 2, that is, at the leaf level. Aggregation is only done at nodes belonging to the same parent node. The results obtained are brought up to level 1 where, in turn, they will be aggregated and brought up to the root. If we represent the bit alternation function by $AB()$ and apply it to the *Impact Model* in Figure 3.6, it will be equivalent to performing the function:

$$AB(\text{AB}(AB(F_{1,1} ; F_{1,2} ; F_{1,3})); \text{AB}(F_{2,1} ; F_{2,2}; F_{2,3}; F_{2,4}))$$

The resulting sequence is translated into a decimal value. This value is compared to the maximum value to get an idea of the magnitude of the impact.

Case study

We take the case of an e-commerce company, whose network consists of three zones (see Figure 3.11): LAN, DMZ and a secure payment zone. The three zones are protected by a firewall at the network entrance. The DMZ zone contains all servers accessible from outside the company, including a web server that is of particular importance to the company. Through this server, you can access the company's online sales website. The payment area is protected by an IPS.

We are studying here the case of a threat of an application attack such as *http flood* on the company's web server.

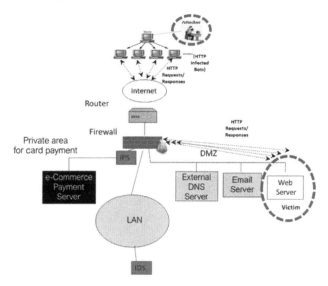

Figure 3.11. *Network architecture of the e-commerce company network*

Such an attack can have a very negative impact on the company. In the following paragraphs, we will use our risk model to estimate the impact of such an attack on the company's web server. To do this, we first assign criticality values to the factors of the *Impact* model (see Figure 3.6) as follows:

– *Financial* ($F_{1,1}$): this attack will cause the web server to stop during the attack period. It will therefore have a very serious financial impact. For this purpose, the critical value '11' is assigned to this factor;

– *Reputation* ($F_{1,2}$): in a world of fierce competition, such an attack will have a great impact on the company's *Reputation*. For this purpose, the critical value '11' is assigned to this factor;

– *Secret* ($F_{1,3}$): this attack will not affect the company's *Secrets*. It will therefore have little impact on the company's *Secrets*. For this purpose, the low value '00' is assigned to this factor;

– *Integrity* ($F_{2,1}$): this attack will not affect the *integrity* of the company's data. It will have no impact on the company. For this purpose, the low value '00' is assigned to this factor;

– *Availability* ($F_{2,2}$): this attack will cause the company's site to be unavailable. For this purpose, the critical value '11' is assigned to this factor;

– *Confidentiality* ($F_{2,3}$): this attack will not affect the confidentiality of the company's data. For this purpose, the low value '00' is assigned to this factor;

– *Accounting* ($F_{2,4}$): this attack will not affect *Accounting*. For this purpose, the low value '00' is assigned to this factor.

The application of our method on the *Impact* model tree with these criticality values involves replacing the values in the function:

$$AB(AB(F_{1,1}; F_{1,2}; F_{1,3}); AB(F_{2,1} ; F_{2,2}; F_{2,3}; F_{2,4})) =$$

$$AB(AB('11';'11';'00');('00';'11';'00';'00')) = '10110010100100'$$

By translating this sequence into decimal values, we obtain an *Impact* value of 11428. If we compare this value with the maximum value 16383 (corresponding to the sequence '11111111111111111'), we deduce that this *Impact* value is quite high.

3.3.2.3. *Assessment of the Probability of occurrence*

The application of the bit alternation method to estimate the *Probability of occurrence* parameter is similar to that of the *Impact* parameter. If we apply the *AB()* function at the level of the *Probability of occurrence* model in Figure 3.6, it will be equivalent to evaluating the function:

$$AB(AB(F_{1,1}; F_{1,2}; F_{1,3}; F_{1,4}) \; ; \; AB(F_{2,1}; F_{2,2}; F_{2,3}; F_{2,4}))$$

Case study

In what follows, we will use our *Risk* model to estimate the *Probability of occurrence* of the *http flood* attack on the company's web server presented earlier (see section 3.3.2.2). As for the *Impact,* we will give criticality values to the *Probability of occurrence* factors (see Figure 3.6):

– *Detection Systems* $(F_{1,1})$: this attack cannot be intercepted by the company's network security devices, which can be summarized as a firewall. Thus, it is assigned the critical value '11';

– *Awareness* $(F_{1,2})$: it is assumed that the company's managers are not fully aware of the seriousness of this threat. For this purpose, it is assigned a fairly high criticality value of '10';

– *Ease of discovery* $(F_{1,3})$: this vulnerability is not very difficult to discover. All you have to do is scan the open ports or simply start the attack to find out if the web server is vulnerable or not. Thus, it is assigned the critical value '11';

– *Ease of operation* $(F_{1,4})$: this vulnerability is very easy to exploit. Thus, it is assigned the critical value '11';

– *Knowledge* $(F_{2,1})$: this attack does not require acute knowledge of the attacker. For this purpose, the critical value '11' is assigned to this factor;

– *Opportunity* $(F_{2,2})$: this factor represents the resources and opportunities necessary to carry out such an attack. Since this attack requires a minimum of resources, the critical value '11' will be assigned to this factor;

– *Motivation* $(F_{2,3})$: it is assumed that the company has many competitors, and therefore, there is a high motivation to interfere with the company's activities. For this purpose, the rather high criticality value '10' is assigned to this factor;

– *Size* $(F_{2,4})$: it is assumed that the size or number of people wanting to carry out such an attack is quite high. For this purpose, the rather high criticality value '10' is assigned to this factor.

The application of our method on the probability of occurrence tree with these criticality values consists of replacing the values in the function:

$$AB(AB(F_{1,1}; F_{1,2}; F_{1,3}; F_{1,4}); AB(F_{2,1}; F_{2,2}; F_{2,3}; F_{2,4})) =$$

$$AB(AB('11';'10';'11'; '11');('11';'11';'10';'10')) = '1111111111011010'$$

By translating this sequence into decimal values, we will have a *Probability of occurrence* value of 65498. If we compare this value with the maximum value 65535, corresponding to the sequence '1111111111111111111111', we can deduce that it is critical.

3.3.2.4. Overall risk assessment

As described in the context setting section (see section 3.3.1.), in order to assess the *Risk*, we must go through the classification of the *Impact* and *Probability of occurrence* parameters.

3.3.2.4.1. Impact classification

To classify the Impact, we must divide the range of *Impact* values into four sub-intervals, each representing a class of the *Impact*. This classification requires the use of the Impact classes' thresholds (see section 3.3.1.3.1.): SI_B, SI_M, and SI_E.

In this chapter, we will adopt the strategy of dividing the range of *Impact* values into four sub-intervals of roughly pre-equivalent size. In our case, knowing that the *Impact* value belongs to the interval [0...16383], we will therefore have classes I_{++} for the interval [0...4096[, I_{-+} for the interval [4096...8192[, I_{+-} for the interval [8192..12288[, and I_{--} for the interval [12288...16383].

Referring to the case study presented in section 3.3.2.2, the *Impact* value of 11428 belongs to the high class I_{--}.

3.3.2.4.2. Classification of the Probability of occurrence

For the ranking of the *Probability of occurrence* parameter, we will adopt the same strategy as for the *Impact*. We will divide the interval of values of the *Probability of occurrence* into four sub-intervals of almost equivalent size. Knowing that the maximum value of the *Probability of occurrence* is 65535, we will therefore have the classes O_{++} for the interval [0...16384[, O_{-+} for the interval [16384...32768[, O_{+-} for the interval [32768...48152[, and O_{--} for the interval [48152..65535].

For our case study in section 3.3.2.2, the value of the *Probability of occurrence* is 65498, which belongs to the critical class O_-.

3.3.2.4.3. Risk assessment

After classifying the *Impact* and *Probability of occurrence*, we can now move on to the Risk Assessment. To do this, decision-makers must specify two global threshold classes *CGSI* and *CGSO* associated with the two parameters *I* and *O* (see section 3.3.1.3.2). These global threshold classes define the value classes of *I* (resp. *O)* that are considered acceptable. For example, if we set $CGSI = I_{++}$ and $CGSO = O_{++}$, we will have the acceptable values of *I* (class I^+) belonging to the interval [0...4096[and those in the interval [4096...16383] belonging to class I^-. Similarly for *O, the* values in [0...16384[belong to O^+ and those in the interval [16384...65535] belong to class O^-. In this way, we obtain the classification presented in section 3.1 (see Figure 3.9).

For our study in section 3.3.2.2, the value of $I=11428$ belongs to class I^- and $O=65498$ belongs to class O^-. This gives us the worst *risk* class I^-O^-.

3.3.3. *Risk treatment*

In defining the actions to be taken to address the *Risk*, it is necessary not only to consider the values of the *Risk* and its two parameters, but also the possible costs of their treatment. There are four alternatives to *risk* treatment:

a) the *Risk* must be eliminated and therefore corrective activities must be undertaken regardless of the cost;

b) the *Risk* is unmanageable at the level of that entity and the data will be transferred to another entity to manage it;

c) the *Risk* must be reduced by reducing these Impacts and its Probability of occurrence;

d) the level of Risk is acceptable.

By analyzing the *risk* assessment results obtained in our case study (see section 3.3.2.2.), we can see that the values of *I*, *O,* as well as the *risk* class are high. For the treatment of *Risk*, we consider that we have chosen the third alternative, that is, the company's managers decide that the *Risk* related to the *http flood* threat on their web server must decrease. To do this, we must try to reduce its *Impacts* and *Probability of occurrence*.

3.3.3.1. *Improvement of risk parameters*

To reduce the *Impact* values and the *Probability of occurrence* of a threat to an important company resource, the factors that alter their respective values must be addressed first. We assume that the person responsible for dealing with the risk or reducing the value of these two parameters is not the one who calculated them and has only the overall values of these parameters and not those of their respective factors. They must therefore first discover the factors causing the failure of these parameters. To achieve this objective, we will rely on two facts. The first is that *Impact* and *Probability Models* have been used, where all attributes and factors are known and ordered by importance. The second fact is that we use the bit alternation (*BA*) method which is completely invertible.

3.3.3.1.1. *Restitution of the factors of the risk parameters*

The *BA* aggregation method makes it possible, from a single value of the *Impact* or *Probability of occurrence*, to find the criticality value of these factors. The inversion is done from an inverse function of $BA()$ noted $BA^{-1}()$. The inversion of the binary sequence I will be done in three steps:

a) $BA^{-1}(M)$ will produce M_1 and M_2, which represent the respective sequences of the attributes of the second level of the tree, that is, *Business* and *Technique* for the *Impact* and *Vulnerability Model* and *Threat Agent* for the *Probability of occurrence*. In our case study, *Impact* M_1 will be equal to '110110' and $M2$ to '01000100'. For the *Probability of occurrence*, $M1$ will be equal to '11111011' and $M2$ to '11111100';

b) $BA^{-1}(M_1)$ will produce the factors of $M1$. For the *Impact* these factors are those of the *Business* attribute: *Financial* ($F_{1,1}$), *Reputation* ($F_{1,2}$) and *Secret* ($F_{1,3}$). For the *Probability of occurrence*, these factors are those of the *Vulnerabilities* attribute: *Detection Systems* ($F_{1,1}$), *Awareness* ($F_{1,2}$), *Ease of discovery* ($F_{1,3}$) and *Ease of use* ($F_{1,4}$). In the case study, for the *Impact* parameter, the criticality of the factors will be: $F_{1,1}$='11', $F_{1,2}$='11' and $F_{1,3}$='00'. For the parameter *Probability of occurrence*, the criticality of the factors will be: $F_{1,1}$='11', $F_{1,2}$='10', $F_{1,3}$='11' and $F_{1,4}$='11';

c) $BA^{-1}(M_2)$ will produce the $M2$ factors for the *Impact* and its *Technical* attributes: *Integrity* ($F_{2,1}$), *Availability* ($F_{2,2}$), *Confidentiality* ($F_{2,3}$) and

Accounting ($F_{2,4}$). For the *Probability of occurrence*, it concerns its attribute *Threat Agent* and the factors *Knowledge, Opportunity, Motivation* and *Size*. In the case study, $F_{2,1}$='00', $F_{2,2}$='11', $F_{2,3}$='00' and $F_{2,4}$='00'.

3.3.3.1.2. Improvement of risk factors

From the set of factors with high criticality value, we will choose a subset of factors that can be acted upon to improve the *Risk*. For example, for the *Probability of occurrence*, we can act on the factors related to the *Vulnerability* attribute and not on the *Threat Agent*. This is because the *Threat Agent* is an external attribute that cannot necessarily be modified. *Vulnerabilities,* on the other hand, are characteristics of the IS and the network that can be treated.

If we look back at our case study and the criticality values of the *Vulnerabilities* attribute that we have restored, we note that practically all the factors of the *Vulnerabilities* attribute have very high values: *Detection Systems* ($F_{1,1}$='11'), *Awareness* ($F_{1,2}$='10'), *Ease of Discovery* ($F_{1,3}$='11') and *Ease of Use* ($F_{1,4}$='11').

We will now illustrate the process of improving these factors. Take, for example, the improvement of the *Detection Systems* factor ($F_{1,1}$='11'), which is very relevant to the company's network architecture and security equipment. Referring to Figure 3.11, we see that the deployed security equipment is not capable of stopping or reducing an attack of the *http flood* type. Indeed, the only security device that protects access to the company's web server (in the DMZ) is the network entry firewall. This equipment is a network and transport-level filtering equipment and is not capable of stopping an application attack. To do this, we propose more secure network architecture as shown in Figure 3.12. In this new architecture, we propose to add, at the DMZ level, a WAF (Web Application Firewall), which stops application attacks, a load balancer (Load Balancer), which (if a DDoS attack ever succeeds in entering through the WAF) prevents automatic blocking of the server since there is load sharing between several equivalent web servers, and finally an IDS, which works in the background to detect other attack scenarios.

By deploying these new devices, the protection of the web server against *http flood* attacks is almost assured. Thus, if we take the evaluation of *the Probability of occurrence* again, we will use a low criticality value '00' for the detection systems factor. If we assume that we only modify this parameter, we will have a *Probability of occurrence* represented by the binary sequence '0111111101011011010', and therefore, a decimal value of 32602. If we set $CGSO = O_{-+}$ and $CGSI = I_{-+}$, by comparing with the initial value of 65498 which belongs to the class O^-, we will have succeeded through our new value in improving the class to O^+. This improves the *risk* classification from IO^- to IO^+.

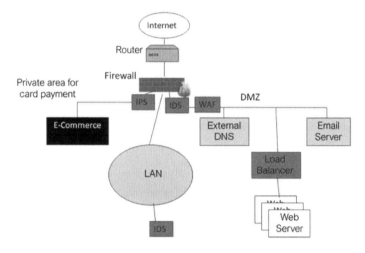

Figure 3.12. *Secure network architecture*

3.3.4. *Acceptance of risks*

Risk assessment, processing and acceptance activities can be considered as an iterative process whose stopping condition is the acceptance of the *risk* level (see Figure 3.13). It is worth noting that a *risk* level of 0 is generally impossible to achieve.

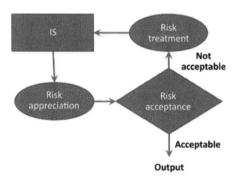

Figure 3.13. *Risk analysis process*

The activity of deciding whether or not to accept the level of *risk* of an IS is done by decision-makers according to the seriousness of a threat, the importance of the resource to be protected and the company's resources. Decision-makers can define for each threat to a resource the threshold of acceptability of the *risk*; this threshold is called *TAR*. Compared to Figure 3.9, *TAR* can be one of the following classes: I^+O^+, I^+O^-, I^-O^+, I^-O^+ or I^-O^-. In our case study, we can, for example, set $TAR = I^+O^-$. In this case, we are below the acceptable *risk* level, since the *risk* class is I^-O^+.

3.3.5. *Risk communication*

To be able to communicate and exchange the expertise acquired through this *risk* analysis process, we must think of an archiving system that can be used by the various stakeholders.

We can think of a database of risk containing two main tables: the important enterprise resource table and the threat table. The index of the resource table can be used in the threat table to search for threats related to this resource.

The threat table contains the following fields: threat index, threat description, company target resource, *I*, *CGSI* (see section 3.3.1.3.2.), *O*, *CGSO* (see section 3.3.1.3.2.) and *TAR* (see section 3.3.4.). If we use this threat table in the context of our case study, for the *http flood* attack, we will have the information:

Threat index=Index$_{\text{Http\_flood}}$, Threat description= « .... », Company target resource=Index$_{\text{web-server}}$», I=65498, CGSI =8, O=32602, CGSO =32768, TAR=I$^+$O$^-$.

By consulting this record, we can see that *O* belongs to O^+ since its value is lower *CGSO*, while *I* belongs to I^- since its value is higher *CGSI*. The Risk class is I^-O^+, it is below the $TAR=I^+O^-$ class, so the Risk treatment process must be repeated. By consulting this record, we can see that *O* belongs to O^+ since its value is lower *CGSO*, while *I* belongs to I^- since its value is higher *CGSI*. The Risk class is I^-O^+, and it is below the $TAR=I^+O^-$ class, so the Risk treatment process must be repeated.

3.3.6. *Risk monitoring*

During the operation of the IS, several functional failures may occur. This forces decision-makers to introduce changes and updates to the IS. These interventions, while necessary, can induce new threats or may increase existing threat risks. In addition, the various network security equipment (such as IDSs) and the analysis of security equipment logs can discover new threats. The Risk Analysis must therefore not be completed following the initial deployment of the IS, but must continue and be on the lookout for changes and additions of new Risks. This ongoing monitoring and vigilant activity is an integral part of Risk Analysis and is called Risk Monitoring. Risk monitoring has other objectives such as ensuring that the risk analysis process remains relevant and adapted to the company's security objectives. For example, to refine the Risk Analysis, it may be decided to add or modify a factor from the *Impact* or *Probability Model*.

3.4. Conclusion

First, we presented to the reader the issue of IS security through risk analysis. We familiarized them with the specificities of risk, presenting the technical vocabulary and the associated definitions. We presented some of the most important methodologies dealing with risk analysis and proposed the attributes that allow them to be compared.

On the other hand, we also devoted a section to show how to analyze IS risk in a network context. We presented a structured methodology based on the different phases of the 27005 standard. We illustrated this methodology by applying it to a case study on the risk of application attacks on an e-commerce company's website. This allows the reader to deepen their knowledge of the subject and to have a basis for further study.

3.5. References

Alberts, C.J. and Dorofee, A. (2002). *Managing Information Security Risks: The OCTAVE Approach*. Addison-Wesley Longman Publishing Co., Boston.

ANSI (2014). *Comparatif des méthodes d'audit et d'analyse des risques*. Available: https://www.nacs.tn/fr/documents/comparatif_methodes_Audit_AR.pdf, accessed February 22, 2018.

Bahtit, H. and Regragui, B. (2012). Modélisation des processus de la norme ISO 27005. *National Days of Network Security and Systems (JNS2)*. IEEE, 1-6.

Bloch, L., Wolfhugel, C., Queinnec, C., Makarévitch, N. and Schauer, H. (2007). *Sécurité informatique. Principes et méthodes*. Eyrolles, Paris.

Bou Nassar, P. (2012). Gestion de la sécurité dans une infrastructure de services dynamique: Une approche par gestion des risques. PhD Thesis, Lyon, INSA.

Brenner, J. (2007). ISO 27001: Risk Management and Compliance. *Risk Management*, 54(1), 24.

Burke, I. and Mouton, F. (2018). *Ethical Hacking*, CSIR, Available: https%3A%2F%2Fwww.snode.com%2Fsnode%2Fwp-content%2Fuploads%2F2017%2F04%2FEthical-Hacking.pdf.

Caralli, R.A., Stevens, J.F., Young, L.R. and Wilson, W.R. (2007). *Introducing Octave Allegro: Improving the Information Security Risk Assessment Process*. Carnegie-Mellon University, Pittsburgh.

Charpentier, J.E. and Torstenson, O. (2013). *Web Application Security*. Network Project. Available: http://hh.diva-portal.org/smash/get/diva2:610574/ FULLTEXT01.pdf, accessed February 22, 2018.

Culioli, M., Libes, M., Mouthuy, T., and Kourilsky. M. (2009). *Elaboration d'une PSSI au sein d'une unité propre du CNRS: Utilisation de la méthode EBIOS*. Available: https://2009.jres.org/planning_files/article/pdf/100.pdf, accessed February 22, 2018.

Défense Nationale, Secrétariat Général (2010). EBIOS-Expression des Besoins et Identification des Objectifs de Sécurité, Méthode de Gestion des risques. Report, Agence nationale de la sécurité des systèmes d'information, Paris.

Eloff, J.H., Labuschagne, L., and Badenhorst, K.P. (1993). A comparative framework for risk analysis methods. *Computers & Security*, 12(6), 597–603.

ENISA. (2013). ENISA Threat Landscape. Report, ENISA, Heraklion. Available: http://www.enisa.europa.eu/activities/risk-management/evolving-threat-environment/ enisa-threat-landscape-mid-year-2013/at_download/fullReport, accessed February 22, 2018.

Ghazouani, M., Faris, S., Medromi, H., and Sayouti, A. (2014). Information security risk assessment – A practical approach with a mathematical formulation of risk. *International Journal of Computer Applications*, 103(8).

Karoui, K. (2016). Security novel risk assessment framework based on reversible metrics: A case study of DDoS attacks on an E-commerce web server. *International Journal of Network Management*, 26(6), 553–578.

Microsoft (2018). Improving Web Application Security: Threats and Countermeasures. Report. Available: http://www.microsoft.com/downloads/ details.aspx?FamilyID=E9C4BAA-AF88-4AA5-88D4-ODEA898C31B9 &displaylang=en, accessed February 22, 2018.

OWASP (2018a). *The OWASP Risk Rating Methodology*. Available: https://www.owasp.org/index.php/OWASP_Risk_Rating_Methodology, accessed February 22, 2018.

OWASP (2018b). *Top 10. The Ten Most Critical Web Application Security Risks*, Available: https://www.owasp.org/images/7/72/OWASP_Top_10-2017_%28en% 29.pdf.pdf, accessed February 23, 2018.

Pons, F. (2014). Etude actuarielle du cyber-risque. Master's dissertation, Institut des Actuaires, France. Available: http://www.ressources-actuarielles.net/EXT/ISFA/1226-02.nsf/d512ad5b22d73cc1c1257052003f1aed/ecd55020616719e1c1257dda0 02ae1fe/$FILE/PONS%20Florian.pdf, accessed February 22, 2018.

Purdy, G. (2010). ISO 31000: 2009 – setting a new standard for risk management. *Risk Analysis*, 30(6), 881–886.

SGDN, Direction Centrale De La Sécurité Des Systèmes D'information Sous-Direction Des Opérations Bureau Conseil. (2017). Guide pour l'élaboration d'une politique de sécurité de système d'information : PSSI Section 3 : Principes de sécurité. Available : https://www.ssi.gouv.fr/uploads/IMG/pdf/pssi-section3-principes-2004-03-03.pdf, accessed December 12, 2017.

Syalim, A., Hori, Y., and Sakurai, K. (2009). Comparison of risk analysis methods: Mehari, magerit, NIST800-30 and Microsoft's security management guide. *IEEE International Conference on Availability, Reliability and Security. ARES'09*, 726–731.

Vasquez, M., Lammari, N., Comyn-Wattiau, I., and Akoka J. (2012). De l'analyse des risques à l'expression des exigences de sécurité des systèmes d'information. *Inforsid*, Montpellier, France, 337–362.

WEF (2012). *Risk and responsibility in a hyperconnected world: pathways to global cyber resilience*. Available: http://www3.weforum.org/docs/WEF_IT_ PathwaysToGlobalCyberResilience_Report_2012.pdf, accessed February 22, 2018.

4

Analytical Overview on Secure Information Flow in Android Systems: Protecting Private Data Used by Smartphone Applications

Malicious third-party applications can leak personal data stored in the Android system by exploiting control dependencies. The information flow tracking mechanism allows us to protect sensitive data. It is based on the data tainting technique used to control the manipulation of private data. In this chapter, we study and discuss the different mechanisms used to protect sensitive data in the Android systems. These mechanisms cannot detect control flows. This can cause an under-tainting problem and therefore a failure to detect a leak of sensitive information. We propose a formal and technical approach based on data tainting mechanisms combining dynamic and static analysis to handle control flow in java and native apps code and to solve the under-tainting problem in the Android systems. We show that our approach can resist code obfuscation attacks in control flow statements that exploit taint propagation to leak sensitive information. We propagate taint in timing, memory cache and GPU channels as well as in meta data (file and clipboard length) to detect software side channel attacks that try to bypass detection mechanisms based on dynamic taint analysis.

Chapter written by Mariem GRAA.

4.1. Introduction

Android devices account for 80.7% of the global smartphone sales in most markets in the world (Gartner 2016). To make smartphones more fun and useful, users generally download third-party applications. The development of Android applications has been growing at a high rate. In May 2016, 65 billion apps had been downloaded from Google Play Statista (2016). These applications are often used to capture, store, manipulate and access data of a sensitive nature. In a study presented in the Black Hat conference, Daswani (Wilson, July 2011) analyzed the live behavior of 10,000 Android applications and showed that more than 800 of them were found to be leaking personal data to an unauthorized server. Therefore, there is a need to provide adequate security mechanisms to control the manipulation of private data. The information flow tracking mechanism is used for monitoring the propagation of sensitive data in Android systems and for providing security against malicious software attacks. The information flow tracking mechanism uses the data tainting technique, which consists of associating taint with sensitive data and then propagating the taint to data for tracking the information flow in the program. It is used for vulnerability detection and protection of sensitive data. However, this technique does not detect control flows, which can cause an under-tainting problem, that is, some values should be marked as tainted, but are not. This can cause a failure to detect a leakage of sensitive information. Thus, malicious applications can bypass the Android system and get privacy sensitive information through control flows.

In this chapter, we provide an analytical overview on secure information flow in smartphones and more specifically in android-based mobile phones. We propose an enhancement of dynamic taint analysis that propagates taint along control dependencies to track control flows in the Google Android operating system. We use a hybrid approach that combines and benefits from the advantages of static and dynamic analyses to defend sensitive data against information flow attacks launched by third-party apps. We begin by categorizing, in section 4.2, information flow. As the data tainting mechanism is used to track information flow and to protect sensitive information, we describe in more detail works based on data tainting in section 4.3. We study related works on securing the Android system in section 4.4. We note that these works cannot detect the control flow attacks that can cause an under-tainting problem (false negative). This problem can cause a leak of sensitive data. We present solutions based on data tainting mechanisms and a hybrid approach that combines dynamic and static analysis to solve this problem in section 4.5. We propose a formal and technical approach that allows us to handle control flow in java and native code and solve the under-tainting problem in section 4.6. We show that our approach can resist code obfuscation attacks in control flow statements that exploit taint propagation to leak sensitive information in the Android system in section 4.7. We propose an enhancement of our approach to detect software side channel attacks that try to bypass detection mechanisms based on dynamic taint analysis in section 4.8. We compare information flow tracking approaches in Android systems in section 4.9. Finally, section 4.10 concludes this chapter.

4.2. Information flow

Information flow is the transfer of information between objects in a given process. It can cause sensitive information leakage. Therefore, not all flows are permitted. The information flows occur in different forms (channels). Two types of flows are defined: explicit and implicit flows (Denning 1976).

4.2.1. *Explicit flows*

```
1.int x;
2.int y;;
3.x:=y
```

Figure 4.1. *Example of an explicit flow*

Explicit information flow is the simplest form of information flow that arises when data is explicitly assigned to memory locations or variables. Here is an example that shows an explicit transfer of a value from y to x. Unlike implicit flows, explicit flows are easy to detect because we must justify, track and give reasons for about explicit assignments.

4.2.2. *Implicit flows*

Implicit flows occur in the control flow structure of the program. When a conditional branch instruction is executed, information about the condition is propagated into each branch. In the implicit flows (control flows) shown in

Figure 4.2, there is no direct transfer of value from x to y. However, when the code is executed, y will contain the value of x.

```
1.boolean x;
2.boolean y;
3.if ( x== true)
4. y = true;
5. else
6. y = false;
7.return(y);
```

Figure 4.2. *Example of an implicit flow*

Function calls, goto loop and statements, switch instructions and exceptions represent other control mechanisms. The most important covert channel is the implicit flow, but there are other covert channels that will be presented as follows.

4.2.3. *Covert channels*

The covert channels (Sabelfeld and Myers 2003) include:

– timing channels that leak information through the time at which an event occurs;

– termination channels that leak information through the non-termination of computation;

– resource exhaustion channels that leak information through exhaustion of a limited resource;

– power consumption channels that leak information through power consumption;

– processor frequency channels that leak information through frequency changes;

– free space on filesystem channels that leak information about the file system usage of the other applications by querying the number of free blocks;

– probabilistic channels that leak information through changing probability distribution of observable data.

4.3. Data tainting

Data tainting is a mechanism used to trace how data is propagated in a system. The principle of this mechanism is to "color" (tag) some of the data in a program and then spread the colors to other related objects to this data according to the execution of the program. It is primarily used for vulnerability detection, protection of sensitive data, and more recently, for analysis of binary malware. To detect vulnerabilities, the sensitive transactions must be monitored to ensure that they are not tainted by outside data. The three operations considered sensitive are the execution of a command, reading or writing to a file and modification of the flow of control. Monitoring the implementation of a program is necessary to propagate data coloration and detect vulnerabilities.

Methods to ensure this follow-up include static analysis during compilation and dynamic analysis during execution. Data tainting is implemented in interpreters and in system simulators to analyze sensitive data.

4.3.1. *Interpreter approach*

One of the most well-known works on data tainting is Perl's taint mode (Wall 2000). Perl is an interpreted language that explicitly marks any outside data as tainted and prevents it from being used in sensitive functions that affect the local system, such as running local commands, creating and writing files and sending data over the network. The Ruby programming language (Hunt and Thomas 2000) presents a taint checking mechanism but with finer-grained taint levels than Perl. It has five safety levels ranging from 0 to 4. At each level, different security checks are performed. Vogt *et al.* (2007) implement a data tainting mechanism in a Javascript interpreter to detect and prevent cross-site scripting vulnerabilities. RESIN (Yip *et al.* 2009) tracks data application developed by a runtime language, such as the Python or PHP interpreter to prevent web application attacks. Xu *et al.* (2006) implement a fine-grained taint analysis in the PHP interpreter to detect SQL injection attacks.

One of the limits of interpreter-based tainting approaches is that they can only protect against vulnerabilities in language-specific source code.

4.3.2. *Architecture-based approach*

Chow *et al.* (2004) develop a tool based on whole-system simulation called TaintBochs for measuring data lifetime. TaintBochs tracks propagation of sensitive data using the tainting mechanism at the hardware level. The authors run a simulation in which sensitive data is identified as tainted. Then, the simulation data is analyzed by the analysis framework. Minos (Crandall *et al.* 2006) proposes a hardware extension that modifies the architecture and the operating system to track the integrity of data. It adds an integrity bit to word of memory at the physical memory level. This bit is set when data is written by the kernel into a user process' memory space. Minos implements Biba's (1977) low water-mark integrity policy to protect control flow when a program moves data and uses it for operations. Suh *et al.* (2004) modify the processor core by implementing dynamic information tracking and security tag checking. They taint inputs from potentially malicious channels and track the spurious information flows to prevent malicious software attacks. RIFLE (Vachharajani *et al.* 2004) translates a binary program into a binary running, on a processor architecture, that supports information flow security. The binary translation converts all implicit flows to explicit flows for tracking all information flows by dynamic mechanisms. The operating system uses the labels defined by the RIFLE architecture to ensure that no illegal flow occurs. Sapper (Li *et al.* 2014) presents a hardware description language for designing security-critical hardware components. It uses static analysis at compile time to automatically insert dynamic checks in the resulting hardware that provably enforce a given information flow policy at execution time. However, it requires the user to redesign the hardware using a new language.

The limit of these architecture-based approaches is that they need hardware modifications and thus cannot be directly used with current systems.

4.3.3. *Static taint analysis*

The static taint analysis allows us to analyze code without executing it. This analysis reviews program code and searches application coding flaws. In general, it is used to find bugs, back doors or other malicious code. In most cases, this analysis requires the source code, which is not always available. Also, it is not sufficient for scanning. More recent static analysis tool scans binary code instead of the source code to make the software test more effective and comprehensive.

Static taint analysis is used in Evans' Splint static analyzer (Evans and Larochelle 2002) and Cqual (Zhang *et al.* 2002) to detect bugs in C programs. The input data is annotated with "tainted" and "untainted" annotations to find security vulnerabilities such as string format vulnerabilities and buffer overflows. Shankar *et al.* (2001) use Cqual to detect format string bugs in C programs at compile time. The major disadvantage of the static analysis-based approach of Splint and Cqual is that they require access to the source code. Denning (Denning 1976, Denning and Denning 1977) defines a certification mechanism using a lattice model at the static analysis phase of compilation. The Denning certification mechanism determines the consistency of the data flow, with the security classes flow relation specified by the programmer. JFlow (Myers 1999) is an extension to the Java language. It implements statically checked information flow annotations to prevent information leaks through storage channels. SFlow (Huang *et al.* 2014) is a type-based taint analysis for Java web applications to secure information flow. Programmers only add a few annotations to specify sources and sinks, and the inference analysis infers a concrete-type or reports-type error, indicating information flow violations.

The static analysis approaches have some limitations due to undecidability problems (Landi 1992). They can never know if the execution of a specific program for a given input will terminate. Another limitation of static analysis tools is the fact that they report problems that are not really bugs in the code, that is, they identify error behaviors that cannot really occur in any run of the program (false positives) (Chess and McGraw 2004).

4.3.4. *Dynamic taint analysis*

In contrast to the static taint analysis, the dynamic taint analysis is performed at run time. It allows us to test and evaluate a program by executing code. The objective of this analysis is to detect potential security vulnerabilities. It does not require an access to the source code, and it traces a binary code to understand the system behavior. Many dynamic taint analysis tools are based on bytecode instrumentation to determine how information flows in the program. TaintCheck (Newsome and Song 2005) uses the Valgrind (Nethercote and Seward 2003) tool to instrument the code and to perform dynamic taint analysis at binary level. It associates taint with input data from an untrusted source. Then, it tracks the manipulation of data in instructions to propagate the taint to the result. TaintCheck allows us to detect overwrite attacks such as jump targets that include return addresses, function pointers or function pointer offsets and format string attacks. To detect jump target attacks, TaintCheck checks whether tainted data is used as a jump target before each UCode jump instruction. It also checks whether tainted data is used as a format string argument to the printf family of standard library functions to detect format strings attacks. TaintTrace (Cheng *et al.* 2006) protects systems against security exploits such as format string and buffer overflow. It uses code instrumentation to dynamically trace the propagation of taint data. TaintTrace is more efficient than TaintCheck because it implements a number of optimizations to keep the overhead low. LIFT (Qin *et al.* 2006) is a software information flow tracking system that reduces the overhead by using optimizations and dynamic binary instrumentation. LIFT allows us to detect security attacks that corrupt control data, such as return addresss and function pointers. Haldar *et al.* (2005) use bytecode instrumentation to implement taint propagation in the Java virtual machine. They instrument Java classes to define untrustworthy sources and sensitive sinks. They mark strings as tainted and propagate taintedness of strings. An exception is raised when a tainted string is used in a sink method. Yin *et al.* (2007) propose an end-to-end prototype called Panorama for malware detection and analysis. They run a series of automated tests to generate events that introduce sensitive information into the guest system. To monitor how the sensitive information propagates within the system, they perform whole-system fine-grained information flow tracking. They generate a taint graph to define various policies specifying the characteristic behavior of different types of malware. Hauser *et al.* (2012) extend Blare, an information flow monitor at the operating system level, to implement an approach for detecting confidentiality violations. They define a confidentiality policy based on dynamic data tainting (George *et al.* 2009). They associate labels with sensitive information and define information that can leave the local system through network exchanges.

The previous dynamic taint analysis approaches instrument application code to trace and maintain information about the propagation. Thus, they suffer from significant performance overhead that does not encourage their use in real-time applications. More recently, Cox (2016) has improved the dynamic taint analysis in the JVM and reduced the performance overhead by instrumenting less of the program. The major limitation of all dynamic taint analysis approaches is that they do not detect control flow (Volpano 1999).

We focus in the following on security of Android systems and study the different mechanisms used to protect users' private data.

4.4. Protecting private data in Android systems

The number of available apps in the Google Play Store has been most recently placed at 2.6 million apps in December 2018, after surpassing 1 million apps in July 2013. (Statista 2018). Third-party smartphone applications have access to sensitive data and can compromise confidentiality and integrity of smartphones.

Several works have been proposed to secure mobile operating systems. We first present approaches that allow us to control data access and then focus on approaches using the information flow tracking mechanism to prevent private data leakage.

4.4.1. *Access control approach*

According to Android Police, any app installed on HTC phones that connects to the Internet can access email addresses, GPS locations, phone numbers and other private information (Klimas 2011). The Android applications can use excessive permissions to access the user data. AhnLab analyzed 178 Android apps using AhnLab Mobile Smart Defense. The analysis shows that 42.6% of all apps examined require excessive permissions for device information access and 39.3% ask for excessive permissions for location information access, followed by personal information access permission at 33.1% and service charging at 8.4% (AhnLab 2012). The excessive permissions to access the user data can provoke the leakage of the victim's private information.

We present in the following approaches based on rule-driven policies to control data access, and works on preventing privilege escalation attacks.

4.4.1.1. *Rule-driven policy approach*

Many works based on new policy languages have been proposed to enhance protection of smartphone systems. The Kirin security service for Android (Enck *et al.* 2009) performs lightweight certification of applications to assure security service for Android at install time. The Kirin certification is based on security rules matching undesirable properties in security configurations bundled with applications. The Kirin policies control the permissions of applications by verifying consistency of the permissions requested by applications and system policy. Kirin cannot make decisions about local security enforcements made by applications; thus, it suffers from false positives. As Kirin does not consider runtime policies, the Secure Application INTeraction (Saint) framework (Ongtang *et al.* 2012) extends the existing Android security architecture with an install-time policy that defines the assignment of permissions to applications, and a runtime policy that controls the interaction of software components within Android middleware framework. Saint policy is defined by application developers; this can result in failure to consider all security threats. Furthermore, Saint cannot control data flow of inter-process communication. Nauman *et al.* (2010) presents Apex, an extension of the Android permission framework, which restricts the usage of phone resources by applications. It allows the user to grant and deny permissions to applications by imposing runtime constraints on the usage of sensitive resources. The Nauman *et al.* model is significantly different from Kirin (Enck *et al.* 2009) since it is user-centric. It allows the user to grant permissions on their device rather than automating the decisions based on the policies of remote owners. Conti *et al.* (2011) include the concept of context-related access control in smartphones. They implement CrePE (Context-related Policy Enforcing) that enforces fine-grained context-based policies. The context depends on the status of some variables and the interaction between the user and the smartphone. CrePE allows the user and trusted third parties to define and activate policies at run time. It proposes a solution, based on environmental constraints, to restrict the permissions of an application by enabling/disabling functionalities. However, it does not address privilege escalation attacks because it does not focus on the transitive permission usage across different applications. Backes *et al.* (2012) extend Android's permission system to prevent malicious behaviors. They propose AppGuard, which enforces fine-grained security policies. It prevents vulnerabilities in the operating system and third-party apps. It allows us to revoke dynamic permissions attributes to malicious apps to protect Android from real-world attacks. Aurasium

(Xu *et al.* 2012) controls the execution of applications to protect private data. It repackages untrusted applications to manage user-level sandboxing and policy enforcement. The concept of security-by-contract (SxC) (Desmet *et al.* 2008) is used to secure untrusted mobile applications. It consists of defining a security contract for the application and matching these contracts with device policies. This allows us to verify that the application will not violate the contractual policy. EasyGuard (Ren *et al.* 2016) automatically provides adaptive access control when the specific context is detected according to the pre-configured policies.

The rule-driven policy approach requires definition and maintenance of policy rules. The application developers define these policy rules; this can result in failure to consider all security threats. CoDRA (Thanigaivelan *et al.* 2017) is an access control system for Android that offers the ability to enforce various policy configurations at different levels of system operation to protect open resources, for example, sensors on user basis through its integration of multi-user support in Android. Apex (Nauman *et al.* 2010) is another solution that allows users to specify policies to protect themselves from malicious applications. However, creating useful and usable policies is difficult.

4.4.1.2. *Privilege escalation prevention approach*

The privilege escalation prevention approach is defined at the application level and the Android kernel level to protect the Android system from privilege escalation attacks. The IPC Inspection (Felt *et al.* 2011) is an operating system mechanism that protects Android system applications from the risk of permission re-delegation introduced by inter-application communication. To avoid permission re-delegation, Felt *et al.* (2011) reduce the privileges of an application after it receives communication from a less privileged application. This allows the permission system to prevent a privileged API call from the deputy when the influenced application has insufficient permission. However, the IPC Inspection cannot prevent collusion attacks launched by malicious developer and attacks through covert channels. Furthermore, the IPC Inspection cannot determine the context of the call provenance. To address this, QUIRE (Dietz *et al.* 2011) provides security to local and remote apps communicating by IPC (inter-process communication) and RPC (remote procedure call), respectively. This security is based on the call-chain and data provenance of requests. It allows apps to observe the full call chain associated with the request by annotated IPCs and to choose the diminished privileges of its callers. Fragkaki *et al.* (2012) implement Sorbet, an enforcement system that allows us to specify privacy and integrity policies. Sorbet improves existing Android permission systems by implementing coarse-grained mechanisms to protect applications from privilege escalation and undesired information flows. To address flaws of Android implementation of permission delegation, Sorbet offers developers the ability to specify constraints that limit the lifespan and re-delegation scope of the delegated permissions. Bugiel *et al.* (2011) propose XManDroid to detect and prevent application-level privilege escalation attacks at runtime. They dynamically analyze communication links among Android applications to verify if they respect security rules imposed by system policy. The major hurdle for this approach is that it cannot detect subsets of covert channels such as Timing Channels Processor Frequencies and Free Space on Filesystems. Also, it reports false-positive results when two non-malicious applications try to share legitimate data. The privilege escalation approach is implemented in the Android kernel. Shabtai *et al.* (2010) reconfigure and deploy an Android kernel that supports SELinux to protect the system from privilege escalation attacks. SELinux enforces low-level access control on critical Linux processes that run under privileged users. SELinux presents a complex policy that makes it harder to act as an administrator on a mobile device. Furthermore, it lacks a coordination mechanism between the Linux kernel and the Android middleware. L4Android (Lange *et al.* 2011) assures kernel integrity when a device is rooted by encapsulating the smartphone operating system in a virtual machine. This provides an isolated environment for securely running applications. Since L4Android and SELinux operate at the kernel level, they cannot prevent privilege escalation attacks at the application level. DroidAuditor (Heuser *et al.* 2016) observes application behavior on real Android devices and generates a graph-based representation that enables users to develop an intuitive understanding of application internals. It allows us to detect application-layer privilege escalation attacks, such as confused deputy and collusion attacks.

These access control approaches, although implementing permission systems and strong isolation between applications, have in practice proved insufficient. They control access to sensitive information but do not ensure end-to-end security because they do not track propagation of input data to the application. The approaches based on faking sensitive information, static analysis and dynamic analysis have addressed these weaknesses from various perspectives, including tracking information flows and developing tools to prevent data leakage.

4.4.2. *Preventing private data leakage approach*

Third-party applications can disseminate private information without smartphone users' authorization. The Duke University, Pennsylvania State University and Intel Labs research show that half of 30 popular free applications from the Android Market send sensitive information to advertisers, including the GPS-tracked location of the user and their telephone number (Wilson 2010). Also, in a study presented in the Black Hat conference, Daswani analyzed the live behavior of 10,000 Android applications and showed that 80% of the scanned apps leaked IMEI numbers (Kerner 2011). Cole and Waugh (Cole and Waugh 2012) affirm that many of the top 50 free apps leak data such as contacts lists to advertisers. We present in the following works based on faking sensitive information, static analysis and dynamic analysis to prevent sensitive data leakage.

4.4.2.1. *Faking sensitive information*

One solution to solve the smartphone data application leakage security problem is to provide fake or "mock" information to applications. This mechanism is achieved by substituting private data with fake information in the data flow. TISSA (Zhou *et al.* 2011) implements a new privacy mode to protect user private data from malicious Android apps. This privacy mode allows the user to install untrusted applications but control their access to different types of private information. The TISSA tool includes three main components: the privacy setting content provider (policy decision point), the privacy setting manager (policy administration point) and the privacy-aware components (policy enforcement points). The application sends an access request to private data to a content provider component that raises a query to the privacy setting content provider to check the current privacy settings for the app. If the application access is not permitted, then the privacy setting returns an empty result (empty option), an anonymized information result (anonymized option) or a fake result (bogus option). AppFence (Hornyack *et al.* 2011) limits the access of Android applications to sensitive data. It retrofits the Android runtime environment to implement two privacy controls: (1) substituting shadow data (fake data) in place of sensitive data that the user does not want applications have an access to and (2) blocking network communications tainted by sensitive data. MockDroid (Beresford *et al.* 2011) revokes access of applications to particular resources. It allows the user to provide fake data to applications. It reduces the functionalities of applications by requesting empty or unavailable resources.

The faking sensitive information approach provides "mock" information to applications instead of private data. This approach successfully prevents private information leakage by untrusted Android applications. However, giving bogus private information can disrupt the execution of applications.

4.4.2.2. *Static analysis of Android applications*

Static analysis is used on smartphone applications to detect leakage of sensitive data and dangerous behavior. Chin *et al.* (2011) present ComDroid, a tool that can be used by developers to statically analyze DEX code (Dalvik Executable files before their installation on a device) of third-party applications in Android. They disassemble application DEX files and parse the disassembled output to log potential component and Intent vulnerabilities. ComDroid detects inter-application communication vulnerabilities such as broadcast theft, activity and service hijacking and broadcast injection. One limitation of ComDroid is that it does not distinguish between paths through *if* and *switch* statements. This can lead to false negatives. SCANDROID (Fuchs *et al.* 2009) facilitates automated security certification of Android applications. It statically analyzes data flows in Java code for Android applications. Based on such flows, SCANDROID checks compliance of required accesses with security specifications and enforces access control. One limitation of this analysis approach is that it cannot be immediately applied to packaged applications on Android devices. Enck *et al.* (2011) design and implement the Dalvik decompiler "ded", dedicated to retrieving and analyzing the Java source of an Android Market application. The decompiler extraction occurs in three stages: retargeting, optimization and decompilation. They identify class and method constants and variables in the retargeting phase. Then, they make bytecode optimization and decompile the retargeted class files. Their analysis is based on automated tests and manual inspection. A slight current limitation of the ded decompiler is that it requires the Java source code to be available to detect potential vulnerabilities.

SCANDAL (Kim *et al.* 2012) is a sound and automatic tool that performs static analysis for detecting privacy leaks in Android applications. It converts

Dalvik bytecode of Android applications to a formally defined intermediate language. It uses an abstract interpretation to detect dangerous flows. The limitation of SCANDAL is that it generates a large number of false positives. AppIntent (Yang *et al.* 2013) provides the sequence of events that leads to the sensitive data transmission in the form of a sequence of UI manipulations. It statically analyzes the target app to identify the possible execution paths leading to the sensitive data transmission. These paths are used to generate all the possible event sequences by considering the call graph and the Android execution model. It designs a new technique, event-space constraint symbolic execution, to distinguish intended and unintended transmission. AppIntent facilitates the discrimination of whether sensitive data transmission is user-intended or not, but it does not handle data transmissions that are not triggered by sequences of GUI manipulations. AndroidLeaks (Gibler *et al.* 2012) creates a call graph of an application's code and then performs a static analysis to identify potential leaks of personal information in Android applications. It defines a set of mappings between Android API methods and the permissions they require to execute using static techniques. A subset of this mapping is used as the sources and sinks of private data for the data flow analysis. LeakMiner (Yang and Yang 2012) uses static taint analysis to detect information leakage before apps are distributed to users, so that malicious apps can be removed from the market before users download them. It transforms apk files of Android apps to Java bytecode and propagates taint sensitive information through call graphs to identify possible leakage paths. LeakMiner produces a large number of false positives due to an insufficient context information. FlowDroid (Arzt *et al.* 2014) is a static taint analysis tool that automatically scans Android apps' bytecode and configuration files for privacy-sensitive data leakage. It is fully context, flow, field and object-sensitive while precisely modeling the complete Android life cycle, including the correct handling of callbacks and user-defined UI widgets within the apps. It uses techniques based on machine learning to identify the sources and sinks of sensitive information in the Android API. FlowDroid does not consider the attack when the attacker obfuscates the code and uses implicit flows to disguise data leaks. Comnoid (Dhavale and Lokhande 2016) is based on FlowDroid and is capable of analyzing the inter-app communication. DroidSafe (Gordon *et al.* 2015) is a static information flow analysis tool that reports potential leaks of sensitive information in Android applications. It uses flow-insensitive points-to and information-flow analyses to consider all possible runtime event orderings that asynchronous callbacks can trigger. DroidSafe analyzes both Intent and

RPC. It is effective for tracking explicit data flows, but it does not detect leaks of sensitive data via side channels or implicit flows.

The static analysis approaches implemented in smartphones allow us to detect data leakage, but they cannot capture all runtime configurations and inputs.

4.4.2.3. Dynamic analysis of Android applications

Many works based on dynamic analysis are implemented in smartphones for detecting and preventing private data leakage.

TaintDroid (Enck *et al.* 2010) improves the Android mobile phone to control the use of privacy sensitive data by third-party applications. It monitors application behavior to determine when privacy sensitive information leaves the phone. It implements dynamic taint analysis to track information dependencies. First, it defines a sensitive source. All input data is tainted with its source taint. Then, TaintDroid tracks propagation of tainted data at the instruction level. The taint propagation is performed by running the native code without instrumentation. To minimize IPC (inter-process communication) overhead, it implements message-level tracking between applications and file-level tracking. Finally, vulnerabilities can be detected when tainted data is used in taint sink (network interface). To be practical, TaintDroid addresses different challenges specific to mobile phones, such as resource limitations. Taint tags are stored adjacent to the corresponding variables on the internal execution stack, and one taint tag per array is defined to minimize overhead.

TaintDroid is used by MockDroid (Beresford *et al.* 2011) and TISSA (Zhou *et al.* 2011) to evaluate their effectiveness. AppFence extends TaintDroid to implement enforcement policies. AndroTaint (Shankar *et al.* 2017) is a malware detection framework based on dynamic taint analysis used to identify information flow leakage in Android systems in two phases: the first phase is a training phase for feature extraction and the second phase is an analysis phase for automatic tagging and tainting.

The dynamic analysis approaches defined in smartphones such as TaintDroid, AndroTaint and AppFence track the information flow in real time and control the handling of private data. However, they do not propagate taint along control dependencies. This can cause an under-tainting problem: some values should be marked as tainted, but are not. This problem causes a failure to detect a leakage of sensitive information.

```
1.x= false;
2.y=false;
3.char c[256];
4.if( gets(c) != user_contact )
5.      x=true;
6.else
7.      y=true;
8.NetworkTransfer (y);
9.NetworkTransfer (x);
```

Figure 4.3. *Attack using indirect control dependency*

Let us consider the attack shown in Figure 4.3, the variables x and y are both initialized to false. On Line 4, the attacker tests the user's input for a specific value. Let us assume that the attacker was lucky and the test was positive. In this case, Line 5 is executed, setting x to true and x is not tainted because TaintDroid does not propagate taint along control dependencies. Variable y keeps its false value, since the assignment on Line 7 is not executed and y is not tainted. As x and y are not tainted, they are leaked to the network without being detected. Since y has not been modified, it informs the attacker about the value of the user private contact. There is a similar effect when x is leaked. Thus, an attacker can circumvent an Android system through the control flows.

A significant limitation of these dynamic taint analysis approaches implemented in Android systems is that they only track explicit flows at the Java code level and they do not check native libraries that can contain sensitive data. Therefore, an attacker can exploit this native code to get private information.

We aim to enhance the TaintDroid approach by tracking control flows in both Java and native Android apps code to solve the under-tainting problem. In the following, we will study existing systems that control native code execution.

4.4.3. *Native libraries approaches*

Fedler *et al.* (2013) assert that all current local root exploits are exclusively implemented as native code and can be dynamically downloaded and run by any app. Since the lack of control mechanisms for the execution of native code poses a major threat to the security of Android devices, Fedler *et al.* propose mechanisms to control native code execution. Some works have been undertaken to consider native libraries in Android applications. DroidRanger (Zhou *et al.* 2012) records any calls to the Android framework APIs for the dynamically loaded Java code and their arguments to provide rich semantic information about an app's behavior. For the dynamically loaded native code, it collects system calls made by the native code using a kernel module that catches the system calls table in the (Linux) kernel. To analyze potential harmful applications for the Android platform, AASandbox (Blasing *et al.* 2010) realizes system and library call monitoring.

```
package com.tuto.attackndk;
public class MainActivity extends Activity {
  static {
    System.loadLibrary("attackndk");
  }
  public static native void invokeNativeFunction(String IMEI);
  @Override
    protected void onCreate(Bundle savedInstanceState) {
      super.onCreate(savedInstanceState);
      setContentView(R.layout.activity_main);
        String device_id = GetDeviceId();
          invokeNativeFunction(device_id);
    }
}
```

Listing 4.1. *Attack exploiting native code based on control dependencies*

Paranoid (Portokalidis *et al.* 2010) and Crowdroid (Burguera *et al.* 2011) intercept system calls and process signals. The dynamic analyzer presented in Spreitzenbarth *et al.* (2013) traces codes included in native shared objects, those included with the app through the NDK and those shipped with Android by intercepting library calls of a monitored application. CopperDroid (Reina *et al.* 2013) instruments the Android emulator to enable system call tracking and support an out-of-the-box system call-centric analysis. DroidScope (Yan and Yin 2012), an emulation-based Android malware analysis engine, is used to analyze the Java and native components of Android applications. It implements several analysis tools to collect detailed native and Dalvik instruction traces, profile API-level activity and track information leakage through both the Java and native components using taint analysis. One of the limitations of DroidScope is that it incurs high overhead. DROIT (Wang and Shieh 2015) is an emulation-based taint tracking system. It tracks data flow at Java object level and switches to instruction-level instrumentation when native code starts to take over.

DROIT is designed to profile the program behavior. Thus, the program is considered as the taint source. On the contrary, in TaintDroid, the data in the program presents the taint sources. NDroid (Qian *et al.* 2014) extends TaintDroid to track explicit flow in native code. The major disadvantage of all approaches that consider native libraries is that they do not propagate taint in control flows, which can cause an under-tainting problem.

Consider the example in Listing 4.2 that presents an under-tainting problem in Android native code. The malicious program written in Java code (see Listing 4.1) obtains the device id and passes it as an argument to a native function (written in C). In the native code presented in Listing 4.2, the attacker compares each character of private data with symbols in AsciiTable (TabAsc). Then, it stores the sequence of characters found in the string Z. The variable Z contains the value of the private data, but it is not tainted using existing dynamic analysis taint systems. TaintDroid taints the returned value of a JNI function if one argument is tainted. In this case, the native function does not return a value.

NDroid under-taints the control flows of native code. Thus, variable Z is leaked through JNI without any warning reports. In this example, the taint sink (network interface) is defined in the native code. Therefore, the variable Z is leaked through the network connection (Send_Data(Z)). The approach cited in Enck *et al.* (2010) does not implement taint sink in the native code. However, NDroid instruments native libraries to define the taint sink. As the variable Z sent through the network connection is not tainted, the leakage of this data cannot be detected.

```c
#include <string.h>
#include <jni.h>
void Java_com_tuto_attackndk_MainActivity_
invokeNativeFunction(JNIEnv* env, jobject thiz, jstring IMEI)
{
  String Private_Data;
  String Z;
    strcpy(Private_Data, IMEI);
      for(int i = 0; i < sizeof(Private_Data); i++)
        {
          char s;
          sprintf(s, "%d", i);
          for(int j = 1; j < sizeof(TabAsc); j++)
              if (strcmp(s,TabAsc[j]) == 0)
                  strcat(Z,TabAsc[j]);
        }
        Send_Data(Z);
}
```

Listing 4.2. *Native malicious function*

The taint sink can be defined in the Java code. In this case, another Java program searches the sensitive information from the native code, or the native method calls and passes the sensitive information to the Java code. Then, the Java code leaks the private data. As it is not tainted, it will be sent without any warning reports.

We study in the following existing approaches that allow us to handle control flows. These approaches propose solutions to the under-tainting problem.

4.5. Detecting control flow

Both static and dynamic analyses have advantages and disadvantages. Static analysis presents limitations due to undecidability problems, but it allows us to track all execution branches of a program. In the case of dynamic analysis, it is not possible to detect all information flows because dynamic tainting occurs only along the branch that is actually executed. This can cause an under-tainting problem. This problem can be solved by using a hybrid approach that combines and benefits from the advantages of static and dynamic analyses.

We present in the following the technical and formal approaches that allow us to detect control flow and solve the under-tainting problem.

4.5.1. *Technical control flow approaches*

Many works exist in the literature to track information flows. Dytan (Clause *et al.* 2007) allows us to perform data-flow and control-flow based tainting. To track control flows, Dytan analyses the binary code and builds the CFG to detect the control dependencies. Based on the CFG, Dytan taints variables in the conditional structure. To track data flows, Dytan identifies the source and destination operands based on the instruction mnemonic. Then, it combines the taint markings associated with the source operands and associates them with the destination operands. The main limitation of this approach is that it generates many false positives. BitBlaze (Song *et al.* 2008) implements a hybrid approach combining static and dynamic taint analysis techniques to track implicit and explicit flows. DTA++ (Kang *et al.* 2011), based on the BitBlaze approach, enhances dynamic taint analysis to limit the under-tainting problem. The DTA++ approach is performed in two phases: first, an offline phase, which looks for branches that cause under-tainting and generates DTA++ propagation rules, then an online phase, which performs taint propagation using these rules to enhance dynamic taint analysis and to solve under-tainting in culprit branches. The DTA++ approach selects more branches than Dytan to reduce over-tainting. However, DTA++ is only evaluated on benign applications, but malicious programs in which an adversary uses implicit flows to circumvent analysis are not addressed. Furthermore, DTA++ is not implemented in embedded applications. Trishul (Nair *et al.* 2008) is an information flow control system. It is implemented in a Java virtual machine to secure execution of Java applications by tracking data flow within the environment. It does not require a change to the operating system kernel because it analyzes the bytecode of an application being executed. Trishul is based on the hybrid approach to correctly handle implicit flows using the compiled program rather than the source code at load time. Trishul correctly identifies implicit flows of information to detect leakages of sensitive information. It solves the under-tainting problem by updating the taint of the condition and maintaining a list of assignments in a basic block of control flow graphs to handle non-executed branches. The aforementioned approaches allow us to handle control flow, but they have not been yet adapted and implemented in Android systems. Gilbert *et al.* (2011) present a vision for implementing a dynamic approach to control the use of sensitive information by an app and to check for suspicious behavior. Their solution is based on a mixed-execution approach that combines symbolic and concrete execution to explore diverse paths of a specific third-party app. To analyze apps, they propose AppInspector, a security validation service that allows us to track actions as well as explicit and implicit flows. Mongiov *et al.* (2015) propose a novel hybrid approach that combines static and dynamic data flow analyses for detecting data leaks in Java applications. Their approach minimizes the overhead by computing a minimal set of "application points" that need to be monitored and injects control code on the target application.

We drew on these prior works and propose a solution based on a hybrid approach that combines static and dynamic analyses to detect control flow and to solve the under-tainting problem in Android systems.

We present in the following a formal approach based on a formal model to detect control flows.

4.5.2. *Formal control flow approaches*

The Data Mark Machine (Fenton 1974) is an abstract model proposed by Fenton to handle control flows. Fenton associates a security class $\underline{p}$ with a program counter p and defines an interaction matrix to track data in the system. The class combining operator "$\oplus$" specifies the class result of any binary function on values from the operand classes. For each object y, $\underline{y}$ defines a security class that is assigned to y. A flow relation "$\rightarrow$" between a pair of security classes A and B means that "information in class A is permitted to flow into class B". When a statement S is conditioned on the value of k condition variables $c_1, \ldots, c_k$, then $\underline{p}$ is set to $\underline{p} = \underline{c_1} \oplus \ldots \oplus \underline{c_k}$ to illustrate the control information flow. Fenton also tracks the explicit flow: if S represents an explicit flow from objects $a_1, \ldots, a_n$ to an object b, then the instruction execution mechanism verifies that $\underline{a_1} \oplus \ldots \oplus \underline{a_n} \oplus \underline{p} \rightarrow \underline{b}$. Fenton proves the correctness of his model in terms of information flow. He (Fenton 1973) asserts that his mechanism ensures security of all implicit flows. However, the Data Mark Machine does not take into account the implicit flow when the branch is not executed because it is based on a runtime mechanism.

```
1.boolean b = false;
2.boolean c = false;
3.if (!a)
4.   c = true;
5.if (!c)
6.   b = true;
```

Figure 4.4. *Implicit flow example*

The implicit flow example shown in Figure 4.4 proposed by Fenton (1974) presents an under-tainting problem. The first branch is not followed ($a = true$), but it contains information that is then leaked using the next if. Thus, at the end of the execution, b attains the value of a, whereas $\underline{b} <> \underline{a}$. Many solutions are proposed to solve the under-tainting problem. Fenton (1973) and Gat and Saal (1975) propose a solution that restores the value and class of objects changed during the execution of a conditional structure to the value and security class it had before entering the branch. However, in practice, existing application code does not modify control structures to consider information flow leakage. Furthermore, Gat and Saal's approach is based on specialized hardware architecture to control information flow and it is difficult to implement. Also, Fenton's approach was never implemented. Aries (Brown and Knight Jr 2001) proposes a solution that disallows the writing to a particular location within a branch when the security class associated with that location is equal or less restrictive than the security class of p. Considering the example shown in Figure 4.4, the program cannot write to c because the security class of c (Low) is less than or equal to the security class of p ($Low \Leftarrow \underline{p}$). Aries' approach is restricted because it is based only on high and low security classes and would preclude many applications from executing correctly (Beres and Dalton 2003).

The Bell–LaPadula model (Bell and LaPadula 1976) defines multilevel security. It associates security level with subjects and objects to indicate their sensitivity or clearance. It considers information flow from a high security classification to a lower security classification illegal.

Denning (1975) enhances the runtime mechanism used by Fenton with a compile time mechanism to solve the under-tainting problem. Denning proposes to insert updating instructions at compile time whether the branch is taken or not. Considering the example shown in Figure 4.4, an instruction is added at the end of the if $(!a)c = true$ code block to update $\underline{c}$ to $\underline{p}$ $(= \underline{a})$.

Denning's solution reflects the information flow exactly. However, this solution is based on informal arguments for the soundness of the compile time mechanism (Denning and Denning 1977). We draw our inspiration from the Denning approach, but we perform the required class update when Java methods are invoked, as we track Java applications instead of performing the update at compile time. We define a set of formally correct and complete propagation rules to solve the under-tainting problem.

These previous works present technical and formal solutions to detect the control flow and to solve the under-tainting problem. However, they are not implemented in Android systems. Thus, to secure a running process of Android systems, we propose to prevent the execution of the malicious code by monitoring transfers of control in a program. Then, we show that this approach is effective to detect control flow attacks and solve the under-tainting problem.

4.6. Handling explicit and control flows in Java and native Android apps' code

In this section, we formally specify the under-tainting problem. As a solution, we provide an algorithm based on a set of formally defined rules that describe the taint propagation. We prove the completeness of those rules and the correctness and completeness of the algorithm. Finally, we present our technical solution that propagates taint along control dependencies using two propagation rules.

4.6.1. *Formal specification of the under-tainting problem*

We formally specify the under-tainting problem based on Denning's information flow model. Denning (1976) defines an information flow model as:

$$F\,M = <\,N, P, SC, \oplus, \rightarrow>$$

where N is a set of logical storage objects (files, program variables, etc.), P is a set of processes that are executed by the active agents responsible for all information flow and SC is a set of security classes that are assigned to the objects in N. SC is finite and has a lower bound L attached to objects in N by default. The class combining operator "$\oplus$" specifies the class result of any binary function with operand classes. A flow relation "$\rightarrow$" between pairs of security classes A and B means that "information in class A is permitted to flow into class B". A flow model $F\,M$ is secure if, and only if, execution of a sequence of operations cannot produce a flow that violates the relation "$\rightarrow$".

We draw our inspiration from the Denning information flow model to formally specify under-tainting. However, we assign taint to the objects instead of assigning security classes. Thus, the class combining operator "$\oplus$" is used in our formal specification to combine taints of objects.

4.6.1.1. *Syntactic definition of connectors* $\{\Rightarrow, \rightarrow, \leftarrow, \oplus\}$

We use the following syntax to formally specify under-tainting (A and B are two logical formulas and x and y are two variables):

$- A \Rightarrow B$: if A then B;

$- x \rightarrow y$: information flow from object x to object y;

$- x \leftarrow y$: the value of y is assigned to x;

$- Taint(x) \oplus Taint(y)$: specifies the taint result of combined taints.

4.6.1.2. Semantic definition of connectors $\{\rightarrow, \leftarrow, \oplus\}$

– The $\rightarrow$ connector is reflexive: if x is a variable, then $x \rightarrow x$.

– The $\rightarrow$ connector is transitive: x, y and z are three variables: if $(x \rightarrow y)$ $\wedge (y \rightarrow z)$, then $x \rightarrow z$.

– The $\leftarrow$ connector is reflexive: if x is a variable, then $x \leftarrow x$.

– The $\leftarrow$ connector is transitive: x, y and z are three variables: if $(x \leftarrow y)$ $\wedge (y \leftarrow z)$, then $x \leftarrow z$.

– The $\rightarrow$ and $\leftarrow$ connectors are not symmetric.

– The $\oplus$ relation is commutative: $Taint(x) \oplus Taint(y) = Taint(y) \oplus Taint(x)$.

– The $\oplus$ relation is associative: $Taint(x) \oplus (Taint(y) \oplus Taint(z)) = (Taint(x) \oplus Taint(y)) \oplus Taint(z)$.

DEFINITION 4.1. Under-tainting.– *Under-tainting refers to when x depends on a condition, the value of x is assigned in the conditional branch and condition is tainted but x is not tainted.*

Formally, an under-tainting occurs when there is a variable x and a formula *condition* such that:

IsAssigned$(x, y) \wedge Dependency(x, condition)$

$\wedge$Tainted(condition) $\wedge \neg$Tainted(x)   [4.1]

where:

– *IsAssigned*(x, y) associates with x the value of y:

$$IsAssigned(x, y) \overset{def}{\equiv} (x \leftarrow y)$$

– *Dependency*$(x, condition)$ defines an information flow from *condition* to x when x depends on the *condition*

$$Dependency(x, condition) \overset{def}{\equiv} (condition \rightarrow x)$$

4.6.2. *Formal under-tainting solution*

We specify a set of formally defined rules that describe the taint propagation. We prove the completeness of these rules. Then, we provide an algorithm to solve the under-tainting problem based on these rules. Afterwards, we analyze some important properties of our algorithm such as correctness and completeness.

4.6.2.1. *Notations, definitions and theorems*

DEFINITION 4.2. Directed graph.– *A directed graph G = (V,E) consists of a finite set V of vertices and a set E of ordered pairs (v,w) of distinct vertices, called edges. If (v,w) is an edge, then w is a successor of v and v is a predecessor of w.*

DEFINITION 4.3. Complete directed graph.– *A complete directed graph is a simple directed graph G = (V,E) such that all pairs of distinct vertices in G are connected by exactly one edge. Therefore, for each pair of distinct vertices, either (x,y) or (y,x) (but not both) is in E.*

DEFINITION 4.4. Control flow graph.– *A control flow graph G = (V,E,r) is a directed graph (V,E) with a distinguished Exit vertex and start vertex r, such that for any vertex v ∈ V there is a path from r to v. The nodes of the control flow graph represent basic blocks, and the edges represent control flow paths. The concept of post-dominators and dominator trees are used to determine dependencies of blocks in the control flow graph.*

DEFINITION 4.5.– Dominator.– *A vertex v dominates another vertex w ≠ v in G if every path from r to w contains v.*

DEFINITION 4.6.– Post-dominator.– *A node v is post-dominated by a node w in G if every path from v to Exit (not including v) contains w.*

THEOREM 4.1.– Every vertex of a flow graph $G = (V,E,r)$ except r has a unique immediate dominator. The edges $\{(idom(w),w)|w \in V - \{r\}\}$ form a directed tree rooted at r, called the dominator tree of G, such that v dominates w if and only if v is a proper ancestor of w in the dominator tree (Lowry and Medlock 1969; Aho and Ullman 1972).

Computing post-dominators in the control flow graph is equivalent to computing dominators (Aho *et al.* 1986) in the reverse control flow graph. Dominators in the reverse graph can be computed quickly by using a fast algorithm (Lengauer and Tarjan 1979) or a linear-time dominators algorithm (Georgiadis and Tarjan 2004) to construct the dominator tree. Using these algorithms, we can determine the post-dominator tree of a graph.

DEFINITION 4.7. Control dependency.– *Let G be a control flow graph. Let X and Y be nodes in G. Y is control-dependent on X noted Dependency(X ,Y) if:*

1) there exists a directed path P from X to Y with any Z in P (excluding X and Y) post-dominated by Y and;

2) X is not post-dominated by Y.

Given the post-dominator tree, Ferrante *et al.* (1987) determine control dependencies by examining certain control flow graph edges and annotating nodes on the corresponding tree paths.

DEFINITION 4.8. Context_Taint.– *Let G be a control flow graph. Let X and Y be basic blocks in G. If Y is control-dependent on X that contains Condition, then we assign to Y a Context_Taint with Context_Taint(Y) = Taint(Condition).*

We use the completeness theorem to prove the completeness of the taint propagation rules, we use the soundness theorem to prove this completeness from left to right, and we use the compactness theorem and Theorem 4.2 to prove completeness from right to left. These theorems are given below (see Hedman (2004) for the proof):

– *Completeness theorem.* For any sentence G and set of sentences $\mathcal{F}$, $\mathcal{F} \models G$ if and only if $\mathcal{F} \vdash G$;

– *Soundness theorem.* For any formula G and set of formulas $\mathcal{F}$, if $\mathcal{F} \vdash G$, then $\mathcal{F} \models G$;

– *Compactness theorem.* Let $\mathcal{F}$ be a set of formulas. $\mathcal{F}$ is unsatisfiable if and only if some finite subset of $\mathcal{F}$ is unsatisfiable.

DEFINITION 4.9. CNF formula.– *A formula F is in conjunctive normal form (CNF) if it is a conjunction of disjunctions of literals. That is:*

$$F = \bigwedge_{i=1}^{n} \left(\bigwedge_{j=1}^{m} L_{i,j} \right)$$

where each $L_{i,j}$ is either an atomic or a negated atomic formula.

THEOREM 4.2.– Let F and G be formulas of first-order logic. Let H be the CNF formula obtained by applying the CNF algorithm (Hedman 2004) to the formula $F \wedge \neg G$. Let $Res^*(H)$ be the set of all clauses that can be derived from H using resolvents. The following are equivalent:

1) $F \vDash G$

2) $F \vdash G$

3) $\emptyset \in Res^*(H)$

– *The taint propagation rules.* Let us consider the following axioms:

$$(x \rightarrow y) \Rightarrow (Taint(y) \leftarrow Taint(x)) \tag{4.2}$$

$$(x \leftarrow y) \Rightarrow (y \rightarrow x) \tag{4.3}$$

$$(Taint(x) \leftarrow Taint(y)) \wedge (Taint(x) \leftarrow Taint(z))$$

$$\Rightarrow (Taint(x) \leftarrow Taint(y) \oplus Taint(z)) \tag{4.4}$$

THEOREM 4.3.– We consider that *Context_Taint* is the taint of the *condition*. To solve the under-tainting problem, we use the two rules that specify the propagation taint policy:

– Rule 1: if the value of x is modified and x depends on the *condition* and the branch is taken, then we will apply the following rule to taint x:

$$\frac{Is\ modified(x) \wedge Dependency(x, condition) \wedge BranchTaken(br, conditionalstatement)}{Taint(x) \leftarrow Context\_Taint \oplus Taint(explicit\ flowstatement)}$$

where the predicate *BranchTaken(br, conditionalstatement)* specifies that branch *br* in the *conditionalstatement* is executed. Therefore, an explicit flow which contains x is executed.

IsModified (x, explicitflowstatement) associates with x the result of an explicit flow statement (assignment statement):

$$Is\ modified(x) \overset{def}{\equiv} Is\ assigned(x,\ explicitflowstatement)$$

– Rule 2: if the value of y is assigned to x and x depends on the *condition* and the branch *br* in the conditional statement is not taken (x depends only on implicit flow and does not depend on explicit flow), then we will apply the following rule to taint x.

$$\frac{Is\ assigned(x,y) \wedge Dependency(x, condition) \wedge \neg BranchTaken(br, conditionalstatement)}{Taint(x) \leftarrow Taint(x) \oplus Context\_Taint}$$

4.6.2.2. Proof of taint propagation rules

To prove completeness of propagation taint rules, we use the basic rules cited in Table 4.1 for derivations.

Premise	Conclusion	Name
G is in F	$F \vdash G$	Assumption
$F \vdash G$ and $F \subset F'$	$F' \vdash G$	Monotonicity
$F \vdash F, F \vdash G$	$F \vdash (F \wedge G)$	$\wedge$-Introduction
$F \vdash (F \wedge G)$	$F \vdash (G \wedge F)$	$\wedge$-Symmetry

Table 4.1. *Basic rules for derivations*

We start by proving completeness of the first rule.

We suppose that $\mathcal{F} = \{IsModified(x, explicitflowstatement), Dependency(x, condition), BranchTaken(br, conditionalstatement)\}$ and $G = Taint(x) \leftarrow Context\_Taint \oplus Taint(explicitflowstatement)$.

We prove soundness, left to right, by induction. If $\mathcal{F} \vdash G$, then there is a formal proof concluding with $\mathcal{F} \vdash G$ (see Table 4.2). Let M be an arbitrary model of $\mathcal{F}$, we will demonstrate that $M \vDash G$. G is deduced by Modus ponens of G_j, $G_j \rightarrow G$, then by induction, $M \vDash G_j$ and $M \vDash G_j \rightarrow G$ and it follows $M \vDash G$.

Conversely, suppose that $\mathcal{F} \vDash G$, then $\mathcal{F} \cup \neg G$ is unsatisfiable. By compactness, some finite subset of $\mathcal{F} \cup \neg G$ is unsatisfiable. Thus, there exists a finite $\mathcal{F}_0 \subset \mathcal{F}$ such that $\mathcal{F}_0 \cup \neg G$ is unsatisfiable and, equivalently, $\mathcal{F}_0 \vDash G$. Since $\mathcal{F}_0$ is finite, we can apply Theorem 4.2 to get $\mathcal{F}_0 \vdash G$. Finally, $\mathcal{F} \vdash G$ by monotonicity.∎

We will now prove completeness of the second rule.

We assume again that $\mathcal{F} = \{IsAssigned(x,y), Dependency(x,condition),$ $\neg BranchTaken(br,conditionalstatement)\}$ and $G = Taint(x) \leftarrow Taint(x) \oplus Context\_Taint$.

Similarly to the first rule, we prove soundness by induction. If $\mathcal{F} \vdash G$, then there is a formal proof concluding with $\mathcal{F} \vdash G$ (see Table 4.3).

Let M be an arbitrary model of $\mathcal{F}$, we will demonstrate that $M \vDash G$. G is deduced by Modus ponens of G_j, $G_j \rightarrow G$, then by induction, $M \vDash G_j$ and $M \vDash G_j \rightarrow G$ and it follows $M \vDash G$.

Statement	Justification
1. $(condition \rightarrow x) \vdash (Taint(x) \leftarrow Taint(condition))$	Axiom (2)
2. $(condition \rightarrow x) \vdash (Taint(x) \leftarrow Context\_Taint)$	$Taint(condition) = Context\ Taint$
3. $F \vdash (Taint(x) \leftarrow ContextTaint)$	Monotonicity applied to 2
4. $(x \leftarrow explicit\ flowstatement) \vdash (explicit\ flowstatement \rightarrow x)$	Axiom (3)
5. $(x \leftarrow explicit\ flowstatement) \vdash (Taint(x) \leftarrow Taint(explicit\ flowstatement))$	Axiom (2)
6. $F \vdash (Taint(x) \leftarrow Taint(explicit\ flowstatement))$	Monotonicity applied to 5
7. $F \vdash ((Taint(x) \leftarrow Context\_Taint) \wedge (Taint(x) \leftarrow Taint(explicit\ flowstatement)))$	$\wedge$-Introduction applied to 3 and 6
8. $F \vdash G$	Modus ponens

Table 4.2. *Formal proof of the first rule*

Statement	Justification
1. $(condition \rightarrow x) \vdash (Taint(x) \leftarrow Taint(condition))$	Axiom (2)
2. $(condition \rightarrow x) \vdash (Taint(x) \leftarrow Context\_Taint)$	$Taint(condition) = Context\_Taint$
3. $\mathcal{F} \vdash (Taint(x) \leftarrow Context\_Taint)$	Monotonicity applied to 2
4. $x \vdash (x \leftarrow x)$	The relation $\leftarrow$ is reflexive
5. $\mathcal{F} \vdash (x \leftarrow x)$	Monotonicity applied to 3
6. $(x \leftarrow x) \vdash (Taint(x) \leftarrow Taint(x))$	Axiom (2)
7. $\mathcal{F} \vdash (Taint(x) \leftarrow Taint(x))$	Modus ponens applied to 5 and 6
8. $\mathcal{F} \vdash ((Taint(x) \leftarrow Context\_Taint) \wedge$ $(Taint(x) \leftarrow Taint(x)))$	$\wedge$-Introduction applied to 3 and 7
9. $\mathcal{F} \vdash ((Taint(x) \leftarrow Taint(x)) \wedge$ $(Taint(x) \leftarrow Context\_Taint))$	$\wedge$-Symmetry applied to 8
10. $\mathcal{F} \vdash G$	Modus ponens

Table 4.3. *Formal proof of the second rule*

Conversely, suppose that $\mathcal{F} \vDash G$. Then, $\mathcal{F} \cup \neg G$ is unsatisfiable. By compactness, some finite subset of $\mathcal{F} \cup \neg G$ is unsatisfiable. Thus, there exists a finite $\mathcal{F}_0 \subset \mathcal{F}$ such that $\mathcal{F}_0 \cup \neg G$ is unsatisfiable and, equivalently, $\mathcal{F}_0 \vDash G$. Since $\mathcal{F}_0$ is finite, we can apply Theorem 4.2 to get $\mathcal{F}_0 \vdash G$. Finally, $\mathcal{F} \vdash G$ by monotonicity. ∎

4.6.2.3. *The algorithm*

The tainting algorithm that we propose, *Taint_Algorithm*, allows us to solve the under-tainting problem. It takes as input a control flow graph of a binary program. In this graph, nodes represent a set of instructions corresponding to basic blocks. First, it determines the control dependency of the different blocks in the graph using *Dependency_Algorithm* (Ferrante *et al.* 1987). Afterwards, we parse the *Dependency_List* generated by *Dependency_Algorithm* and we set the context taint of blocks to include the taint of the condition that depends on whether the branch is taken or not. Finally, using the context taint and the two propagation rules, we taint all variables to which a value is assigned in the conditional branch.

Algorithm 1 Taint_Algorithm (Control flow graph G)

Input: $G = (V, E, r)$ is a control flow graph of a binary program
Output: *Tainted_Variables_List* is the list of variables that are tainted.

$x \in V$
$y \in V$
Dependency_List $\leftarrow$ *Dependency_Algorithm(G)*
while $(x, y) \in$ *Dependency_List* **do**
    Set_Context_Taint(y, List_Context_Taint)
    Tainted_Variables_List $\leftarrow$ *Taint_Assigned_Variable(y)*
end while

4.6.2.4. Proof of the algorithm correctness

We want to prove the correctness of the *Taint_Algorithm*. Let us assume that the control flow graph is correct (Amighi *et al.* 2012). The proof consists of three steps: first prove that *Dependency_Algorithm* is correct, then prove that *Set_Context_Taint* is correct and finally prove that *Taint_Assigned_Variable* is correct. Each step relies on the result from the previous step.

4.6.2.5. Correctness proof for Dependency_Algorithm

The *Dependency_Algorithm* is defined by Ferrante *et al.* (1987) to determine dependency of blocks in the graph. This algorithm takes as input the post-dominator tree for an augmented control flow graph (ACFG). Ferrante *et al.* add to the control flow graph a special predicate node ENTRY, which has one edge labeled "T" going to START node and another edge labeled "F" going to STOP node. ENTRY corresponds to the external condition that causes the program to begin execution. The post-dominator tree of ACFG can be created using the algorithms defined in Georgiadis and Tarjan (2004) and Lengauer and Tarjan (1979). These algorithms are proven to be correct.

4.6.2.6. Basic steps in Dependency_Algorithm

Given the post-dominator tree, Ferrante *et al.* (1987) determine control dependencies as follows:

– find S, a set of all the edges (*A,B*) in the ACFG such that *B* is not an ancestor of *A* in the post-dominator tree (i.e. *B* does not post-dominate *A*);

– for each edge (*A,B*) in S, find L, the least common ancestor of *A* and *B* in the post-dominator tree.

CLAIM.– Either L is A or L is the parent of A in the post-dominator tree.

Ferrante *et al.* consider these two cases for L and show that one method of marking the post-dominator tree with the appropriate control dependencies accommodates both cases:

– case 1. L = parent of A. All nodes in the post-dominator tree on the path from L to B, including B but not L, should be made control-dependent on A;

– case 2. $L = A$. All nodes in the post-dominator tree on the path from A to B, including A and B, should be made control-dependent on A.

Given (A,B) in S and its corresponding L, the algorithm given by Ferrante *et al.* traverses backwards from B in the post-dominator tree until they reach L and mark all nodes visited; mark L only if $L = A$.

Statements representing all marked nodes are control-dependent on A with the label that is on edge (A,B).

They prove that the correctness of the construction directly follows from the definition of control dependency (see section 4.6.2).

Referring back to this definition, for any node M on the path in the post-dominator tree from (but not including) L to B, (1) there is a path from A to M in the control flow graph that consists of nodes post-dominated by M, and (2) A is not post-dominated by M. Condition (1) is true because the edge (A, B) gives us a path to B, and B is post-dominated by M. Condition (2) is true because A is either L, in which case it post-dominates M, or A is a child of L not on the path from L to B.

We can therefore conclude that *Dependency_Algorithm* is correct.

4.6.2.7. *Correctness proof for Set_Context_Taint*

We include the taint of the condition in the context taint of the dependent blocks. As the condition taint is valid, the inclusion operation is also valid. We can conclude that *Set_Context_Taint* is correct.

4.6.2.8. *Correctness proof for Taint_Assigned_Variable*

We use the two propagation rules to taint variables to which a value is assigned. We have proved the completeness of the two propagation rules in section 4.6.2; thus, we can conclude that *Taint_Assigned_Variable* is complete. Therefore, we can conclude the completeness of the *Taint_Algorithm*.

4.6.2.9. *Proof of the algorithm completeness*

Let us assume that the control flow graph is complete (see Definition 4.3). To prove the completeness of the *Taint_Algorithm*, we will prove the completeness of *Dependency_Algorithm* and *Taint_Assigned_Variable*.

The *Dependency_Algorithm* takes as input the post-dominator tree of the control flow graph. The post-dominator tree can be constructed using the complete algorithm defined in Georgiadis and Tarjan (2004). The *Dependency_Algorithm* is based on the set of the least common ancestor (L) of A and B in the post-dominator tree for each edge (A, B) in S. According to the value of L, Ferrante *et al.* (1987) define two cases to determine the control dependency. To prove the completeness of the *Dependency_Algorithm*, we show that Ferrante *et al.* prove that there does not exist another value of L (either A as parent or A itself) to consider.

PROOF.– Let us assume that X is the parent of A in the post-dominator tree. Therefore, X is not B because B is not an ancestor of A in the post-dominator tree (by construction of S). Ferrante *et al.* perform a proof *reductio ad absurdum* to demonstrate that X post-dominates B. If it does not, there would be a path from B to *STOP* that does not contain X. However, by adding edge (A,B) to this path, a path from A to *STOP* does not pass through X (since, by construction, X is not B). This contradicts the fact that X post-dominates A. Thus, X post-dominates B and it must be an ancestor of B in the post-dominator tree. If X, immediate post-dominator of A, post-dominates B, then the least common ancestor of A and B in the post-dominator tree must be either X or A itself. ■

As only two values of L exist, there does not exist another case to compute the control dependency. Case 2 captures loop dependency, and all other dependencies are determined according to Case 1. Thus, *Dependency_Algorithm* is complete.

We proved the completeness of the two propagation rules in section 4.6.2; thus, we can conclude that *Taint_Assigned_Variable* is complete. Therefore, we can conclude the completeness of the taint algorithm.

4.6.2.10. *Time complexity of the algorithm*

Dependency_Algorithm performs with a time complexity of $O(N^2)$ at most, where N is the number of nodes in the control flow graph. A linear time algorithm to calculate control dependencies was proposed by Johnson and Pingali (1993), but no proof of correctness of this algorithm was given. For each (X,Y) examined in the *Dependency_List*, setting context taint and tainting variables can be done in constant time $O(N)$. Thus, *Taint_Algorithm* requires linear time using the algorithm defined in Johnson and Pingali (1993) and at most $O(N^2)$ using the Ferrante *et al.* algorithm.

4.6.3. *System design*

Our approach allows us to track information flows (explicit and control flows) in Java and native Android applications to detect leakage of sensitive data. It enhances the TaintDroid system based on dynamic taint analysis to control the manipulation of private data by third-party Android applications. First, we assign taint to sensitive data. Then, we track propagation of tainted data in the Java components. We issue warning reports when the tainted data are leaked by malicious applications.

As TaintDroid cannot detect control flows, we combine the static and dynamic taint analyses to solve the under-tainting problem. The static analysis is used to detect control dependencies and to have an overview of all conditional branches in the program. We use information provided by static analysis to propagate taint along all control dependencies in the dynamic analysis phase.

Components colored in gray (see Figure 4.5) present the Java Taint Instruction Tracer module implemented in the Dalvik VM for tracking information flows at Java level.

To ensure the proper propagation of the native code, we implement the Native Taint Instruction Tracer module (see Figure 4.5) that instruments the ARM/Thumb instructions. Also, we use static analysis to enumerate the information flows (control flows) for all JNI methods.

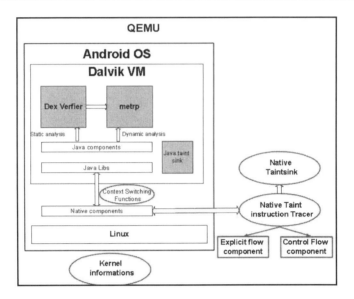

Figure 4.5. *Modified architecture to handle control flow in native code*

In addition, when a native function is invoked in TaintDroid, the corresponding taint is not stored in the native runtime stack. Therefore, they do not correctly receive and set taints when the context (Java and native) switches. Therefore, we define the Context Switching Functions module (see Figure 4.5). This module instruments JNI-related functions, through which information flows a cross the boundary between the Java context and the native context to maintain taints between the two contexts.

Moreover, we implement the Native Taint sink module (see Figure 4.5) which hooks a selected system call. Finally, we get Android Linux kernel information of processes and memory maps (Information Kernel modules). We detail these modules in the following section.

4.6.4. *Handling explicit and control flows in Java Android apps' code*

Our Java Taint Instruction Tracer module is composed of two main components: the *StaticAnalysis* component and the *DynamicAnalysis* component (see Figure 4.6). We implement our proposed approach in the TaintDroid operating system. We add a *Static Analysis* component in the

Dalvik virtual machine verifier that statically analyzes instructions of third-party application Dex code at load time. Also, we modify the Dalvik virtual machine interpreter to integrate the *DynamicAnalysis* component. We implement the two additional rules using native methods that define the taint propagation.

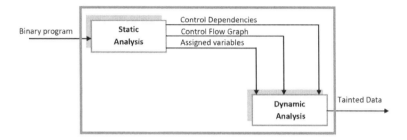

Figure 4.6. *Our approach architecture*

4.6.4.1. *Static analysis component*

The static verification is performed in the file DexVerify.c. In this file, there are three levels of verification: class level, method level and instruction level. In order to add the static analysis component, DexVerify.c is modified by adding three functions: *contextAnalysisBeginAnalyze*, *contextAnalysisControlFlowInstruction* and *contextAnalysisE ndAnalyze* in the function *verifyInstructions*.

In the *contextAnalysisBeginAnalyze* function, we initialize global variables for method analysis. Then, we check the method instructions. When control flow instructions (if, switch, goto, catch, etc.) are detected, the *contextAnalysisControlFlowInstruction* function is called to signal a jump instruction. This function takes as input arguments the program counter *pc*, *pc_target*, the length and the type of block. The *pc_target* presents the jump target if this is a jump instruction or the number of cases if this is a switch instruction. In this function, we create a basic block, or several if forward branches were defined at the end of the basic blocks list. Then, we specify the target of the basic blocks. Also, we allocate a *BitmapBits* for tracking condition dependency.

When we achieve the analysis of a single method, we call the *contextAnalysisisEnd Analyze* function to create the control flow graph

(CFG). A CFG is composed of basic blocks and edges. We allocate the last basic block in the basic blocks list. We call the *dumpGraph* function that uses this list to determine blocks of the graph. The basic blocks represent nodes of the graph. The directed edges represent jumps in the control flow. Edges of the CFG are defined using the *BitmapBits* structure. *BitmapBits* is composed of bits. Setting all bits indicates that the flow of control is merged and the basic block is not controlled by control condition. When one bit is set, the basic block depends on the control condition. The basic block represents the conditional instruction when no bit is set. We store the control flow graph in graphviz format (Research 2016) in the smartphone data directory.

4.6.4.2. *Dynamic analysis component*

The dynamic analysis is performed at run time by instrumenting the Dalvik virtual machine interpreter. The *DynamicAnalysis* component uses information provided by the *StaticAnalysis* component such as *BitmapBits*. *BitmapBits* allows us to detect the condition dependencies from variables in basic blocks of the graph. We assign a *context_taint* to each basic block, which includes the taint of the condition on which the block depends. By referencing to *BitmapBits*, we set the *context_taint* of each basic block. We start by exploring the branches that are not taken. The *StaticAnalysis* component provides the type and the number of instructions in these branches (in basic block). Then, we force the processor to taint variables to which a value is assigned in these instructions. To taint these variables, we use the *context_taint* of the basic block containing these variables and apply the second rule defined in section 4.6.2.

We compare arguments in the condition using the following instruction: *res_cmp* = $((s4)GET\_REGISTER(vsrc1)\_cmp(s4)GET\_REGISTER(vsrc2))$. Based on the comparison result, we verify whether the branch is taken or not. We combine the taints of different variables of the condition as follows: *SET_REGISTER_TAINT* (*vdst,* (*GET_REGISTER_TAINT* (*vsrc1*)|*GET_REGISTER_TAINT* (*vsrc2*))) to obtain *Context_Taint*. If *res_cmp* is not null, then the branch is not taken. Thus, we adjust the ordinal counter to point to the first instruction of the branch by using the function *ADJUST_PC*(2). Otherwise, it is the second branch (else) that is not taken; thus, we adjust the ordinal counter to point to the first instruction in this branch by using the function *ADJUST_PC*(*br*), where *br* represents the branch pointer.

We instrument different instructions in the interpreter to handle conditional statements. For each instruction, we check if it is a conditional statement or not. Then, we test if the condition is tainted (*Context_Taint* is not null). In this case, we taint the variable with which we associate a value (destination register) as follows: *SET_REGISTER_TAINT* (*vdst,* (*GET_REGISTER_TAINT* (*vsrc*1)| *GET_REGISTER_TAINT* (*vsrc*2)|*taintcond*)).

If the conditional branch contains multiple instructions, then we verify each time that (*pc_start* < *pc*) and (*pc* < *pc_end*) to handle all the instructions (we increment the ordinal counter when we execute an instruction).

In the case of *f or* and *while* loops, we process by the same way, but we test whether the condition is still true or not in each iteration.

We reserve special treatment for *Switch* instructions. We deal with all case statements and all instructions that are defined inside *Switch* instructions. Note that we only taint variables and do not modify their values. Once we handle all not taken branches, we restore the ordinal counter to treat the taken branches. We assign taints to modified variables in this branch using the first rule presented in section 4.6.2. We modify the native methods of TaintDroid to implement the two additional rules that propagate taint in the control flow.

4.6.4.3. *Exception handling*

TaintDroid does not detect exceptions used in control flow. Thus, an attacker can successfully leak sensitive information by throwing exceptions to control flow. For this reason, we make a special exception when handling to avoid leaking information. The catch block depends on the type of exception object raised in the throw statement. If the type of exception that occurred is listed in a catch block, then the exception is passed to the catch block. Therefore, an edge is added in the CFG from the throw statement to the catch block to indicate that the throw statement will transfer control to the appropriate catch block. If an exception occurs, then the current context taint and the exception's taint are stored. The variables assigned in any of the catch blocks will be tainted depending on the exception's taint. Each catch block has an entry in the context taint for this purpose.

4.6.5. *Handling explicit and control flows in native Android apps' code*

The Android system runs on top of an emulator QEMU (Wiki 2015), which provides information about all generated ARM/Thumb Android instructions (see Figure 4.5). Thus, we made a number of modifications to QEMU to handle native Android apps' code. We define four modules: (1) Native Taint Instruction Tracer module that handles explicit and control flows at native level; (2) Context Switching Functions module; (3) Native Taint sink module and (4) Information Kernel module.

4.6.5.1. *Native Taint Instruction Tracer*

The Native Taint Instruction Tracer module is composed of (1) an explicit flow component that tracks direct flows and (2) a control flow component that tracks indirect flows at the native level.

We instrument the ARM/Thumb instructions of native libraries invoked by Android applications to propagate taint in explicit flow. We handle unary, binary and move operations. For these operations, we add taint propagation instructions that assign to the destination register (R_d) the combination of all taints of source registers (R_n, R_m). We propagate taint tags in explicit flow referencing data flow rules presented in Table 4.4. *#imm* represents the immediate number with a null value of taint. $t(M[addr])$ is the taint of memory at address *addr* that is calculated using R_n and *#imm* ($Cal(R_n, \#imm)$). *LDM* and *ST M* represent the load and store instructions, respectively. The operator "$\oplus$" is used to combine taints of objects. The operator "$\otimes$" indicates a binary operation between two registers. Listing 4.3 and Listing 4.4 present the instrumentation code to handle explicit flow of, respectively, move and binary operations.

It is more difficult to handle control flows because it is necessary to detect all conditional branches. Thus, to track control flow at the native level, we use a static analysis that checks instructions of native methods at load time. This analysis is based on the control flow graphs (Aho *et al.* 1986, Allen 1970), which are analyzed to determine branches in the conditional structure.

Instruction Format	Instruction Semantics	Taint Propagation
mov R_d,#imm	$R_d \leftarrow$ #imm	$Taint(R_d) \leftarrow \emptyset$
mov R_d,R_m	$R_d \leftarrow R_m$	$Taint(R_d) \leftarrow Taint(R_m)$
unary-op R_d,R_m	$R_d \leftarrow \otimes R_m$	$Taint(R_d) \leftarrow Taint(R_m)$
binary-op R_d,R_n,R_m	$R_d \leftarrow R_n \otimes R_m$	$Taint(R_d) \leftarrow Taint(R_n) \oplus Taint(R_m)$
binary-op R_d,R_m	$R_d \leftarrow R_d \otimes R_m$	$Taint(R_d) \leftarrow Taint(R_d) \oplus Taint(R_m)$
binary-op R_d,R_m,#imm	$R_d \leftarrow R_m \otimes$ #imm	$Taint(R_d) \leftarrow Taint(R_m)$
STR R_d,R_n,#imm	$addr \leftarrow Cal(R_n,\#imm), M[addr] \leftarrow R_d$	$Taint(M[addr]) \leftarrow Taint(R_d)$
LDR R_d,R_n,#imm	$addr \leftarrow Cal(R_n,\#imm), R_d \leftarrow M[addr]$	$Taint(R_d) \leftarrow Taint(M[addr]) \oplus Taint(R_n)$
STM(PUSH) regList,R_n,#imm	$startAddress/endAddress \leftarrow Cal(R_n,\#imm),$ $\{M[startAddress],M[endAddress]\} \leftarrow \{R_i,R_j\}$	$Taint(\{M[startAddress],M[endAddress]\}) \leftarrow Taint(\{R_i,R_j\})$
LDM(POP) regList,R_n,#imm	$startAddress/endAddress \leftarrow Cal(R_n,\#imm),\{R_i,R_j\} \leftarrow \{M[startAddress],M[endAddress]\}$	$Taint(\{R_i,R_j\}) \leftarrow Taint(R_n) \oplus Taint(\{M[startAddress],M[endAddress]\})$

Table 4.4. *Explicit flow propagation logic*

The control flow graph is composed of nodes that represent basic blocks and directed edges that represent jumps in the control flow. A basic block is assigned to each control flow branch. We detect the flow of the condition dependencies from blocks in the graph using the *BitmapBits*, which is an array of bits. Setting all bits indicates that the flow of control is merged and the basic block does not depend on control condition. When one bit is set, the basic block depends on the control condition. The basic block represents the conditional instruction when no bit is set.

```
case I_MOV:

d->Rd = (w >> 8) & b111;
/* CONTROL FLOWS START */
if(context_cond)
{
setRegTaint(d->Rd,( getRegTaint(d->Rn)|taint_cond));
}
/* CONTROL FLOWS END */
else
/* EXPLICIT FLOWS START */
{
setRegToReg(d->Rd, d->Rn);
}
/* EXPLICIT FLOWS END */
return 0;
```

Listing 4.3. *Instrumenting I_MOV instruction to propagate taint in control flows*

Also, we detect variable assignment in a basic block of the control flow graph. When we run the native methods, we taint these variables if the condition is tainted. To do this, we use dynamic analysis and instrument third-party native libraries conditional instructions (see Listing 4.3 and Listing 4.4 for move and binary instructions, respectively, in a conditional statement). This analysis uses information provided by the static analysis, such as *BitmapBits*, to detect condition dependencies from block in the graph and variable assignment. Then, we define a context taint as condition taint. We taint modified variables that exist in the conditional instruction according to the rules of taint propagation defined and proven in the previous section. If the branch is taken, then $Taint(x) = ContextTaint \oplus Taint(explicitflowstatement)$.

```
case  T_THUMB_3REG:
    d->Rd = (w >> 0) & b111;
    d->Rn = (w >> 3) & b111;
    d->Rm = (w >> 6) & b111;
/* CONTROL FLOWS START */
if (context_cond)
{
setRegTaint(d->Rd,(getRegTaint(d->Rn) | getRegTaint(d->d->Rm) | taint_cond))
}
/* CONTROL FLOWS END */
else
/* EXPLICIT  FLOWS START */
{
setRegTaint(d->Rd,(getRegTaint(d->Rn) | getRegTaint(d->d->Rm)));
}
/* EXPLICIT  FLOWS END */
return 0;
```

Listing 4.4. *Instrumenting T_THUMB_3REG instruction to propagate taint in control flows*

4.6.5.2. *Context switching functions*

When the context switches from Java to native, we store the taint in the native runtime stack for tracking information flow at native level. The Context Switching Functions module instruments JNI-related functions that ensure switching between the two contexts.

These functions allow Java code to invoke native code. We hook the JNI call bridge (dvmCallJNIMethod) to detect native invoked methods. Then, we assign to each invoked native method a SourcePolicy structure where argument taints of this method are stored. Finally, we add taints to the corresponding native context registers and memories.

Moreover, these functions allow native code to call Java methods through the dvmCallMethod function. We save taints in shadow registers and memory at native level and use them to set taints in the Dalvik virtual machine stack when native codes invoke Java codes by instrumenting the dvmInterpret method. In addition, we maintain taint of a new Java object that can be created in the native codes through JNI functions. Furthermore, we instrument functions that allow native code to access the Java objects' fields to assign taint to these object fields. Finally, we taint exceptions thrown by native code to communicate with Java code by instrumenting functions, including "ThrowNew", "initException", "dvmCallMethod" and "dvmInterpret".

4.6.5.3. Information Kernel

The Information Kernel module provides Android Linux kernel information of processes and memory maps. We use the virtual machine introspection technique described in Droidscope for reconstructing the OS-level view. The QEMU emulator disassembles and translates a basic block of guest instructions into an intermediate representation called TCG (Tiny Code Generator). Then, it compiles the TCG code block down to a block of host instructions and stores it in a code cache. To extract OS-level information (running processes and the memory map), we instrument translated code blocks and add TCG instructions at the code translation phase.

Third-party applications
The Weather Channel; Cestos; Solitaire; Babble; Manga Browser; Box2D[*]; Libgdx[*];
Knocking; Coupons; QQPhoneBook[*]; Fruit Ninja[*]; Bump; Traffic Jam; Find It[*];
Hearts; Blackjack; Alchemy; Horoscope; Bubble Burst Free; Wisdom Quotes Lite; Paper Toss[*];
ePhone[*]; Classic Simon Free; Astrid; Angry Birds[*]; Subway Surfer[*]; Layar; Cocos2D[*]; Unity[*];
Trapster; ProBasketBall; Grindr[*]; HeyWire[*]; Wertago;
Dastelefonbuch[*]; RingTones; Yellow Pages; Contact Analyzer; Hike[*]; TextPlus[*]

Table 4.5. Third-party analyzed applications

4.6.5.4. Native Taint sink

Sensitive data can be leaked through native code. Thus, it is necessary to implement taint sink at the native level. The Native Taint sink module hooks a selected system call to detect the leakage of private information. To make system calls, we use the service zero instruction $svc\#0$. Thus, we instrument this instruction to get system call information. We hook file open ($f\,open$), close ($f\,close$), read ($f\,read$), write ($f\,write, f\,put\,c, f\,put\,s$) and connect ($send, sendto$) system calls to implement the native sinks.

4.6.6. *Evaluation*

In this section, we evaluate effectiveness and performance of our approach. First, we analyze real popular Android applications using our system. Then, we evaluate our taint tracking approach overhead using CF-Bench. We use a Dell laptop (Latitude E6420) with a core i5 @ 2.6 GHz and 4GiB of RAM running Debian 7. Experiments were performed on an Android emulator version 4.1 that running on the laptop.

4.6.6.1. *Effectiveness*

We download and analyze 40 free, frequently used Android applications from the Google Play Store (see Table 4.5). These applications access and handle private data such as location, contacts, phone state, camera and SMS. As shown in Table 4.5, 16 applications (marked with *) invoke native libraries.

We use dex2jar tool (Google 2015) to translate dex files of different applications to jar files. Then, we use jd-gui (Java 2015) to obtain the Java source code that will be analyzed. For native code, we disassemble the libraries object code and we get the assembler mnemonics for the machine instructions by executing objdump (part of the GNU Binutils; sourceware 2015).

We found that 23 Android applications (see Table 4.6) leak private data through information flows:

– six applications use explicit flow in Java context and cause the leakage of sensitive information such as location, phone state, contact and camera;

Application	Java context		Native context		Type of leaked data
	Explicit flow	*Control flow*	*Explicit flow*	*Control flow*	
Wisdom Quotes Lite	x				L, P
The Weather Channel		x			L
Knocking		x			L, Ca, P
Coupons	x				L, Ca, P
QQPhoneBook			x		Co, SMS
Fruit Ninja				x	Co

Find It		x		x	L, P
Horoscope		x			L, P
Paper Toss		x		x	L, P
ePhone			x		Co
Astrid	x				L, P
Angry Birds				x	L
Subway Surfer				x	L
Layar	x				L, Ca, P
Trapster	x				L, Ca, P
Grindr				x	L, SMS
HeyWire				x	L, SMS
Wertago		x			L, Co, P
Dastelefonbuch		x		x	L, Co, P
RingTones	x				L, Co, P
Yellow Pages		x			L, Co, P
Hike				x	L, SMS
TextPlus				x	L, SMS

Table 4.6. *Third-party applications leaking sensitive data (L: location, Ca: camera, Co: contacts, P: phone state, SMS: messages) through information flows*

– eight applications use control flow in the Java context and cause the leakage of sensitive information such as location, phone state, contacts and camera;

– two applications use explicit flow in native context and cause the leakage of sensitive information such as contact and SMS;

– 10 applications use control flow in native context and cause the leakage of sensitive information such as location, phone state, contact and SMS. Most of these applications belong to the game category (Fruit Ninja, Angry Birds, Subway Surfer) and the communication category (Grindr; HeyWire, Hike, TextPlus). These 10 applications were detected only by our approach.

TaintDroid detects 26% of malicious applications that cause leakage of sensitive data, NDroid and Droidscope 35%, Graa *et al.* (2016) implementation 61% and our approach detects all applications. Therefore, our approach identifies more malicious applications than the existing approaches in Android systems.

4.6.6.2. *False negatives*

TaintDroid using its simple JNI tainting policy generates 74%, NDroid 65%, Droidscope 65% and the Graa *et al.* approach 39% of false negatives. Our approach solves the under-tainting problem. It has successfully propagated taint in control instructions at Java and native levels and detected leakage of tainted sensitive data that is reported in the alert messages.

4.6.6.3. *Performance*

To evaluate the performance of our approach, we study our static and dynamic analysis overhead. We perform the static analysis at load and verification times. Our approach adds 37% and 30% overhead with respect to the unmodified system, respectively, at load and verification times. This is due to the verification of method instructions and the construction of the control flow graphs used to detect the control flows.

We use CF-Bench (Bench 2011), which is a CPU and memory benchmark tool to study our taint tracking approach overhead. We choose CF-Bench because it produces a fairly stable score and tests both native and managed code performances.

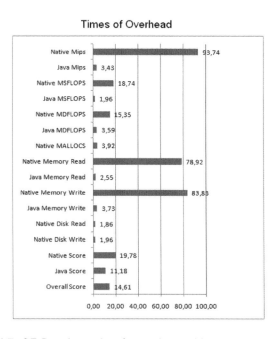

Figure 4.7. *CF-Bench results of our taint tracking approach overhead*

As shown in Figure 4.7, our approach incurs in average a slowdown of 14.9 times. This time of overhead is greater than the result of NDroid (5.45 times slowdown) because we propagate taint in the conditional branches at Java and native levels. This time of overhead is greater than the result of Droidscope (11 times slowdown) performed in a real machine and not in a Google Android Emulator that is prohibitively slow. Despite the proposed approach having additional speed loss, it gives more accurate detection results than NDroid and Droidscope.

4.6.6.4. *False positives*

Our approach generates 30% of false positives. We detected leakage of IMSI and IMEI that was really used as a configuration parameter in the smartphone. Therefore, we cannot consider these applications as malicious.

4.6.7. *Discussion*

Cavallaro *et al.* (2008) describe evasion techniques that can easily defeat dynamic information flow analysis. These evasion attacks can use control dependencies. They demonstrate that a malware writer can propagate an arbitrarily large amount of information through control dependencies. Cavallaro *et al.* see that it is necessary to reason about assignments that take place on the unexecuted program branches. We implement the same idea in our taint propagation rules. Unfortunately, this will lead to an over-tainting problem (false positives). The problem has been addressed in Kang *et al.* (2011) and Bao *et al.* (2010) but was not solved though. Kang *et al.* (2011) use a diagnosis technique to select branches that could be responsible for under-tainting and propagate taint only along these branches in order to reduce over-tainting. However, a smaller amount of over-tainting occurs even with DTA++. Bao *et al.* (2010) define the concept of strict control dependencies (SCDs) and introduce its semantics. They use a static analysis to identify predicate branches that give rise to SCDs. They do not consider all control dependencies to reduce the number of false positives. Their implementation gives similar results to DTA++ in many cases, but it is based on the syntax of a comparison expression. Contrarily, DTA++ uses a more general and precise semantic-level condition, implemented using symbolic execution.

We showed in section 4.8.5 that our approach generates significant false positives. However, it provides more security because all confidential data are tainted. Therefore, the sensitive information cannot be leaked. We are interested in solving the under-tainting because we consider that the false negatives are much more dangerous than the false positives, since the former can lead to a leakage of data. It is possible to reduce the over-tainting problem by considering expert rules. Also, we can ask the user at the moment when the sensitive data is going to be leaked to authorize or not the transmission of the data outside of the system.

4.7. Protection against code obfuscation attacks based on control dependencies in Android systems

In this section, we show how our approach can resist code obfuscation attacks based on control dependencies in the Android system. We use the rules that define the taint propagation presented in section 4.6.2 to avoid these code obfuscation attacks.

4.7.1. *Code obfuscation definition*

In general, the obfuscation consists of making something more difficult to understand. Collberg *et al.* (1997, 1998) define the obfuscation process as a transformation of a computer program into a program that has the same behavior but is much harder to understand.

DEFINITION 4.10. Obfuscating transformation.– *Let* $\Gamma(P)$ *be a program, obtained by transformation of program P. Γ is an obfuscating transformation, if $\Gamma(P)$ has the same observable behavior as P. In addition, Γ must enforce the following two conditions:*

– if program P fails to terminate or terminates with an error condition, then $\Gamma(P)$ may or may not terminate;

– otherwise P terminates and $\Gamma(P)$ must terminate and produce the same output as P.

DEFINITION 4.11. Complexity formulas.– *If program P and $\Gamma(P)$ are identical except that $\Gamma(P)$ contains more of property q than P, then $\Gamma(P)$ is more complex than P.*

According to Definition 4.10, an obfuscating transformation adds more of the q property to the initial program to increase its obscurity.

4.7.2. *Types of program obfuscations*

The obfuscation transformations can be classified into the following four categories and can affect many parts of a program (Collberg *et al.* 1997):

– source and/or binary structure;

– control obfuscation (control flow structure);

– data obfuscation (local and global data structures);

– preventive obfuscation that is used to protect from decompilators and debuggers.

The program obfuscations can be performed at different levels:

– layout obfuscation, which transforms a source code into another source code unreadable by humans;

– intermediate-level obfuscation, which transforms a program at intermediate representation (IR) level;

– binary obfuscation, which is performed at binary level to obfuscate the layout and control flow of binary code.

In this chapter, we focus only on binary obfuscation.

4.7.3. *Obfuscation techniques*

Several specific techniques are used to obfuscate a program, as described in more detail in Wroblewski (2002):

– storage and encoding obfuscations that modify the representation of variables: split variables, promote scalars to objects, convert static data to procedure, change encoding and change a local variable to global variable;

– aggregation obfuscation that merges independent data and splits dependent data: merges scalar variables, modifies inheritance relations and split or merge arrays;

– ordering obfuscation: reorder variables, reorder methods and reorder arrays.

There are three groups of control obfuscation methods (Wroblewski 2002):

– computation obfuscation methods that modify the structure of control flow. For example, extending the loop condition (like the addition of conditions that do not change the behavior of a program);

– aggregation obfuscation methods that split and merge fragments of code. For example, inline methods that consist of inserting the complete code of the function when the function is called, rather than generating a function call;

– ordering obfuscation methods that reorder blocks, loops and expressions, with preservation of dependencies.

We describe in section 4.7.5 our obfuscation attack model based on storage and encoding obfuscation techniques and computation obfuscation methods.

4.7.4. Code obfuscation in Android system

Obfuscation techniques are used in the Android platform to protect applications against reverse engineering (Schulz 2012). In order to achieve this protection, the obfuscation methods such as identifier mangling and string obfuscation modify the bytecode during runtime and reduce meta information within the applications. The obtained code is hard to analyze and makes it difficult to have information about the application and its functionalities. Identifiers are names for packages, classes, methods, and fields. Identifier mangling is the act of replacing any identifier with a meaningless string representation while maintaining consistency (the semantics of the source code). These strings do not contain any information about the object or its behavior. The string obfuscation method consists of transforming an arbitrary string into another string using injective invertible function (xor function or encryption). This method reduces the amount of extractable meta information. However, it is defeated by dynamic analysis.

ProGuard (Lafortune 2006), an open-source tool, is integrated in the Android build system. It is applied to obfuscate Android application code by removing unused code and renaming methods, fields and classes. The resulting code is much harder to reverse-engineer.

Allatori (Smardec 2017) is a Java obfuscator developed by the Russian company Smardec. It is used to protect Android applications and to make reverse engineering of the code impossible. It offers protection methods like flow obfuscation, name obfuscation, debug information obfuscation and string encryption. Finally, Allatori does not just obfuscate but is also designed to reduce the size and processing time of Android applications. It is more powerful than ProGuards, but it does not prevent an analyst from disassembling an Android application.

Cavallaro *et al.* (2008) argue that code obfuscation can be employed by malware developers to avoid detection. Cavallaro *et al.* (2007) describe dynamic anti-taint techniques that can be used to obfuscate code and to leak sensitive data.

We study, in the following, the obfuscation techniques used in malware context that can easily defeat dynamic information flow analysis to evade detection of private data leakage in the Android system.

4.7.5. Attack model

The dynamic taint analysis process is summarized in Figure 4.8. First, the dynamic taint tracking system like TaintDroid assigns taint to sensitive data (Device id, contacts, SMS/MMS) (2).

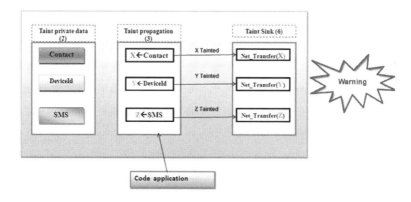

Figure 4.8. *Dynamic taint analysis process without obfuscation attack*

Then, it tracks the propagation of tainted data (3). Finally, it issues warning reports when the tainted data is leaked by malicious applications. This can be detected when sensitive data is used in a taint sink (network interface) (6).

Consider the attack model presented in Figure 4.9. The third-party application is installed by the smartphone user (1). Then, it will be running under a dynamic taint tracking system to detect the transmission of private data to the network. Sensitive data is tainted by the dynamic taint tracking system (2). The developer of the malicious application exploits the limitation of the dynamic taint tracking system such as TaintDroid. The taint propagation rules defined in this system cannot propagate taint in the control flows. The developer interferes in the taint propagation level and uses obfuscation techniques (adding control flows and code encoding) to deceive the taint mechanism. They remove taint of sensitive data that should be tainted (4). Thus, leakage of this data is not detected (5).

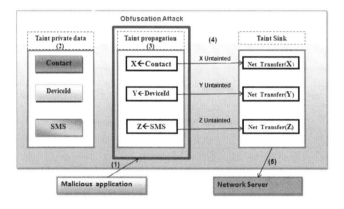

Figure 4.9. *The attack model against dynamic taint analysis*

Next, we present different examples of code obfuscation attacks based on control flows that a dynamic taint tracking system, such as TaintDroid, cannot detect.

4.7.6. *Code obfuscation attacks*

Sarwar *et al.* (2013) introduce the control dependence class of attacks against taint-based data leak protection. They experimentally evaluate the success rates for these attacks to circumvent taint tracking with TaintDroid. We present in this section examples of these obfuscated code attacks based on control dependencies that TaintDroid cannot detect. The taint is not propagated in the control flow statements. The attacker exploits untainted variables that should be tainted to leak private data.

Algorithm 2 presents the first attack. The variable X contains the private data. The attacker obfuscates the code and tries to get each character of X by comparing it with symbols s in *AsciiTable*. He/she stores the right character founded in Y. At the end of the loop, the attacker succeeds in knowing the correct value of the *Private_Data* stored in Y. The variable Y is not tainted because TaintDroid does not propagate taint in the control flows. Thus, Y is leaked through the network connection.

Algorithm 3 presents the second attack. The attacker saves the private data in variable X. Then, he/she reads each character of X and converts it to integer. In the next loop, he/she tries to find the value of the integer by incrementing y. He/she converts the integer to character and concatenates all characters in Y to find the value of X. Thus, Y contains the *Private_Data* value, but it is not tainted because TaintDroid does not track control flow. Therefore, the attacker succeeds in leaking the *Private_Data* value without any warning reports.

Algorithm 2 Code obfuscation attacks 1

$X \leftarrow Private\_Data$
for each $x \in X$ **do**
   for each $s \in AsciiTable$ **do**
      if $(s == x)$ **then**
         $Y \leftarrow Y + s$
      end if
   end for
end for
$Send\_Network\_Data(Y)$

Algorithm 3 Code obfuscation attacks 2

$X \leftarrow Private\_Data$
for each $x \in X$ **do**
   $n \leftarrow CharToInt(x)$
   $y \leftarrow 0$
   for $i = 0$ to n **do**
      $y \leftarrow y + 1$
   end for
   $Y \leftarrow Y + IntToChar(y)$
end for
$Send\_Network\_Data(Y)$

Algorithm 4 presents an obfuscated code attack based on an exception. The variable n contains an integer value that corresponds to the conversion of a character in private data. The attacker raises an exception n times in the try bloc. He/she handles the thrown exception in the catch bloc by incrementing y to achieve the correct value of each character in *Private_Data*. By concatenating the characters, Y contains the value of private data and it is not tainted because TaintDroid does not detect exceptions used in control flow. Thus, an attacker can successfully leak sensitive information by throwing exceptions to control flow. We show, in the following, how our approach can successfully detect these obfuscated code attacks.

4.7.7. Detection of code obfuscation attacks

To launch code obfuscation attacks, the attacker exploits untainted variables that should be tainted. Thus, there is an under-tainting problem, which is defined in section 4.6.1. We use rules that describe the taint propagation presented in section 4.6.2 to solve it and to detect the obfuscated code attacks based on control dependencies. By using these rules, all variables to which a value is assigned in the conditional branch are tainted, whether the branch is taken or not. The taint of these variables reflects the dependency on a condition.

Let us consider the first obfuscated code attack. The variable x is tainted because it belongs to the tainted character string X. Thus, the condition ($x ==$ $TabAsc[\ j]$) is tainted. Our system allows us to propagate the taint in the control flow. Using the first rule, Y is tainted and $Taint(Y) = Taint(x ==$ $TabAsc[\ j]) \oplus Taint(Y + TabAsc[\ j])$. Thus, the leakage of Y that contains the value of private data is detected using our approach.

Algorithm 4 Code obfuscation attacks 3

```
X ← Private_Data
for each x ∈ X  do
    n ← CharToInt(x)
    y ← 0
    while y < n  do
        Try{
        Throw_New_Exception()}
        Catch(Exception e){
        Y ← Y + 1}
    end while
    Y ← Y + IntToChar(y)
end for
Send_Network_Data(Y)
```

In the second obfuscated code attack, the attacker tries to get secret information X. The variable x is tainted because it belongs to the character string X, which is tainted. The result n of converting x to integer is tainted. Thus, the condition ($j = 0$ to n) is tainted. Using the first rule, y is tainted and $Taint(y) = Taint(j = 0$ to $n) \oplus Taint(y + 1)$. In the first loop, the condition x

$\in X$ is tainted. We apply the first rule, Y is tainted and $Taint(Y) = Taint(x \in X) \oplus Taint(Y + (char)y)$. Thus, the attacker cannot succeed in this obfuscated code attack detected using our approach

In the third obfuscated code attack, the attacker exploits exception to launch obfuscated code attacks and to leak sensitive data. The exception is tainted, and its taint depends on the while condition $y < n$. Also, the while condition $(y < n)$ is tainted because the variable n that corresponds to the conversion of a character in private data is tainted. Then, we propagate the exception's taint in the catch block. We apply the first rule to taint y. We obtain $Taint(y) = Taint(exception) \oplus Taint(y + 1)$. Finally, the string Y, which contains the private data, is tainted and $Taint(Y) = Taint(x \in X) \oplus Taint(Y + (char)y)$.

Thus, an attacker cannot leak sensitive information by throwing exceptions to control flow.

4.7.8. Obfuscation code attack tests

We have implemented and run the three obfuscated code attacks based on control dependencies presented in section 4.7.6 to test the effectiveness of our approach in detecting these attacks.

We have tested these attacks using a Nexus One mobile device running Android OS version 2.3 modified to track control flows.

We use the Traceview tool to evaluate the performance of these attacks. We present both the inclusive and exclusive times. Exclusive time is the time spent in the method. Inclusive time is the time spent in the method plus the time spent in any called functions. We install the TaintDroidNotify application to enable notifications on the device when tainted data is leaked.

Let us consider the first obfuscated code attack (see Figure 4.10). The first loop is used to fill the table of ASCII characters. The attacker tries to get the private data (user contact name = "Graa Mariem") by comparing it with symbols of the ASCII table in the second loop. The taint of the user contact name is $((u4)0 \times 00000002)$.

```
String X = contact_name;
String Y="";
char[] TabAsc;
 int k=0;
TabAsc = new char [96];

while (codeAsc < 0x80) {

    for (column = 0; column < 16; column++) {
        TabAsc[k] = codeAsc;
        codeAsc++;
        k++;
    }
    row++;
}

for (int i = 0;i< X.length(); i++)
{
    char x=X.charAt(i);

    for (int j=1;j<TabAsc.length;j++)
    {
        if (x==TabAsc[j])
        Y=Y+TabAsc[j];
    }

}

NetworkTransfer(Y);
```

Figure 4.10. *Code obfuscation attack 1*

The variable x is tainted because it belongs to the tainted character string X. Thus, the condition ($x == TabAsc[j]$) is tainted. Our system allows us to propagate the taint in the control flow. Using the first rule, Y is tainted and $Taint(Y) = Taint(x == TabAsc[j]) \oplus Taint(Y + TabAsc[j])$. We can show in the log file given in Figure 4.11(a) that Y is tainted with the same taint as the user contact name. A notification appears, reporting the leakage of Y that contains the value of private data. The execution of the first algorithm takes 88 ms as Inclusive CPU Time using TaintDroid modified to track control flows and 36 ms in unmodified Android.

The second obfuscated code attack is illustrated in Figure 4.12. The attacker tries to get a secret information X that is the IMEI of the smartphone. The taint of the IMEI is ($(u4)0 \times 00000400$). The variable x is tainted because it belongs to the character string X, which is tainted. The result n of converting x to integer is tainted. Thus, the condition ($j = 0$ *to* n) is tainted. Using the first rule, y is tainted and $Taint(y) = Taint(j = 0$ *to* $n) \oplus Taint(y + 1)$. In the first loop, the condition $x \in X$ is tainted. We apply the first rule, Y is tainted and $Taint(Y) = Taint(x \in X) \oplus Taint(Y + (char)y)$. This result is shown in the log file shown in Figure 4.11(b). The leakage of the private data event is presented in the notification. The execution of the second algorithm takes 101 ms as Exclusive CPU Time using TaintDroid modified to track control flows and 20 ms in unmodified Android. The execution time in our approach is more important because it includes the time of the taint propagation in the control flow.

```
W/dalvikvm( 1209): TaintLog: OSNetworkSystem.write(10.35.131.42) received data with tag
0x2 data=[00
            Mariem Graa]
```

(a)

```
W/dalvikvm(  712): TaintLog: OSNetworkSystem.write(10.35.131.42) received data with
 tag 0x400 data=[00354957033679070]
```

(b)

```
W/dalvikvm(  488): TaintLog: OSNetworkSystem.write(10.35.131.42) received data with tag
0x10008 data=[00
W/dalvikvm(  488): 3627890380]
```

(c)

Figure 4.11. *Log files of code obfuscation attacks*

```
String X = Get_IMEI();
String Y="";
 for (int i = 0;i<X.length(); i++)
 {
        char x=X.charAt(i);
        int n =x;
        int y=0;
            for (int j=0;j<n;j++)
            {
                  y=y+1;
            }

        char c = (char) y;

        Y=Y+c;
 }

 NetworkTransfer(Y);
```

Figure 4.12. *Code obfuscation attack 2*

The third obfuscated code attack is illustrated in Figure 4.13. The attacker exploits exception to launch obfuscated code attacks and to leak sensitive data (phone number). The division by zero throws an *ArithmeticException*. This exception is tainted and its taint depends on the while condition $y < n$. Also, the while condition ($y < n$) is tainted because the variable n that corresponds to the conversion of a character in *Phone_Number* is tainted. TaintDroid does not assign taint to exception. We define taint of exception (*Taint_Exception* = $((u4)0 \times 00010000)$). Then, we propagate exception's taint in the catch block. We apply the first rule to taint y. We obtain $Taint(y)$ = $Taint(exception) \oplus Taint(y + 1)$. Finally, the string Y, which contains the private data, is tainted and $Taint(Y) = Taint(x \in X) \oplus Taint(Y + (char)y)$. In the log file shown in Figure 4.11(c), we show that the taint of Y is the combination of the taint of the exception $(((u4)0 \times 00010000))$ and the taint of the phone number $(((u4)0 \times 00000008))$. A warning message appears indicating the leakage of sensitive information. The execution of the third algorithm takes 1,385 ms as Inclusive CPU Time using TaintDroid modified to track control flows and 1,437 ms in unmodified Android. This difference is due to the taint propagation in the control flow. The sizes of control flow graphs obtained of the three algorithms are about 1,200 bytes.

```
String X = Phone_Number;
String Y="";
 for (int i = 0;i<X.length(); i++)
 {
     char x=X.charAt(i);
     int n =x;
     int y=0;
     int w;
     int v1=2;
     int t=0;
         while (y<n)
             {

             try {
                 w = v1/t;

                 } catch (ArithmeticException e) {

                 y = y+1;

                 }

             }

         char c = (char) y;
             Y=Y+c;
 }

NetworkTransfer(Y);
```

Figure 4.13. *Code obfuscation attack 3*

4.8. Detection of side channel attacks based on data tainting in Android systems

Malicious applications aim to steal personal data that is stored in the device or potentially available through side channels such as timing and storage channels. Side channel attacks (Cai and Chen 2011, Schlegel *et al.* 2011, Jana and Shmatikov 2012) exploit the use of medium to infer private information (SMS, contacts, location, phone number, pictures, etc.) by analyzing side channels. Sarwar *et al.* (Babil *et al.* 2013) propose side channel attacks such as bypass timing, bitmap cache, meta data and graphical properties attacks that create taint free variables from tainted objects to circumvent the dynamic taint analysis security technique. Kim *et al.* (2015) utilize a screen bitmap memory attack proposed by Sarwar *et al.* to propose a collection system that retrieves sensitive information through a screenshot image. The Android security model is based on application sandboxing, application signing and a permission framework. The side channel attack runs in its own process, with its own instance of the Dalvik virtual machine. It accesses side channels that are a public medium. Consequently, the application sandboxing technique cannot detect these attacks. The malicious application that implements side channel attacks is digitally signed with a certificate. Therefore, it can be installed on Android systems. The standard Android permission system controls access to sensitive data but does not ensure end-to-end security because it does not track information flow through side channels. As the core security mechanisms of Android cannot detect side channel attacks, new approaches that extend the Android OS have been proposed. XManDroid (Bugiel *et al.* 2011), a security framework, extends the monitoring mechanism of Android to detect side channel attacks such as Soundcomber. However, it cannot detect a subset of side channels such as the timing channel, processor frequency and free space on filesystem. TaintDroid (Enck *et al.* 2010), an extension of the Android mobile phone platform, uses dynamic taint analysis to detect a direct buffer attack. The dynamic analysis approach (Enck *et al.* 2010, Hornyack *et al.* 2011, Spreitzenbarth *et al.* 2015) defined in smartphones cannot detect software side channel attacks presented in Babil *et al.* (2013) and Kim *et al.* (2015). Thus, we modify the Android OS to detect software side channel attacks that try to bypass detection mechanisms based on dynamic taint analysis. We propagate taint in timing, memory cache and GPU channels and in meta data (file and clipboard length) using taint propagation rules. We present in the following side channel class of attacks that TaintDroid cannot detect.

4.8.1. *Target threat model*

Consider the attack model presented in Figure 4.14. The adversary's goal is to extract sensitive data from the Android third-party system. He/she develops a malicious application that will be executed on this system and sends sensitive data through the network to a system that the adversary controls. We assume that the smartphone user installs the malicious application on their phone.

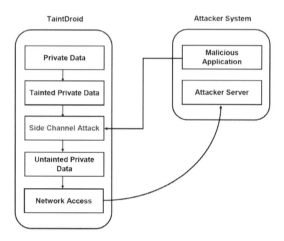

Figure 4.14. *Target threat model*

Also, we assume that he/she uses a dynamic taint tracking system such as TaintDroid to protect his/her private data. Therefore, the malicious application will be executed under this system. The adversary exploits the limitation of the dynamic taint analysis mechanism that it cannot propagate taint through side channels. He/she interferes in the taint propagation level and removes the taint of sensitive data that should be tainted. Therefore, this data will be leaked without being detected. Next, we present different examples of side channel attacks that a dynamic taint tracking system such as TaintDroid cannot detect.

4.8.2. *Side channel attacks*

Sarwar *et al.* (Babil *et al.* 2013) present side channel class of attacks such as bypass timing, bitmap cache, meta data and graphical properties attacks using a medium that might be overlooked by the taint-checking mechanism to extract sensitive data. They test and evaluate the success rate and time of these attacks with the TaintDroid system. We are interested in these attacks because they are the most important attacks presented by Sarwar *et al.* and the other attacks are already detected (Graa *et al.* 2014). We present in this section examples of these side channel attacks.

4.8.2.1. *Timing attack*

The timing attack is an example of a side channel attack in which the attacker attempts to compromise a cryptosystem by analyzing the time taken to gain information about the keys. A similar concept can be used to leak tainted data when running a program with taint analysis approach. Algorithm 5 presents the timing attack in the taint tracking system. This attack exploits the system clock that is not tainted. The *sleep*() function suspends the execution of the current program until the waiting period, which depends on the value of a tainted variable, has elapsed. Therefore, the difference in time readings before and after a waiting period indicates the value of sensitive data. This difference is not tainted because there is no taint propagation in the system clock. Consequently, it can be assigned to the taint-free output variable and leaked through the network without being detected.

Algorithm 5 Timing Attack

$X_{Tainted} \leftarrow Private\_Data$
$n \leftarrow CharToInt(X)$
$StatTime \leftarrow ReadSystemTime()$
$Sleep(n)$
$StopTime \leftarrow ReadSystemTime()$
$y \leftarrow (StopTime - StartTime)$
$Y_{Untainted} \leftarrow IntToChar(y)$
$Send\_Network\_Data(Y_{Untainted})$

4.8.2.2. *Cache memory attack*

The cache memory attack is another example of a side channel attack that can be used to extract sensitive data. This attack exploits the fact that graphical output can be obtained from a cache of the currently displayed screen. Algorithm 6 presents the bitmap cache attack. The graphical widget contains the private data. The attacker successfully extracts it from the bitmap cache without any warning reports because the taint is not propagated in the cache memory. He/she sends the bitmap data to a cloud and uses the optical character recognition (OCR) techniques (Kay 2007) to read the value of sensitive data.

Algorithm 6 Bitmap Cache Attack

$X_{Tainted} \leftarrow Private\_Data$
$W \leftarrow CreateNewTextWidget()$
$B \leftarrow CreateNewBitmap()$
$WriteText(X_{Tainted} \rightarrow W)$
$B \leftarrow CaptureBitmapCache(W)$
$Y \leftarrow OpticalCharacterRecognition(B)$
$Send\_Network\_Data(Y_{Untainted})$

4.8.2.3. *Bitmap pixel attack*

An attacker can extract private data by exploiting bitmap cache pixels as shown in Algorithm 7. He/she modifies an arbitrarily chosen pixel to represent the private data value. Then, he/she reads the value contained in this pixel at specific coordinates.

Algorithm 7 Bitmap Pixel Attack

$X_{Tainted} \leftarrow Private\_Data$
$B \leftarrow CreateNewBitmap()$
$SetPixel([10;10], X_{Tainted} \rightarrow B)$
$Y_{Untainted} \leftarrow GetPixel(B;[10;10])$
$Send\_Network\_Data(Y_{Untainted})$

4.8.2.4. *Meta data attacks*

Taint analysis systems such as TaintDroid associate taint with the object containing sensitive data. However, these systems do not propagate taint to object size. We present side channel attacks that exploit meta data to evade taint tracking.

4.8.2.5. *File length attack*

Algorithm 8 File Length Attack

$X_{Tainted} \leftarrow Private\_Data$
$F \leftarrow CreateNewFileHandle()$
$z \leftarrow 0$
while $z < X_{Tainted}$ **do**
    $WriteOneByte(F)$
    $z \leftarrow z + 1$
end while
$Y_{Untainted} \leftarrow ReadFileLength(F)$
$Send\_Network\_Data(Y_{Untainted})$

As the file size is not tainted, an attacker can exploit this meta data to leak sensitive data, as shown in Algorithm 8. Each character in private data is represented by an arbitrary file size. One byte is written to a file until its size equals the character private data value. Then, the attacker obtains the file size, which corresponds to the sensitive data without any warning reports.

4.8.2.6. *Clipboard length attack*

An attack similar to the file length attack can be performed if an application required a clipboard to exchange data. In the clipboard length attack, the size of the file is replaced with the size of the content of the clipboard, as shown in Algorithm 9.

Algorithm 9 Clipboard Length Attack
$X_{Tainted} \leftarrow Private\_Data$
$z \leftarrow 0$
while $z < X_{Tainted}$ **do**
    $WriteOneByte(Clipboard)$
    $z \leftarrow z + 1$
end while
$Y_{Untainted} \leftarrow ReadFileLength(Clipboard)$
$Send\_Network\_Data(Y_{Untainted})$

4.8.2.7. *Graphics processing unit attacks*

We are interested in a graphics processing unit class of attacks that exploits the properties of a graphical element to evade the taint tracking mechanism.

For example, in the text scaling attack presented in Algorithm 10, the attacker sets an arbitrary property of a graphical widget (the scaling) with the value of private data. Then, he/she extracts and sends this property through the network.

Algorithm 10 Text Scaling Attack
$X_{Tainted} \leftarrow Private\_data$
$T \leftarrow TextViewWidget()$
$T \leftarrow SetTextScalingValue(X_{Tainted})$
$Y_{Untainted} \leftarrow GetTextScalingValue(T)$
$Send\_Network\_Data(Y_{Untainted})$

4.8.3. *Propagation rules for detecting side channel attacks*

Our approach is based on dynamic taint analysis to overcome side channel attacks as attacks presented in section 4.8.2. We specify a set of formally defined rules that propagate taint in different side channels to detect leakage of sensitive data.

4.8.3.1. *Timing side channel propagation rule*

The timing attack exploits the system clock, which is available without tainting. The attacker reads the system clock after the waiting period. We define *Timing Context_Taint*, which is activated when the argument (*arg*) of the *Sleep*() function is tainted.

Sleep(arg) ∧ Istainted(arg) ⇒ Activate (Timing_Context_Taint)

In this case, we propagate taint in timing side channel. Therefore, the system clock is tainted and the attacker cannot leak sensitive information through timing side channel.

Isactivated(Timing_Contex_Taint) ⇒ Taint(system clock)

4.8.3.2. *Memory cache side channel propagation rules*

The bitmap cache attack exploits the cache memory of the currently displayed screen. The attacker captures the bitmap cache of a graphical object containing private data. We define *Bitmap_Context_Taint*, which is activated when the graphical object is tainted.

Istainted(graphical object) ⇒ Activate(Bitmap_Context_Taint)

In this case, we propagate taint in the bitmap cache side channel and associate taint with the bitmap object.

Isactivated(Bitmap_Context_Taint) ⇒ Taint(Bitmap)

For the bitmap pixel attack, the attacker exploits the bitmap cache pixels that are modified to get the private data value. We define *Pixels_Context_Taint*, which is activated when the argument parameter of the set pixel function is tainted. Therefore, an arbitrarily chosen pixel is changed to represent the value of the private data

setPixel(arg) ∧ Istainted(arg) ⇒ Activate (Pixels_Context_Taint)

In this case, we assign taint to the return value of *getPixel*() function.

Isactivated(Pixels_Context_Taint) ⇒ Taint(return_getPixel)

By using these memory cache side channel propagation rules, the attacker cannot leak sensitive information through bitmap cache memory.

4.8.3.3. *Meta data propagation rule*

The meta data attacks exploit the size of the object which is available without tainting. We define *Meta_Data_Context_Taint*, which is activated when the application gets private data.

get_private_data() ⇒ *Activate (Meta_Data_Context_Taint)*

In this case, we define the meta data propagation rule and associate taint with the return value of the *length*() method.

Isactivated(Meta_Data_Context_Taint) ⇒ Taint(length_object)

Therefore, by applying the meta data propagation rule, the attacker cannot leak sensitive information using meta data.

4.8.3.4. *GPU propagation rule*

The graphics processing unit class of considered attacks exploits the properties of the graphical elements (scaling, text size, etc.). The attacker sets an arbitrary property of a graphical widget to the value of private data. Therefore, we define *GPU_Context_Taint*, which is activated when the argument parameter of the *Set property* function is tainted.

setProperty(arg) ∧ Istainted(arg) ⇒ Activate (GPU_Context_Taint)

In this case, we assign taint to the return value *getProperty*() function to prevent this attack.

Isactivated(GPU_Context_Taint) ⇒ Taint(getProperty())

By using the GPU propagation rule, the attacker cannot leak sensitive information by exploiting properties of the graphical elements.

4.8.4. *Implementation*

We modify the TaintDroid system to implement the taint propagation rules defined in section 4.8.3. Figure 4.15 presents the modified components (blue components) to detect side channel attacks in TaintDroid system. We modify the Dalvik virtual machine to detect timing attacks. We implement the memory cache and the GPU propagation rules at the framework level to prevent bitmap cache and the GPU class of attacks. We instrument the core libraries to associate taint with meta data.

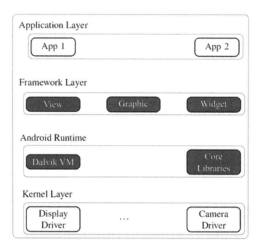

Figure 4.15. *The modified components (blue) to detect side channel attacks. For a color version of this figure, see www.iste.co.uk/tounsi/cyber.zip*

4.8.4.1. *Timing attack detection*

The *VMT hread_sleep*(*constu*4 * *args, JValue * pResult*) function in Dalvik virtual machine native code suspends the execution of the current thread until the value of a tainted variable has elapsed. Then, the attacker reads the system clock after the waiting period. We test the argument of *VMT hread_sleep*() to implement *Timing_Context_Taint*. We modify the *currentTimeMillis*(*constu*4 * *args, JValue * pResult*) function in the Dalvik virtual machine native code to propagate taint in the system clock if *Timing_Context_Taint* is activated. Therefore, the difference in time readings before and after a waiting period that indicates the value of sensitive data is tainted.

4.8.4.2. *Cache memory attack detection*

We verify if the graphical object contains a private data to implement the *GPU_Taint_Context*. All of the graphical objects defined in the Android framework extend the view. Therefore, we check if the view is tainted. The *getDrawingCache*() function in the view class creates and returns a bitmap object that contains the private data. Therefore, we taint the return value of the *getDrawingCache*() function if the *GPU_Taint_Context* is activated. For the bitmap pixel attack, the bitmap is created first and then modified by exploiting the bitmap cache pixels. We verify if the argument parameter of the set pixel function in the bitmap class (Graphic package) is tainted to implement *Pixels_Taint_Context*. In this case, we assign taint to the return value of the *getPixel*() function in the bitmap class.

4.8.4.3. *Meta data attacks detection*

TaintDroid implements taint source placement where privacy sensitive information types are acquired (low-bandwidth sensors, e.g. location meter and accelerometer; high-bandwidth sensors e.g. microphone and camera; information databases, e.g. address books and SMS messages and device identifiers, e.g. SIM card identifiers (IMSI, ICC-ID) and device identifier (IMEI)). In each taint source placement, we implement *Meta_Data_Context_Taint*, which is activated if private data is acquired. To detect the meta data class of attacks, we associate taint with the return value of the *length*() method at libcore level in File and String classes if *Meta_Data_Context_Taint* is activated.

4.8.4.4. *Graphics processing unit attacks detection*

To launch the graphics processing unit class of considered attacks, the attacker sets an arbitrary property of a graphical widget with the value of private data. Therefore, we verify if the argument parameter of the SetProperty (*SetTextScalingValue* function) in graphical widget class is tainted to implement *GPU_Taint_Context*. Then, we taint the return value of *getProperty*(*GetTextScaling Value* function) if *GPU_Taint_Context* is activated to prevent this attack.

4.8.5. *Evaluation*

We install our system in a Nexus 4 mobile device running Android OS version 4.3. We analyze a number of Android applications to test the effectiveness of our approach. Then, we evaluate the false positives that could occur. We study our taint tracking approach overhead using standard benchmarks.

4.8.5.1. *Effectiveness*

To evaluate the effectiveness of our approach, we analyze the 100 most popular free Android applications downloaded from the Android Market (Android 2017). These applications are categorized as games, shopping, device information, social, tools, weather, music and audio, maps and navigation, photography, productivity, lifestyle, reference, travel, and sports and entertainment applications. We observe that all applications use bitmap cache channel, 50% use timing channel, 30% use GPU channel (get and set graphic properties) and 20% use meta data (file and clipboard sizes). We found that 66% of these applications manipulate confidential data. Our approach has successfully propagated taint in side channels and detected leakage of tainted sensitive data by checking the content of network packets sent by applications.

(a)   (b)   (c)

Figure 4.16. *Leakage of private data through the bitmap cache side channels*

We found that 35% of applications leaked private data through timing and bitmap cache side channels. For example, the IMEI application takes and sends a screenshot of IMEI information through the network by exploiting the bitmap cache side channel (see Figure 4.16 (a)). Other applications copy the SIM card and device information from the screen to the clipboard and send them through the network, SMS or Bluetooth using the bitmap cache side channel (see Figure 4.16 (c)). Some applications get the drawing cache to implicitly leak private data. For example, the IMEI Analyzer application gets the drawing cache to implicitly send the IMEI outside the smartphone (see Figure 4.16 (b)). Games applications implicitly leaked the devices' ID through the timing side channel at the time of score sharing. In addition, we successfully implemented and detected side channels class of attacks presented in section 4.8.2.

4.8.5.2. False positives

We found that 35 of the 100 tested Android applications leaked sensitive data through side channels. We detected three device information (Android id, device serial number, device model, phone number, etc.) leakage vulnerabilities. Also, we detected that the IMEI is transmitted outside of smartphone by two different forms (digital and by another application that takes a screenshot of IMEI). In addition, we detected four SIM card information leakage vulnerabilities (SIM provider's country, SIM contacts, SimState, etc.). As the user is sent this information by email, SMS or Bluetooth, we cannot treat these applications as privacy violators. Therefore, our approach generates 9% of false positives.

4.8.5.3. Performance

We use the CaffeineMark (Corporation 1997) to study our approach overhead. The CaffeineMark scores roughly correlate with the number of Java instructions executed per second and do not significantly depend on the amount of memory in the system or on the speed of the computer's disk drives or Internet connection. Figure 4.17 presents the execution time results of a Java microbenchmark.

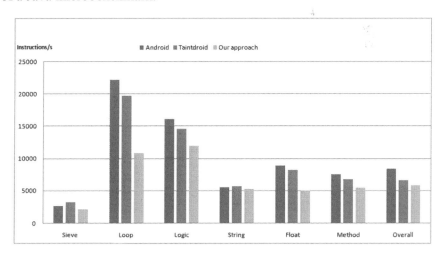

Figure 4.17. *Microbenchmark of Java overhead. For a color version of this figure, see www.iste.co.uk/tounsi/cyber.zip*

The unmodified Android system had an overall score of 8,401 Java instructions executed per second, and the TaintDroid system measured 6,610 Java instructions executed per second. Therefore, TaintDroid has a 21% overhead with respect to the unmodified Android system. Our approach had an overall score of 5,873 Java instructions executed per second. Therefore, our approach has a 9% overhead with respect to the TaintDroid system. It gives a lower execution speed because we propagate taint in side channels. However, the overhead given by our approach is acceptable in comparison to the one obtained by TaintDroid.

4.9. Tracking information flow in Android systems approaches comparison: summary

In this section, we discuss tracking information flow in Android systems approaches. The features on which we are based to make this comparison are summarized in Table 4.7.

We note that most static analysis approaches (Fuchs *et al.* 2009, Enck *et al.* 2011, Kim *et al.* 2012, Arzt *et al.* 2014, Gibler *et al.* 2012, Dhavale and Lokhande 2016) can track explicit and control flows but cannot consider code obfuscation and side channel attacks. In addition, these static analysis systems generate a high number of false positives. We reported that dynamic taint analysis approaches (Enck *et al.* 2010, Hornyack *et al.* 2011, Yan and Yin 2012, Shankar *et al.* 2017, Qian *et al.* 2014, Wang and Shieh 2015) only detect explicit flow in java or native code but do not detect control flow. Therefore, they cannot detect code obfuscation and side channel attacks based on control dependencies in Android systems and they generate false negatives. Also, we note that most hybrid approaches (Spreitzenbarth *et al.* 2015, Graa *et al.* 2016) cannot detect side channel attacks. In this chapter, our proposed approach allows us to track explicit and control flows in java and native android applications code. Also, we can detect code obfuscation and side channel attacks by using taint propagations rules.

Year	System	Technique	Description	Data flow	Java or native code	Detect obfuscation and side channel attacks	False +/−
2009	ScanDoid (Fuchs et al. 2009)	S.A	Extract security specifications + Check data flows + Security certification	Explicit and control flows	Java code	Not tested	Not evaluated
2011	ded (Enck et al. 2011)	S.A	Automated tests and manual inspection	Explicit and control flows	Java code	Not detected	False negatives and positives
2012	ScanDal (Kim et al. 2012)	S.A	Abstract interpretation + Path-insensitive + Context-sensitive analysis + Flow-sensitive and flow-insensitive analyses	Explicit and control flows	Java code	Not tested	False positives
2012	AndroidLeaks (Gibler et al. 2012)	S.T.A	- Create a call graph + A reachability analysis + Permission mapping	Explicit and control flows	Java code	Not tested	False positives
2012	LeakMiner (Yang and Yang 2012)	S.T.A	- Sensitive data identification - Call graph construction and pointer analysis	Explicit flow	Java code	Not tested	False positives
2014	FlowDroid (Arzt et al. 2014)	S.T.A	- Fully context, flow, field and object + Modeling the complete Android life cycle	Explicit and control flows	Java and native code	Excluded	False positives

Year	System	Technique	Description	Data flow	Java or native code	Detect obfuscation and side channel attacks	False +/−
2015	DroidSafe (Gordon *et al.* 2015)	S.T.A	Model callback context, life cycle events, data flows, heap object instantiations, native methods and aliasing	Explicit flow	Java and native code	Not detected	False positives
2016	Comnoid (Dhavale and Lokhande 2016)	S.T.A	Based on FlowDroid + Analyzing the inter-app communication	Explicit and control flows	Java and native code	Not tested	Not evaluated
2010	TaintDroid (Enck *et al.* 2010)	D.T.A	Dynamic taint tracking and analysis system + Leverage Androids virtualized execution environment + Monitor the behavior of Android app	Explicit flow	Java code	Not detected	False positives and negatives
2011	AppFence (Hornyack *et al.* 2011)	D.T.A	- Dynamic taint tracking and analysis system + Substituting shadow data + Blocking network transmissions	Explicit flow	Java code	Not detected	False negatives

Year	System	Technique	Description	Data flow	Java or native code	Detect obfuscation and side channel attacks	False +/−
2014	Graa et al. (2012), Graa et al. (2014)	S.T.A + D.T.A	Taint propagation rules + Information flow tracking	Explicit and control flows	Java code	Obfuscation code attacks detected	False positives
2017	AndroTaint (Shankar et al. 2017)	D.T.A	- Training phase for feature extraction – The analysis phase for automatic tagging and tainting	Explicit flow	Java and native code	Not detected	Less false positive and false negative
2012	DroidScope (Yan and Yin 2012)	D.T.A	Reconstructs OS level and DVM level information	Explicit flow	Java and native code	Not detected	Not tested
2014	NDroid (Qian et al. 2014)	D.T.A	Virtualization + Instruction tracer + DVM and system lib hook + Taint propagation	Explicit flow	Java and native code	Not detected	False negatives
2015	Droit (Wang and Shieh 2015)	D.T.A	Switching between object and instruction levels	Explicit flow	Java and native code	Not detected	False negative and false positives

Year	System	Technique	Description	Data flow	Java or native code	Detect obfuscation and side channel attacks	False +/−
2015	DroidBox (Spreitzenbarth et al. 2015)	S.T.A + D.T.A	Sandbox, tainting, machine learning techniques	Explicit and control flows	Java and native code	Obfuscation attacks detected	False positives
2016	Graa et al. 2016 approach (Graa et al. 2016)	S.T.A + D.T.A	Based on Graa et al. 2014 approach + Instrument native libraries + Hook the JNI call bridge + Virtual machine introspection + Hook a selected system call	Explicit and control flows	Java and native code	Obfuscation code attacks detected	False positives
2017	TaintMan (You et al. 2017)	S.T.A + D.T.A	Statical instrumentation + Reconstruction of a new execution environment + Android runtime analysis	Explicit and control flows	Java code	Not tested	No false positives
2017	Graa et al. 2017 approach (Graa et al. 2017)	D.T.A	Side channel propagation rules	Explicit and control flows	Java code	Side channel attacks detected	False positives

Table 4.7. *Tracking information flow in Android systems approaches comparison*

4.10. Conclusion and highlights

Android systems use data of a sensitive nature. Many mechanisms are defined to control access to and the manipulation of private information. We have presented an overview and analysis of current approaches, techniques and mechanisms used to ensure security properties in Android systems. We observe that Android system security is an area of growing interest and research work. We note that third-party applications are responsible for most attacks in Android systems. These applications use excessive permissions, privilege escalation and advertisement libraries to access private data. The access control approaches define policy rules. However, creating useful and usable policies is difficult. Thus, future research must balance between security and usability. These approaches control access to sensitive information but do not ensure end-to-end security because they do not track the propagation of input data in the application. However, third-party applications exploit information flow for leaking private data. The faking sensitive information approach gives bogus private information. This can disrupt the execution of applications. One possible enhancement is to provide more contextual information to justify the need for the access and to help users make the decision. The static and dynamic taint analysis approaches implemented in Android systems allow us to detect data leakage. These techniques are useful but have limitations. The dynamic taint analysis approaches such as Taintdroid and AppFence track the information flow in real time and control the handling of private data. However, they cannot detect control flows and they are limited by scalability. These approaches and most static analysis approaches cannot detect code obfuscation attacks based on control dependencies in Android systems. Therefore, hybrid approaches enhance dynamic taint analysis by propagating taint along control dependencies using static analysis in Android systems. Most tracking information flows do not consider native code. We show in this chapter that malicious Android applications can exploit native code to leak sensitive data. In addition, these approaches dot not propagate taint in side channels. Thus, an attacker can use a covert channel to obtain private information. In this chapter, we have proposed an approach that uses the static analysis to guide the dynamic analysis in Android systems. We track information flow in java and native Android applications code. Using our approach, we can detect code obfuscation and side channel attacks exploiting control flow and protecting sensitive information.

4.11. References

AhnLab, I. (2012). Ahnlab reports the analysis of the best apps in the android market. Available: http://www.businesswire.com/news/home/20120430005670/ en/AhnLabReports-Analysis-Apps-Android-Market.

Aho, A.V. and Ullman, J.D. (1972). *The Theory of Parsing, Translation, and Compiling*. Prentice-Hall, Inc.

Aho, A.V., Sethi, R., and Ullman, J.D. (1986). *Compilers: Principles, Techniques, and Tools*. Addison-Wesley Longman Publishing Co., Inc., Boston, MA.

Allen, F.E. (1970). Control flow analysis. *ACM Sigplan Notices*, 5(7), 1–19.

Amighi, A., de Carvalho Gomes, P., Gurov, D., and Huisman, M. (2012). Provably correct control-flow graphs from java programs with exceptions. *Formal Verication of Object-oriented Software, Volume 26 of Karlsruhe Reports in Informatics, October 2011*. Karlsruhe Institute of Technology, Germany, pp 31–48.

Android (2017). Android. Available: http://www.android.com/.

Arzt, S., Rasthofer, S., Fritz, C., Bodden, E., Bartel, A., Klein, J., Le Traon, Y., Octeau, D., and McDaniel, P. (2014). Flowdroid: precise context, flow, field, objectsensitive and lifecycle-aware taint analysis for android apps. *Proceedings of the 35th Annual ACM SIGPLAN Conference on Programming Language Design and Implementation (PLDI 2014)*. ACM, pp. 259–269.

Babil, G.S., Mehani, O., Boreli, R., and Kaafar, M.-A. (2013). On the effectiveness of dynamic taint analysis for protecting against private information leaks on androidbased devices. *2013 International Conference on Security and Cryptography (SECRYPT)*. IEEE, pp. 1–8.

Backes, M., Gerling, S., Hammer, C., Maffei, M., and Styp-Rekowsky, P. (2012). Appguard-real-time policy enforcement for third-party applications. *Universitats- und Landesbibliothek, Postfach 151141, 66041 Saarbracken*, Technical Report, Available: http://scidok.sulb.uni-saarland.de/volltexte/2012/ 4902.

Bao, T., Zheng, Y., Lin, Z., Zhang, X., and Xu, D. (2010). Strict control dependence and its effect on dynamic information flow analyses. *Proceedings of the 19th International Symposium on Software Testing and Analysis*. ACM, pp. 13–24.

Bell, D.E. and LaPadula, L.J. (1976). Secure computer system: unified exposition and multics interpretation, Technical report, DTIC Document. Available: http://bench.chainfire.eu/.

Beres, Y. and Dalton, C. (2003). Dynamic label binding at run-time. *Proceedings of the 2003 Workshop on New Security Paradigms*. ACM, pp. 39–46.

Beresford, A.R., Rice, A., Skehin, N., and Sohan, R. (2011). Mockdroid: trading privacy for application functionality on smartphones. *Proceedings of the 12th Workshop on Mobile Computing Systems and Applications*. ACM, pp. 49–54.

Biba, K.J. (1977). Integrity considerations for secure computer systems, Technical report, DTIC Document.

Blasing, T., Batyuk, L., Schmidt, A.-D., Camtepe, S.A., and Albayrak, S. (2010). An android application sandbox system for suspicious software detection. *2010 5th International Conference on Malicious and Unwanted Software (MALWARE)*. IEEE, pp. 55–62.

Brown, J. and Knight Jr, T. (2001). A minimal trusted computing base for dynamically ensuring secure information flow. Project Aries TM-015. Technical report, MIT.

Bugiel, S., Davi, L., Dmitrienko, A., Fischer, T., and Sadeghi, A.-R. (2011). Xman-droid: a new android evolution to mitigate privilege escalation attacks. Technische Universität Darmstadt, Technical Report TR-2011-04.

Burguera, I., Zurutuza, U., and Nadjm-Tehrani, S. (2011). Crowdroid: behaviour-based malware detection system for android. *Proceedings of the 1st ACM Workshop on Security and Privacy in Smartphones and Mobile Devices*. ACM, pp. 15–26.

Cai, L. and Chen, H. (2011). Touchlogger: inferring keystrokes on touch screen from smartphone motion. *HotSec*, 11, 9–9.

Cavallaro, L., Saxena, P., and Sekar, R. (2007). *Anti-taint-analysis: Practical Evasion Techniques Against Information Flow Based Malware Defense*. Stony Brook University, Stony Brook, New York.

Cavallaro, L., Saxena, P., and Sekar, R. (2008). On the limits of information flow techniques for malware analysis and containment. *Detection of Intrusions and Malware, and Vulnerability Assessment*. Springer, pp. 143–163.

Cheng, W., Zhao, Q., Yu, B., and Hiroshige, S. (2006). Tainttrace: efficient flow tracing with dynamic binary rewriting. *Proceedings. 11th IEEE Symposium on Computers and Communications (ISCC'06)*. IEEE, pp. 749–754.

Chess, B. and McGraw, G. (2004). Static analysis for security. *Security & Privacy, IEEE*, 2(6), 76–79.

Chin, E., Felt, A.P., Greenwood, K., and Wagner, D. (2011). Analyzing inter-application communication in android. *Proceedings of the 9th International Conference on Mobile Systems, Applications, and Services*. ACM, pp. 239–252.

Chow, J., Pfaff, B., Garfinkel, T., Christopher, K., and Rosenblum, M. (2004). Understanding data lifetime via whole system simulation. *Proceedings of the 13th Conference on USENIX Security Symposium Volume 13, SSYM'04.* USENIX Association, Berkeley, CA, pp. 22–22.

Clause, J., Li, W., and Orso, A. (2007). Dytan: a generic dynamic taint analysis framework. *Proceedings of the 2007 International Symposium on Software Testing and Analysis.* ACM, pp. 196–206.

Cole, R. and Waugh, R. (2012). Top 'free Android apps' secretly leak users' private contact lists' to advertising companies. Available: http://www.dailymail.co.uk/sciencetech/article-2110599/.

Collberg, C., Thomborson, C., and Low, D. (1997). A taxonomy of obfuscating transformations, Technical report, Department of Computer Science, University of Auckland, New Zealand.

Collberg, C., Thomborson, C., and Low, D. (1998). Manufacturing cheap, resilient, and stealthy opaque constructs. *Proceedings of the 25th ACM SIGPLAN-SIGACT Symposium on Principles of Programming Languages.* ACM, pp. 184–196.

Conti, M., Nguyen, V., and Crispo, B. (2011). Crepe: context-related policy enforcement for android. *Proceedings of the 13th International Conference on Information Security (Berlin, Heidelberg, 2011), ISC'10,* Springer-Verlag, pp. 331–345.

Corporation, P.S. (1997). Caffeinemark 3.0. Available: http://www.benchmarkhq.ru/cm30/.

Cox, J. (2016). Improved partial instrumentation for dynamic taint analysis in the JVM, PhD thesis, University of California, Los Angeles.

Crandall, J.R., Wu, S.F., and Chong, F.T. (2006). Minos: architectural support for protecting control data. *ACM Transactions on Architecture and Code Optimization (TACO),* 3(4), 359–389.

Denning, D. (1975). Secure information flow in computer systems, PhD thesis, Purdue University, Indiana.

Denning, D. (1976). A lattice model of secure information flow. *Communications of the ACM,* 19(5), 236–243.

Denning, D. and Denning, P. (1977). Certification of programs for secure information flow. *Communications of the ACM,* 20(7), 504–513.

Desmet, L., Joosen, W., Massacci, F., Philippaerts, P., Piessens, F., Siahaan, I., and Vanoverberghe, D. (2008). Security-by-contract on the net platform. *Information Security Technical Report,* 13(1), 25–32.

Dhavale, S. and Lokhande, B. (2016). Comnoid: information leakage detection using data flow analysis on android devices. *International Journal of Computer Applications*, 134(7), 15–20.

Dietz, M., Shekhar, S., Pisetsky, Y., Shu, A., and Wallach, D.S. (2011). Quire: lightweight provenance for smart phone operating systems. *Proceedings of the 20th USENIX Security Symposium, USENIX Security '11*. USENIX Security Symposium, p. 3.

Enck, W., Gilbert, P., Chun, B., Cox, L., Jung, J., McDaniel, P., and Sheth, A. (2010). Taintdroid: an information-flow tracking system for realtime privacy monitoring on smartphones. *Proceedings of the 9th USENIX Conference on Operating Systems Design and Implementation*. USENIX Association, pp. 1–6.

Enck, W., Ongtang, M., and McDaniel, P. (2009). On lightweight mobile phone application certification. *Proceedings of the 16th ACM Conference on Computer and Communications Security*. ACM, pp. 235–245.

Enck, W., Octeau, D., McDaniel, P., and Chaudhuri, S. (2011). A study of android application security. *Proceedings of the 20th USENIX Security Symposium. USENIX Association, August 2011*. USENIX Association, p. 2.

Evans, D. and Larochelle, D. (2002). Improving security using extensible lightweight static analysis. *Software, IEEE*, 19(1), 42–51.

Fedler, R., Kulicke, M., and Schütte, J. (2013). Native code execution control for attack mitigation on android. *Proceedings of the Third ACM Workshop on Security and Privacy in Smartphones & Mobile Devices*. ACM, pp. 15–20.

Felt, A.P., Wang, H.J., Moshchuk, A., Hanna, S., and Chin, E. (2011). Permission re-delegation: attacks and defenses. *Proceedings of the 20th USENIX Security Symposium*. USENIX Security Symposium, pp. 22–37.

Fenton, J. (1973). Information protection systems, PhD thesis, University of Cambridge.

Fenton, J. (1974). Memoryless subsystem. *Computer Journal*, 17(2), 143–147.

Ferrante, J., Ottenstein, K.J., and Warren, J.D. (1987). The program dependence graph and its use in optimization. *ACM Transactions on Programming Languages and Systems (TOPLAS)*, 9(3), 319–349.

Fragkaki, E., Bauer, L., Jia, L., and Swasey, D. (2012). Modeling and enhancing android's permission system, *ESORICS*, pp. 1–18.

Fuchs, A.P., Chaudhuri, A., and Foster, J.S. (2009). *Scandroid: Automated Security Certification of Android Applications*. University of Maryland.

Gartner (2016). Gartner says worldwide smartphone sales grew 3.9 percent in first quarter of 2016. Available: http://www.gartner.com/newsroom/id/3323017.

Gat, I. and Saal, H. (1975). Memoryless execution: a programmers viewpoint. IBM Israeli Scientific Center, IBM tech. rep. 025.

George, L., Viet Triem Tong, V., and Mé, L. (2009). Blare tools: a policy-based intrusion detection system automatically set by the security policy. *Recent Advances in Intrusion Detection*. Springer, pp. 355–356.

Georgiadis, L. and Tarjan, R.E. (2004). Finding dominators revisited. *Proceedings of the Fifteenth Annual ACM-SIAM Symposium on Discrete Algorithms*. Society for Industrial and Applied Mathematics, pp. 869–878.

Gibler, C., Crussell, J., Erickson, J., and Chen, H. (2012). Androidleaks: automatically detecting potential privacy leaks in android applications on a large scale. *Trust*, 12, 291–307.

Gilbert, P., Chun, B.-G., Cox, L.P., and Jung, J. (2011). Vision: automated security validation of mobile apps at app markets. *Proceedings of the Second International Workshop on Mobile Cloud Computing and Services*. ACM, pp. 21–26.

Google (2015). dex2jar. Available: http://code.google.com/p/dex2jar/.

Gordon, M.I., Kim, D., Perkins, J.H., Gilham, L., Nguyen, N., and Rinard, M.C. (2015). Information flow analysis of android applications in droidsafe. *Proceeding of the Network and Distributed System Security Symposium (NDSS)*. *The Internet Society*. NDSS, p. 110.

Graa, M., Cuppens-Boulahia, N., Cuppens, F., and Cavalli, A. (2012). Detecting control flow in Smarphones: combining static and dynamic analyses. *CSS 2012: The 4th International Symposium on Cyberspace Safety and Security*, pp. 33–47.

Graa, M., Boulahia, N.C., Cuppens, F., and Cavalliy, A. (2014). Protection against code obfuscation attacks based on control dependencies in android systems. *2014 IEEE Eighth International Conference on Software Security and Reliability-Companion (SERE-C)*. IEEE, pp. 149–157.

Graa, M., Cuppens-Boulahia, N., Cuppens, F., and Lanet, J.-L. (2016). Tracking explicit and control flows in Java and native Android apps code. *ICISSP 2016: 2nd International Conference on Information Systems Security and Privacy*. ICISSP, pp. 307–316.

Graa, M., Cuppens-Boulahia, N., Cuppens, F., Moussaileb, R., and Lanet, J.-L. (2017). Detection of side channel attacks based on data tainting in Android systems. *IFIP SEC 2017: 32nd International Conference on ICT Systems Security and Privacy Protection*. Vol. 502 IFIPAICT, pp. 1–14.

Haldar, V., Chandra, D., and Franz, M. (2005). Dynamic taint propagation for java. *21st Annual Computer Security Applications Conference*. IEEE, p. 9.

Hauser, C., Tronel, F., Reid, J., and Fidge, C. (2012). A taint marking approach to confidentiality violation detection, *Proceedings of the 10th Australasian Information Security Conference (AISC 2012)*. Vol. 125, Australian Computer Society.

Hedman, S. (2004). *A First Course in Logic: an Introduction to Model Theory, Proof Theory, Computability, and Complexity*. Oxford University Press, Oxford and New York.

Heuser, S., Negro, M., Pendyala, P.K., and Sadeghi, A.-R. (2016). Droidauditor: forensic analysis of application-layer privilege escalation attacks on android. *Proceedings of the 20th International Conference on Financial Cryptography and Data Security*. TU Darmstadt, Springer, pp. 260–268.

Hornyack, P., Han, S., Jung, J., Schechter, S., and Wetherall, D. (2011). These aren't the droids you're looking for: retrofitting android to protect data from imperious applications. *Proceedings of the 18th ACM Conference on Computer and Communications Security*. ACM, pp. 639–652.

Huang, W., Dong, Y., and Milanova, A. (2014). Type-based taint analysis for java web applications. *FASE*, pp. 140–154.

Hunt, A. and Thomas, D. (2000). *Programming Ruby: the Pragmatic Programmer's Guide*. Vol. 2. Addison-Wesley Professional, New York.

Jana, S. and Shmatikov, V. (2012). Memento: learning secrets from process footprints. *2012 IEEE Symposium on Security and Privacy*. IEEE, pp. 143–157.

Java (2015). Java decompiler. Available: http://jd.benow.ca/.

Johnson, R. and Pingali, K. (1993). Dependence-based program analysis, *ACM SigPlan Notices*. Vol. 28, ACM, pp. 78–89.

Kang, M., McCamant, S., Poosankam, P., and Song, D. (2011). Dta++: dynamic taint analysis with targeted control-flow propagation. *Proceedings of the 18th Annual Network and Distributed System Security Symposium*. San Diego, CA.

Kay, A. (2007). Tesseract: an open-source optical character recognition engine. *Linux Journal*, 2007(159), 2.

Kerner, S.M. (2011). Android leaking private info. Available: http://www. esecurityplanet.com/trends/article.php/3938056/AndroidLeaking-Private-Info.

Kim, J., Yoon, Y., Yi, K., and Shin, J. (2012). Scandal: static analyzer for detecting privacy leaks in android applications. *MoST: Mobile Security Technologies*, Chen, H., Koved, L., and Wallach, D.S. (eds). IEEE, Los Alamitos, CA.

Kim, Y.-K., Yoon, H.-J., and Lee, M.-H. (2015). Stealthy information leakage from android smartphone through screenshot and ocr. *International Conference on Chemical, Material and Food Engineering*. Atlantis Press.

Klimas, L. (2011). Video shows how htc android phones leak private info. Available: http://www.theblaze.com/stories/2011/10/03/video-shows-how-htc-androidphones-leak-private-info-left-and-right/.

Lafortune, E. (2006). Proguard. Available: http://proguard.sourceforge.net.

Landi, W. (1992). Undecidability of static analysis. *ACM Letters on Programming Languages and Systems (LOPLAS)*, 1(4), 323–337.

Lange, M., Liebergeld, S., Lackorzynski, A., Warg, A., and Peter, M. (2011). L4android: a generic operating system framework for secure smartphones, *Proceedings of the 1st ACM Workshop on Security and Privacy in Smartphones and Mobile Devices*. ACM, pp. 39–50.

Lengauer, T. and Tarjan, R.E. (1979). A fast algorithm for finding dominators in a flowgraph. *ACM Transactions on Programming Languages and Systems (TOPLAS)*, 1(1), 121–141.

Li, X., Kashyap, V., Oberg, J.K., Tiwari, M., Rajarathinam, V.R., Kastner, R., Sherwood, T., Hardekopf, B., and Chong, F.T. (2014). Sapper: a language for hardware-level security policy enforcement. *ACM SIGARCH Computer Architecture News*. Vol. 42, ACM, pp. 97–112.

Lowry, E.S. and Medlock, C.W. (1969). Object code optimization. *Commun. ACM*, 12(1), 13–22.

Mongiovi, M., Giannone, G., Fornaia, A., Pappalardo, G., and Tramontana, E. (2015). Combining static and dynamic data flow analysis: a hybrid approach for detecting data leaks in java applications. *Proceedings of the 30th Annual ACM Symposium on Applied Computing*. ACM, pp. 1573–1579.

Myers, A. (1999). Jflow: practical mostly-static information flow control. *Proceedings of the 26th ACM SIGPLAN-SIGACT Symposium on Principles of Programming Languages*. ACM, pp. 228–241.

Nair, S., Simpson, P., Crispo, B., and Tanenbaum, A. (2008). A virtual machine based information flow control system for policy enforcement. *Electronic Notes in Theoretical Computer Science*, 197(1), 3–16.

Nauman, M., Khan, S., and Zhang, X. (2010). Apex: extending android permission model and enforcement with user-defined runtime constraints. *Proceedings of the 5th ACM Symposium on Information, Computer and Communications Security*. ACM, pp. 328–332.

Nethercote, N. and Seward, J. (2003). Valgrind: a program supervision framework. *Electronic Notes in Theoretical Computer Science*, 89(2), 44–66.

Newsome, J. and Song, D. (2005). Dynamic taint analysis for automatic detection, analysis, and signature generation of exploits on commodity software. *Proceedings of the 12th Annual Network and Distributed System Security Symposium (NDSS '05)*.

Ongtang, M., McLaughlin, S., Enck, W., and McDaniel, P. (2012). Semantically rich application-centric security in android. *Security and Communication Networks*, 5(6), 658–673.

Portokalidis, G., Homburg, P., Anagnostakis, K., and Bos, H. (2010). Paranoid android: versatile protection for smartphones. *Proceedings of the 26th Annual Computer Security Applications Conference*. ACM, pp. 347–356.

Qian, C., Luo, X., Shao, Y., and Chan, A.T. (2014). On tracking information flows through jni in android applications. *2014 44th Annual IEEE/IFIP International Conference on Dependable Systems and Networks (DSN)*. IEEE, pp. 180–191.

Qin, F., Wang, C., Li, Z., Kim, H., Zhou, Y., and Wu, Y. (2006). Lift: a low-overhead practical information flow tracking system for detecting security attacks. *Proceedings of the 39th Annual IEEE/ACM International Symposium on Microarchitecture*. IEEE Computer Society, pp. 135–148.

Reina, A., Fattori, A., and Cavallaro, L. (2013). A system call-centric analysis and stimulation technique to automatically reconstruct android malware behaviors. *Proceeding of the Sixth European Workshop on System Security (EUROSEC)*. Prague, Czech Republic.

Ren, B., Liu, C., Cheng, B., Hong, S., Zhao, S., and Chen, J. (2016). Easyguard: enhanced context-aware adaptive access control system for android platform: poster. *Proceedings of the 22nd Annual International Conference on Mobile Computing and Networking*. ACM, pp. 458–459.

Research, A. (2016). Graphviz. Available: http://www.graphviz.org/.

Sabelfeld, A. and Myers, A. (2003). Language-based information-flow security. *IEEE Journal on Selected Areas in Communications*, 21(1), 5–19.

Sarwar, G., Mehani, O., Boreli, R., and Kaafar, D. (2013). On the effectiveness of dynamic taint analysis for protecting against private information leaks on android (SECRYPT). *Proceedings of the 10th International Conference on Security and Cryptography*, pp. 461–467.

Schlegel, R., Zhang, K., Zhou, X.-Y., Intwala, M., Kapadia, A., and Wang, X. (2011). Soundcomber: a stealthy and context-aware sound trojan for smartphones. *NDSS*, 11, 17–33.

Schulz, P. (2012). Code protection in android. Technical report, University of Bonn, Germany.

Shabtai, A., Fledel, Y., and Elovici, Y. (2010). Securing android-powered mobile devices using selinux. *Security & Privacy, IEEE*, 8(3), 36–44.

Shankar, U., Talwar, K., Foster, J.S., and Wagner, D. (2001). Detecting format string vulnerabilities with type qualifiers. *USENIX Security Symposium*, pp. 201–220.

Shankar, V.G., Somani, G., Gaur, M.S., Laxmi, V., and Conti, M. (2017). Androtaint: an efficient android malware detection framework using dynamic taint analysis. *Asia Security and Privacy (ISEASP), 2017 ISEA*. IEEE, pp. 1–13.

Smardec (2017). Allatori obfuscator. Available: http://www.allatori.com/doc.html.

Song, D., Brumley, D., Yin, H., Caballero, J., Jager, I., Kang, M., Liang, Z., Newsome, J., Poosankam, P., and Saxena, P. (2008). Bitblaze: a new approach to computer security via binary analysis. *Information Systems Security*, pp. 1–25.

Sourceware (2015). Objdump. Available: https://sourceware.org/binutils/docs/binutils/objdump.html.

Spreitzenbarth, M., Freiling, F., Echtler, F., Schreck, T., and Hoffmann, J. (2013). Mobile-sandbox: having a deeper look into android applications. *Proceedings of the 28th Annual ACM Symposium on Applied Computing*. ACM, pp. 1808–1815.

Spreitzenbarth, M., Schreck, T., Echtler, F., Arp, D., and Hoffmann, J. (2015). Mobilesandbox: combining static and dynamic analysis with machine-learning techniques. *International Journal of Information Security*, 14(2), 141–153.

Statistica (2016). Cumulative number of apps downloaded from the Google Play as of May 2016 (in billions). Avaialble: http://www.statista.com/statistics/281106/number-of-android-app-downloads-from-google-play/.

Statistics (2018). Number of available applications in the Google Play Store from December 2009 to December (2018). Available: https://www.statista.com/statistics/266210/number-of-available-applications-in-the-google-play-store/.

Suh, G., Lee, J., Zhang, D., and Devadas, S. (2004). Secure program execution via dynamic information flow tracking. *ACM SIGPLAN Notices*. Vol. 39, ACM, pp. 85–96.

Thanigaivelan, N.K., Nigussie, E., Hakkala, A., Virtanen, S., and Isoaho, J. (2017). Codra: context-based dynamically reconfigurable access control system for android. *Journal of Network and Computer Applications*, 101(2018), 1–17.

Vachharajani, N., Bridges, M.J., Chang, J., Rangan, R., Ottoni, G., Blome, J.A., Reis, G.A., Vachharajani, M., and August, D.I. (2004). Rifle: an architectural framework for user-centric information-flow security. *37th International Symposium on Microarchitecture, 2004. MICRO-37 2004*. IEEE, pp. 243–254.

Vogt, P., Nentwich, F., Jovanovic, N., Kirda, E., Kruegel, C., and Vigna, G. (2007). Cross site scripting prevention with dynamic data tainting and static analysis. *NDSS'07*, Vol. 42, Citeseer.

Volpano, D. (1999). *Safety versus Secrecy*. Springer, London, UK.

Wall, L. (2000). *Programming Perl*. 3rd edition, O'Reilly & Associates, Inc., Sebastopol, CA.

Wang, C. and Shieh, S.W. (2015). Droit: dynamic alternation of dual-level tainting for malware analysis. *Journal of Information Science and Engineering*, 31, 111–129.

Wiki (2015). Qemu open source processor emulator. Available: http://wiki.qemu. org/Main_Page/.

Wilson, D. (2010). Many android apps send your private information to advertisers. Available: http://news.techeye.net/mobile/many-android-apps-send-your-privateinformation-to-advertisers.

Wilson, T. (2011). Many android apps leaking private information. Available: http://www.informationweek.com/security/mobile/many-android-apps-leakingprivate-inform/231002162.

Wroblewski, G. (2002). General method of program code obfuscation (draft), PhD thesis, Citeseer.

Xu, W., Bhatkar, E., and Sekar, R. (2006). Taint-enhanced policy enforcement: a practical approach to defeat a wide range of attacks. *15th USENIX Security Symposium*. pp. 121–136.

Xu, R., Saïdi, H., and Anderson, R. (2012). Aurasium: practical policy enforcement for android applications. *Proceedings of the 21st USENIX Security Symposium*. USENIX Association, pp. 27–27.

Yan, L.-K. and Yin, H. (2012). Droidscope: seamlessly reconstructing the os and dalvik semantic views for dynamic android malware analysis. *USENIX Security Symposium*. pp. 569–584.

Yang, Z. and Yang, M. (2012). Leakminer: detect information leakage on android with static taint analysis. *2012 Third World Congress on Software Engineering (WCSE)*. IEEE, pp. 101–104.

Yang, Z., Yang, M., Zhang, Y., Gu, G., Ning, P., and Wang, X.S. (2013). Appintent: analyzing sensitive data transmission in android for privacy leakage detection. *Proceedings of the 2013 ACM SIGSAC Conference on Computer & Communications Security*. ACM, pp. 1043–1054.

Yin, H., Song, D., Egele, M., Kruegel, C., and Kirda, E. (2007). Panorama: capturing system-wide information flow for malware detection and analysis. *Proceedings of the 14th ACM Conference on Computer and Communications Security*. ACM. pp. 116–127.

Yip, A., Wang, X., Zeldovich, N., and Kaashoek, M.F. (2009). Improving application security with data flow assertions. *Proceedings of the ACM SIGOPS 22nd Symposium on Operating Systems Principles*. ACM, pp. 291–304.

You, W., Liang, B., Shi, W., Wang, P., and Zhang, X. (2017). Taintman: an ART-compatible dynamic taint analysis framework on unmodified and non-rooted android devices. *IEEE Transactions on Dependable and Secure Computing*. Available: doi.ieeecomputersociety.org/10.1109/TDSC.2017. 2740169.

Zhang, X., Edwards, A., and Jaeger, T. (2002). Using cqual for static analysis of authorization hook placement. *Proceedings of the 11th USENIX Security Symposium*, pp. 33–48.

Zhou, Y., Zhang, X., Jiang, X., and Freeh, V. (2011). Taming information-stealing smartphone applications (on android). *International Conference on Trust and Trustworthy Computing*. Springer, pp. 93–107.

Zhou, Y., Wang, Z., Zhou, W., and Jiang, X. (2012). Hey, you, get off of my market: detecting malicious apps in official and alternative android markets. *NDSS*, pp. 50–52.

List of Authors

Mariem GRAA
IMT Atlantique
Rennes
France

Kamel KAROUI
INSAT
University of Carthage
Tunis
Tunisia

Wiem TOUNSI
Axians Cybersecurity
Paris
France

Reda YAICH
IRT SystemX
Palaiseau
France

Index

Other titles from

in

Networks and Telecommunications

2018

ANDIA Gianfranco, DURO Yvan, TEDJINI Smail
Non-linearities in Passive RFID Systems: Third Harmonic Concept and Applications

BOUILLARD Anne, BOYER Marc, LE CORRONC Euriell
Deterministic Network Calculus: From Theory to Practical Implementation

PEREZ André
Wi-Fi Integration to the 4G Mobile Network

2017

BENSLAMA Malek, BENSLAMA Achour, ARIS Skander
Quantum Communications in New Telecommunications Systems

HILT Benoit, BERBINEAU Marion, VINEL Alexey, PIROVANO Alain
Networking Simulation for Intelligent Transportation Systems: High Mobile Wireless Nodes

JUMIRA Oswald, ZEADALLY Sherali
Energy Efficiency in Wireless Networks

KRIEF Francine
Green Networking

PEREZ André
Mobile Networks Architecture

2011

BONALD Thomas, FEUILLET Mathieu
Network Performance Analysis

CARBOU Romain, DIAZ Michel, EXPOSITO Ernesto, ROMAN Rodrigo
Digital Home Networking

CHABANNE Hervé, URIEN Pascal, SUSINI Jean-Ferdinand
RFID and the Internet of Things

GARDUNO David, DIAZ Michel
Communicating Systems with UML 2: Modeling and Analysis of Network Protocols

LAHEURTE Jean-Marc
Compact Antennas for Wireless Communications and Terminals: Theory and Design

PALICOT Jacques
Radio Engineering: From Software Radio to Cognitive Radio

PEREZ André
IP, Ethernet and MPLS Networks: Resource and Fault Management

RÉMY Jean-Gabriel, LETAMENDIA Charlotte
Home Area Networks and IPTV

TOUTAIN Laurent, MINABURO Ana
Local Networks and the Internet: From Protocols to Interconnection

Printed and bound by CPI Group (UK) Ltd, Croydon, CR0 4YY

28/10/2024

14581340-0001